IMAGES
of America

HUMBOLDT COUNTY

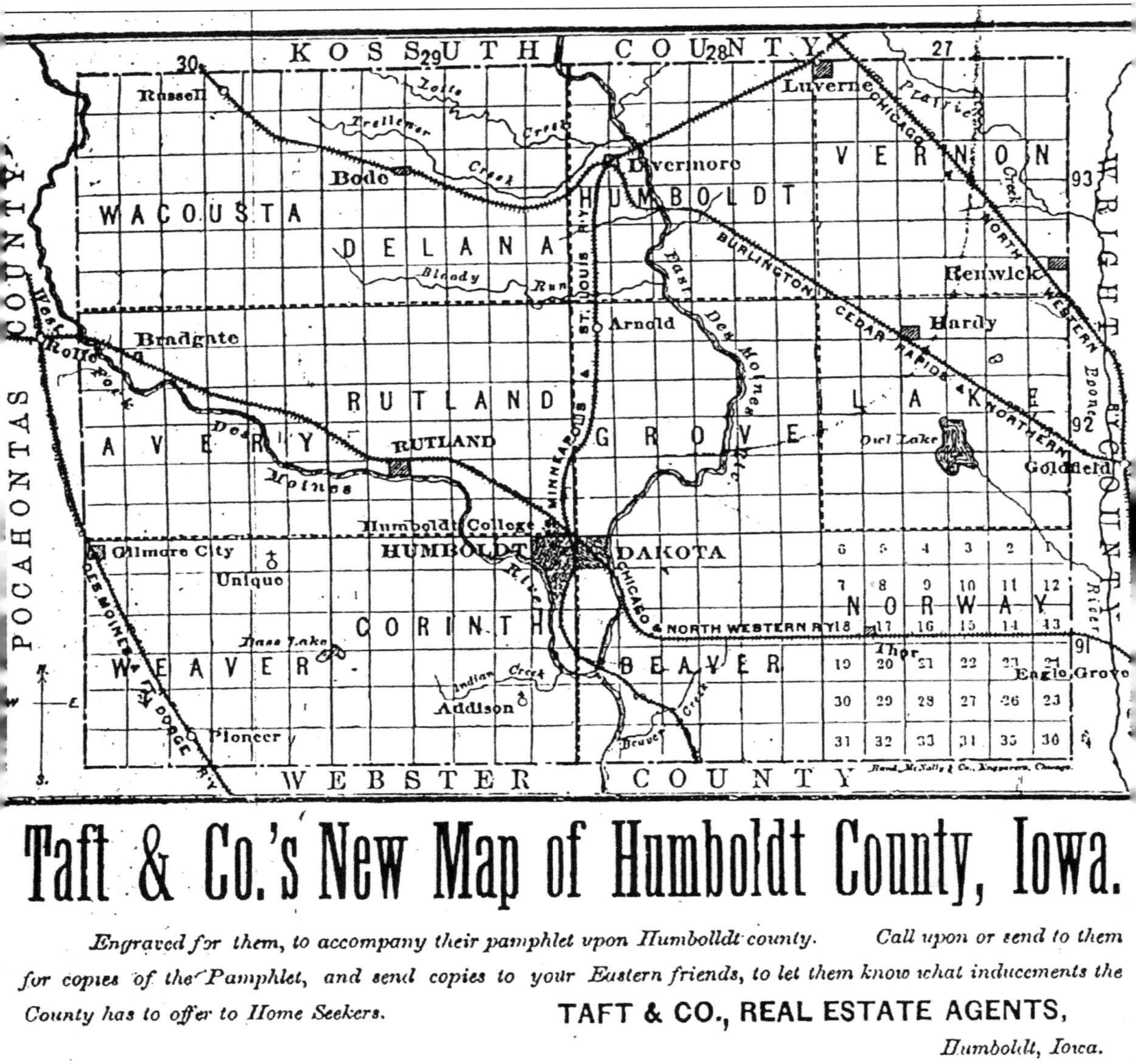

Above is a map of Humboldt County, Iowa, as it was in 1888. The area opened for settlement in 1852. Hardy pioneers ploughed up the prairie and drained the wetlands, transforming them into the richest farmland in the nation. Solitary log cabins gradually grew into flourishing settlements. Trails used by early trappers and hunters gave way to roads and railways. (Courtesy of the Humboldt County Historical Museum.)

On the Cover: The south side of Sumner Avenue is shown in 1905 after curbs and hitching posts were put in. From left to right are Peoples State Bank, Ward Hardware, C.J. White Clothing, Rogers and Kurth Meats, Morgan Restaurant, Stone Grocery, Mathies Jewelry, Windrath Hardware, Rundlet Flour, Tuckey Shoes, Reed Jewelry, Pinney Lumber, Preble Restaurant, and Gotch Billiards. (Courtesy of Pete Holt.)

IMAGES
of America

HUMBOLDT COUNTY

Pat Baker and Martha Schmidt

ARCADIA
PUBLISHING

ISBN 978-0-7385-7649-7

Published by Arcadia Publishing
Charleston, South Carolina

Printed in the United States of America

Library of Congress Control Number: 2011931588

For all general information, please contact Arcadia Publishing:
Telephone 843-853-2070
Fax 843-853-0044
E-mail sales@arcadiapublishing.com
For customer service and orders:
Toll-Free 1-888-313-2665

Visit us on the Internet at www.arcadiapublishing.com

Behold the Work of the Old...
Let your Heritage not be Lost.
But bequeath it as a Memory,
Treasure and Blessing...
Gather the Lost and the Hidden
And preserve it for thy Children.
Christian Metz 1846
(Courtesy Amana Heritage Society)

Contents

ACKNOWLEDGMENTS

Since the Humboldt County Historical Association was founded in 1962, hundreds of volunteers have contributed thousands of hours to preserve the history of Humboldt County. It is impossible to thank all of these volunteers individually, but without their hard work and their love of local history, this book would not have been possible. The Humboldt County Historical Museum's research library, archives, and photograph collections offer a treasure trove of fascinating stories and information about the community's history. The board members, museum directors, and volunteers who maintain these collections have earned our immeasurable gratitude. Unless otherwise noted, all images appearing in this book were graciously provided by the Humboldt County Historical Museum.

We wish to thank our editor at Arcadia Publishing, Winnie Rodgers, for her expert guidance. Also, thanks go to Nancy Kellner and Cheri Waechter, who generously helped us scan the images for this book. We give our thanks to the Humboldt County Genealogical Society, the Humboldt Women's Club, the Humboldt Public Library, and centennial yearbooks from local Humboldt County communities that have contributed photographs for this book. We would like to express our appreciation to several individuals, including Ronald Stone, Peter Holt, Laurie Carlson, Bill Verbrugge, Marilyn Dodgen, Elwyn Weible, Mona Sawyer Hill, Carolyn Logan, Connie Overby, Norm Caldwell, Tom Baker, John Baker, and Robert Baker for their encouragement and support of this project.

INTRODUCTION

Humboldt County was named after Alexander von Humboldt (1769–1859), a German scientist and explorer. His name was given to mountains, rivers, and many of the towns and counties being drawn on the maps in the 1840s.

Two Frenchmen engaged in trading furs with Native Americans in 1825 at Fort Confederation, now Gotch Park. About 10 years later, Lt. Col. Stephen Kearney, Capt. Nathan Boone, Lt. Col. Albert Lea, and 160 mounted foot soldiers, called Dragoons, explored parts of the county along the rivers.

The Dakota Sioux retained legal claim to the areas between the forks of the Des Moines River until 1851. Not wanting to move on, some renegade bands stayed. In 1853, unlicensed trader Henry Lott shot Sioux chief Sidominadotah and murdered six of his family members at a spot near what is now called Bloody Run Creek. It is said by some that the Spirit Lake Massacre in 1857 was a result. Lott was long gone before the first permanent settlers arrived in 1854, taking advantage of the woodlands along the rivers.

Humboldt was the last county to be organized in Iowa, due to greedy manipulation of land by those intent on placing Fort Dodge closer to the center of Webster County. When the dust settled in 1857, Humboldt County was one tier of townships short of what it had been in 1852. These lost townships include Kennedy Park, the Community Apple Orchard, and the towns of Badger, Clare, and Vincent.

The county organized itself in 1857, and although more people lived north in Humboldt Township, the centrally located Dakota City was made the county seat. Stagecoach stops, mills, and schools were built across the county. Dakota City grew slowly under the leadership of Charles Bergk and Edward McKnight.

When the Rev. Stephen H. Taft arrived with his religious colony in 1863, they belittled Dakota City, hoping to build a larger town more in keeping with Taft's values. He wanted his town, first called Springvale, later Humboldt, to be the county seat. Thus began a rivalry as Humboldt built itself up at the expense of its neighbor. Humboldt prospered, but Dakota City remained the seat of government.

Taft oversaw the platting of his town, built at least two dams for his mill, and started erecting commercial buildings from limestone taken from the millrace. The 1870s were hard years, with grasshoppers destroying crops, the financial panic of 1874 forcing settlers to repay loans, fire destroying a block of downtown businesses, and the failure in obtaining a railroad all causing dismay. Finally, in 1879, the Minneapolis & St. Louis Railway arrived, along with the Chicago & Northwestern Railroad to Dakota City in 1881. A boomtown economy set in.

Reverend Taft's vision included establishing a college on the hill in 1872, a "Harvard of the West." Each year, about 100 students attended, taking grammar school, high school, college preparatory, and normal training classes. In 1881, it closed because of debts but reopened in 1895 under Prof. J.P. Peterson's leadership. Two dormitories were built, and about 400 students came each year from 25 states to take business and teacher courses. As high schools began to provide these, enrollment decreased. A small disagreement with the Humboldt County Board of Supervisors caused Peterson to move his college to Minneapolis in 1915.

Attracted by the rich soil for their farms, land-starved immigrants from Scandinavia and Northern Europe came to Humboldt County. Settlers arrived in groups of families and brought their religious preferences with them. Churches were built, often relying on circuit-riding pastors. The population doubled between 1870 and 1880, and again by 1890. Education was important, so schoolhouses were placed every two miles, with as many as 15 children in each building. Country schoolteachers taught grades one through eight and earned $25 per month.

After the railroads came, grain and livestock could be shipped to Chicago, and coal and lumber delivered faster. Villages sprung up along the railway, and markets were established close to farms. Each town provided a grain elevator, a school, churches, retail stores, and a doctor's office.

The city of Humboldt rapidly developed. Several large business buildings were erected of native stone along Sumner Avenue for banks and dry goods and grocery stores. Smaller wood-framed shops lined the streets, providing space for locally owned newspapers, lumberyards, blacksmith shops, implement dealers, hardware stores, restaurants, butchers, carpenters, jewelers, milliners, barbers, doctors, lawyers, and real estate offices.

Civic improvements included board sidewalks, hitching posts, a fire station, water systems, telephones, and electric service. Churches of every denomination served the needs of citizens. Humboldt built a magnificent limestone school in 1893 for kindergarten through the 12th grade. The Northern Roller Milling Company, Humboldt Gravel and Tile (later Concrete Products), cigar factories, icehouses, poultry plants, and a cooperative creamery provided employment.

By 1900, the county population reached 12,000. A new fire station, with city offices, was erected next to the Humboldt Carnegie Public Library in 1912. Automobiles and tractors could be purchased on Main Street, and gas stations provided services. The Humboldt Electric Light and Power Company built the hydroelectric power plant and transmission lines. In 1927, Iowa Public Service, now known as MidAmerican Energy, purchased it.

In 1919, the city paved Sumner Avenue and built the attractive bridge and curved avenue up Johnston Hill. A new school provided needed classrooms, laboratories, home economics and manual training rooms, a gymnasium, and an auditorium. The Legion Building provided retail spaces, meeting rooms, a public restroom, and apartments. New industries included the DeKalb Grain Processing Plant and the Coca-Cola Bottling Company.

Humboldt County's population reached a maximum of 13,459 in 1940. During World War II, the Hemp Plant provided work for many. High schools in small towns consolidated into regional centers as transportation improved. Humboldt's Stephen H. Taft Elementary School was built in 1953, and Humboldt got its swimming pool in 1954.

Retail businesses developed on Highway 169 and Highway 3, along with expanded facilities for Humboldt County Rural Electric and Corn Belt Power Cooperative, Dodgen Industries, Knight's Cottage Cheese, the Sale Barn, Sande Construction, Hadar Manufacturing, ADF Systems Ltd., and the Agrico Chemical Plant. Gunder Manufacturing built in Dakota City. The Humboldt County Historical Museum began to take shape in 1967.

Dakota City and Humboldt schools began to share facilities as country schools closed. The Humboldt Community High School was built on the hill in 1964, with additions of the Wesley Carlson Auditorium and new Humboldt Middle School. Always one of the best school districts in the state, the Humboldt Community School District provides students with the latest high-tech facilities, academics, music, the arts, and outstanding athletic teams.

The Humboldt County Memorial Hospital and Doctor's Park Medical Clinic were built in 1970, providing services and employment to the area, which now includes Springvale Independent Living and Assisted Living facilities.

The Humboldt County Development Association attracted industries to industrial parks surrounding Humboldt, including Jet Company, Schuster Trailers, Hotsy Equipment Company, Chantland-MHS, Hy-Capacity Engineering, Hog Slat, and Liguria Foods. Now, Humboldt County has 10,000 residents, with almost half of the population residing in the city of Humboldt. A new aquatic center and art museum in downtown Humboldt draw visitors to our many parks, hiking trails, and recreational facilities.

One

EARLY SETTLEMENT BEGINS

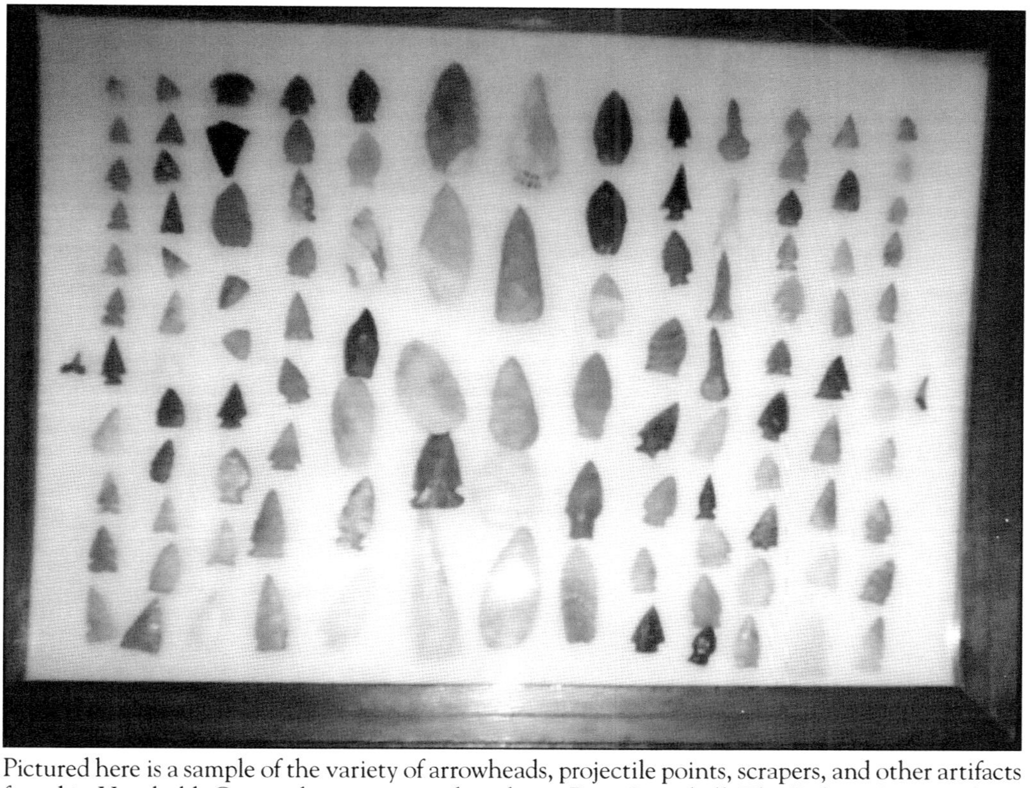

Pictured here is a sample of the variety of arrowheads, projectile points, scrapers, and other artifacts found in Humboldt County by amateur archaeologist Russ Campbell. The Dakota Sioux Indians were still roaming north central Iowa in the early 1850s, using the East and West Forks of the Des Moines River as their highways. The earliest settlers traded furs and learned ways of coping with the wilderness from them.

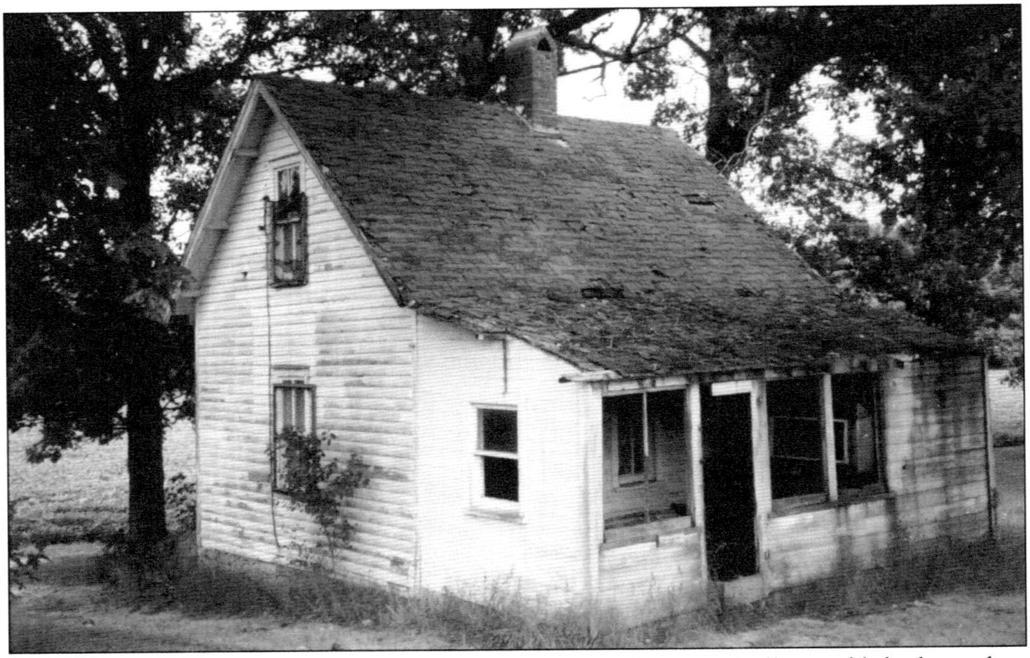

Many of the earliest settlements did not become towns. William R. Miller established a trading post at the forks of the Des Moines River, translated for the Dakotas, and sold goods that he hauled in from Dubuque. Early settlers helped him build a log cabin in 1854. In 1855, Miller built the first wood-frame house in Humboldt County for his family of 12 children. The first school classes met there, and the county was organized in one of his cabins. In 1868, he moved away and sold the place to Lucy and N.R. Jones, who named it Glen Farm. The big barn was built in 1877. The Jones's daughter Faith married William B. West, and the land remains in the family, although others farm it. These images show what are believed to be Miller's wood-frame house (above) and an ice house (below) built at the same time as the barn.

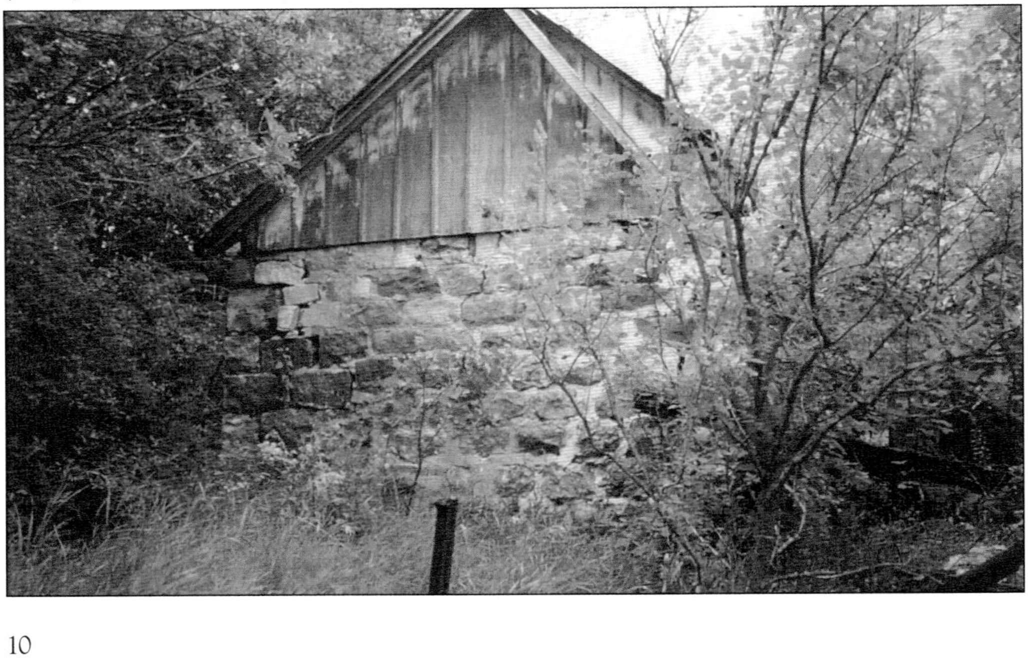

In 1854, Edward McKnight, esquire, son of a wealthy family with a good education, owned land in Wacousta Township that he named McKnight's Point. He helped organize Dakota City and built the first mill on the East Fork of the Des Moines River. McKnight served in the Northern Border Brigade during the Civil War and in the Iowa House of Representatives. (*Annals of Iowa*, Vol. V, No. 7, third series.)

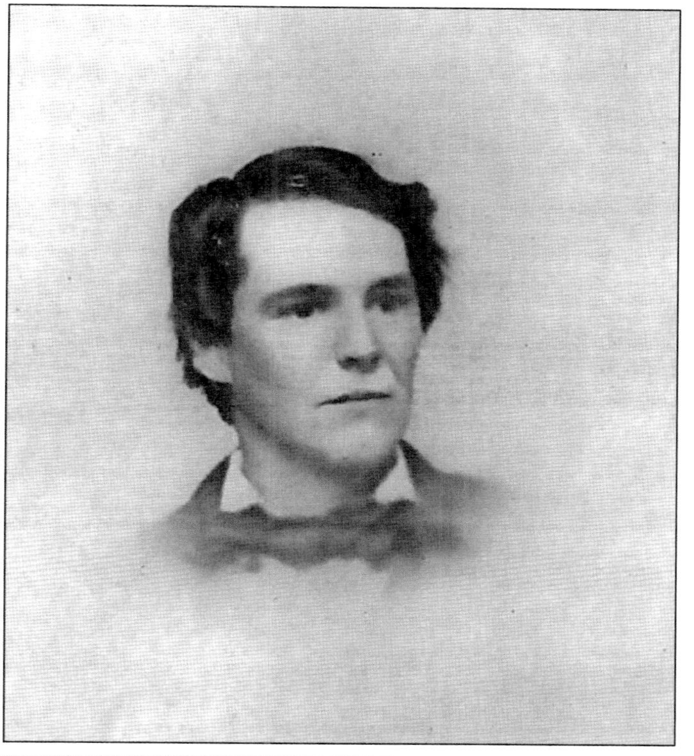

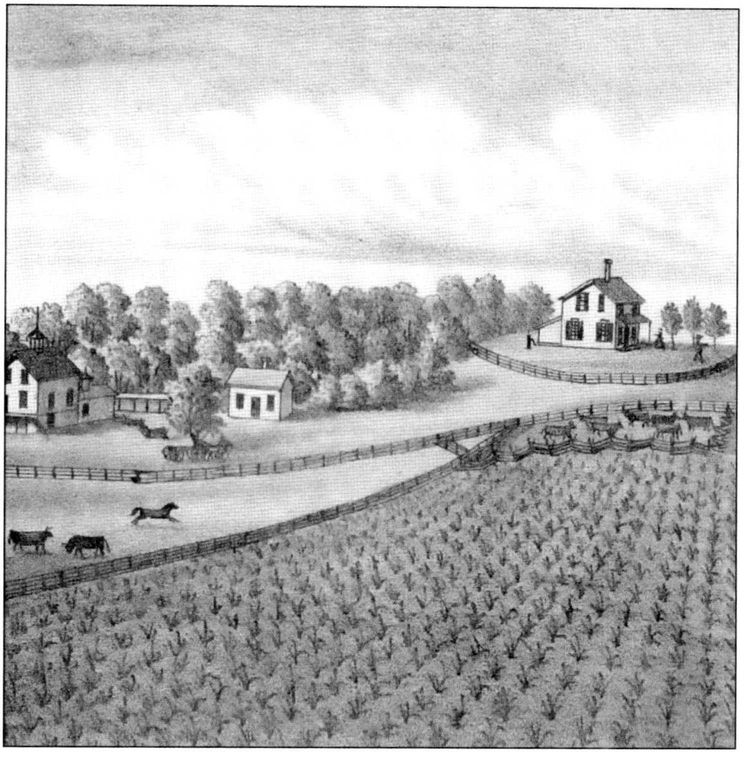

During the summer of 1854, McKnight met Charles Bergk, Christian Hackman, and August Zahlten in Dakota City. All but McKnight spent the winter in a cave in the ravine below the town. Hackman and Zahlten sold their interest in Dakota City to Bergk and moved north to Kossuth County. Bergk's farm was north of Dakota City. (A.T. Andreas's 1875 *Atlas of Iowa.*)

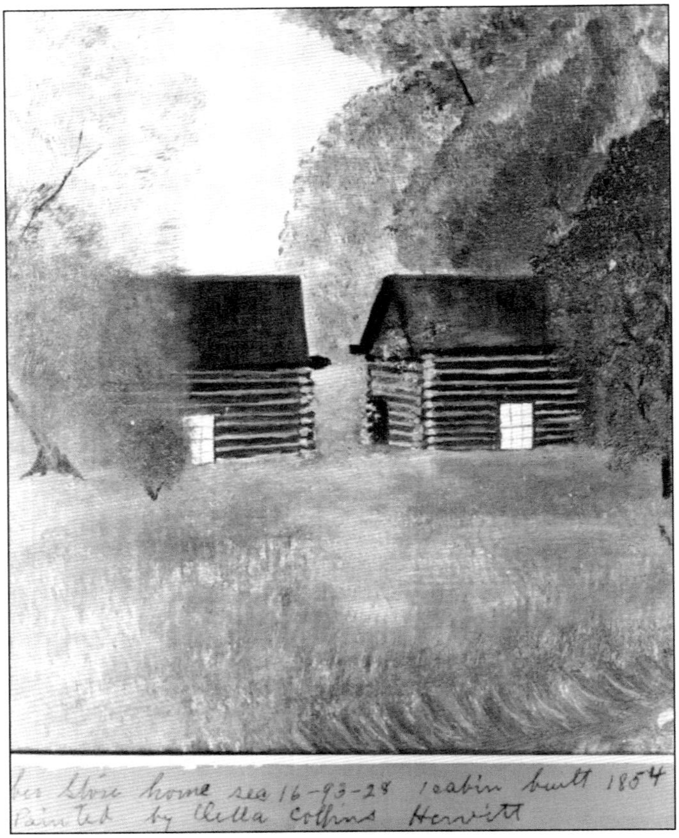

Eber Stone, noted educator and agricultural specialist, pioneered in Grove Township in 1854, first living in a dugout and planting an orchard. He soon settled in Section 16 of Humboldt Township, and he and his 16-year-old sister Lucy A. moved Henry Lott's old cabin next to theirs (shown left). In 1857, his parents, Samuel and Electra St. John Stone (below), and another sister Martha joined them. His father died the next year. In 1868, Eber married teacher Lucy L. Knowles, and three children were born to them. The Stone family lived in the log cabins for 20 years. Soon after building a wood-frame house, Eber died. The painting was done by Oella Collins Hewitt. (Both, courtesy of Ronald H. Stone)

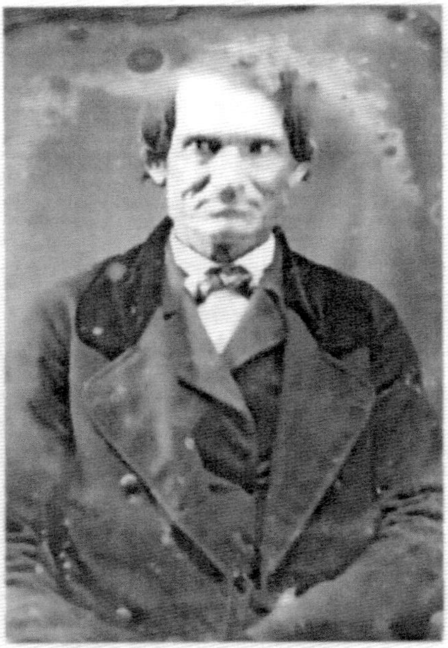

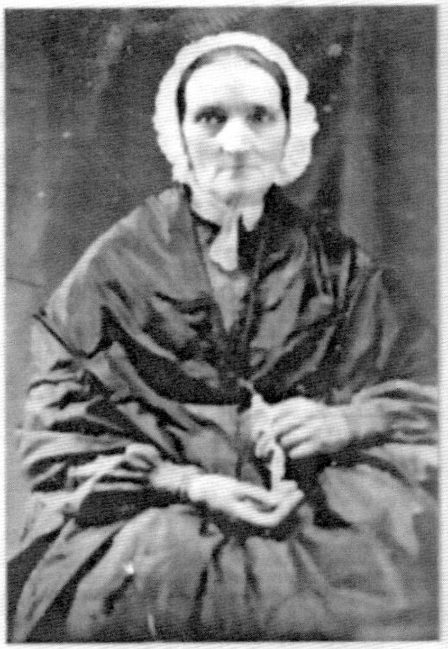

In 1854, brothers Solomon Hand, William Fletcher Hand, and George Washington "Wash" Hand located to the Hand settlement in Grove Township near the Foster Bridge. Solomon helped another settler stay alive while hunting and trapping and froze his feet and hands so severely that it was necessary to amputate them. Hands Grove became a camp meeting place for Methodists in 1856. The second Humboldt County Fair was held there in 1861. Thomas Scurlock, I.B. McCormick, and Michael and John Johnson also made claims in the area. The W.F. Hand family homesteaded the farm in 1855 and erected the hand-hewn native-timber buildings shown here. William Foster purchased it in 1868, and his son Clayton Foster (1873–1968) was born on this farm.

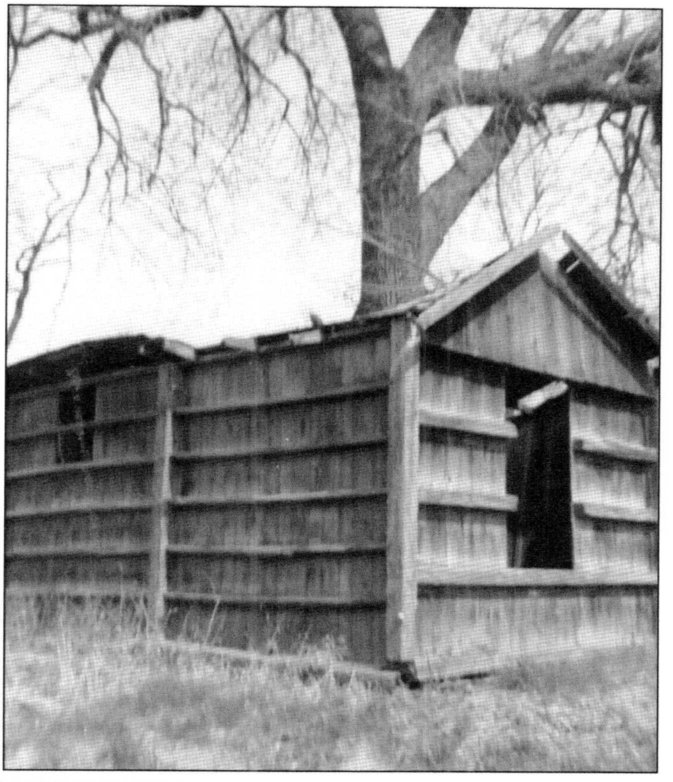

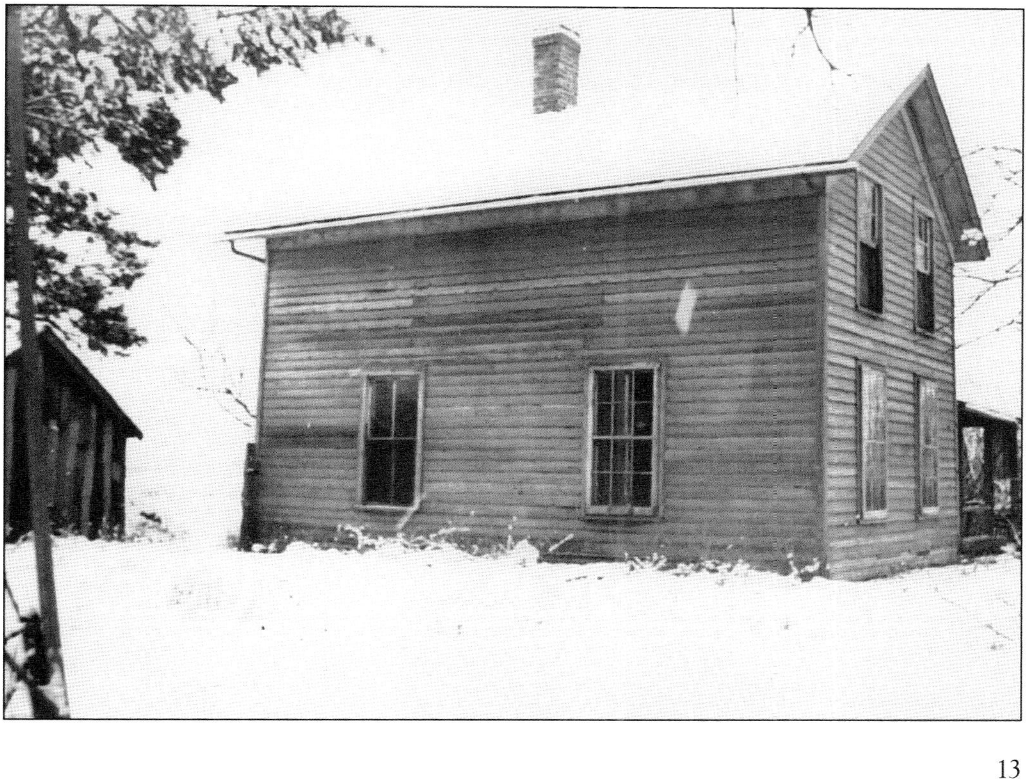

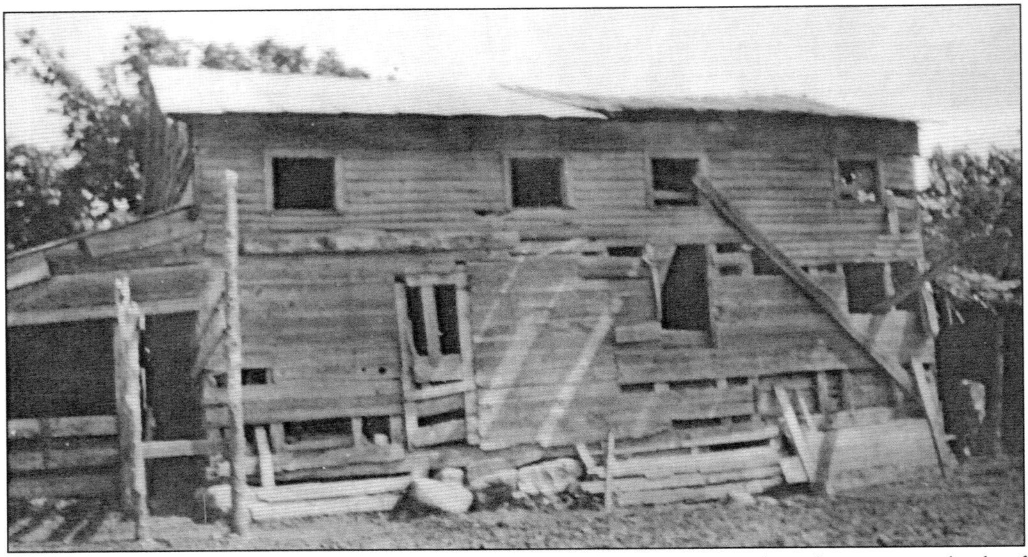

The "Wash" Hand–Taylor place (above), which was a part of the Hand settlement, was built of "real lumber." The two-story building was called the "mansion of the northwest." Other 1855 settlers were George and William Basam; Enos, Abel, and Reuben Bond; George and Thomas Steward; Samuel Church; Henry McLean; Hugh Johnson; Harlow Miner; David H. Niver; William Hamilton; Pat Burns; Martin G. Williams; George Ellis; J.C. Elias; and H.C. Cusey.

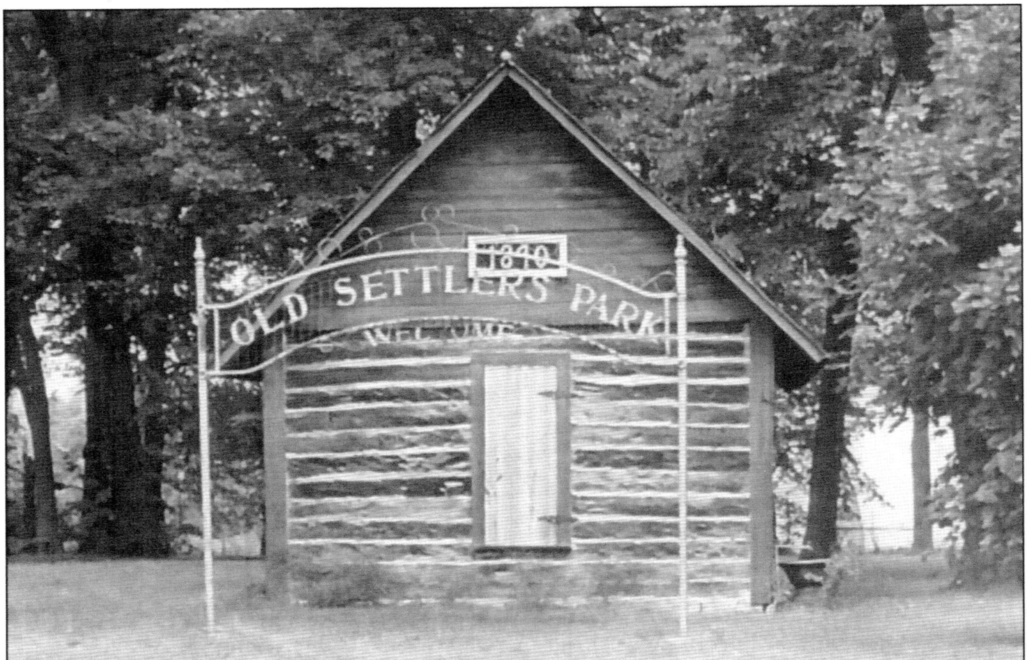

The log cabin in Old Settlers Park in Livermore was built in 1890 from logs donated by the founding members of the Humboldt County Old Settlers Association. The association was formed in 1885 and still meets annually. The cabin stands as a symbol of the early settlers in the area.

The Addison settlement was located on Section 26 of Corinth Township. Morehouse Sherman settled there in 1855. The house known as the "Addison stagecoach stop and post office" (below) was built in 1857 upon the arrival of Sherman's nephew Roswell Flower and family. George L. Cruikshank (right) took a claim near the forks of the Des Moines River in 1857. He ran a general merchandise store in Fort Dodge, served in the Civil War, and married Flower's daughter Esther. In 1868, the Cruikshanks built a home and general store in Dakota City. He was instrumental in building the Dakota City Methodist Church. After selling out in 1875 because of the default of Charles Bergk, the Cruikshanks moved to the Addison stagecoach stop.

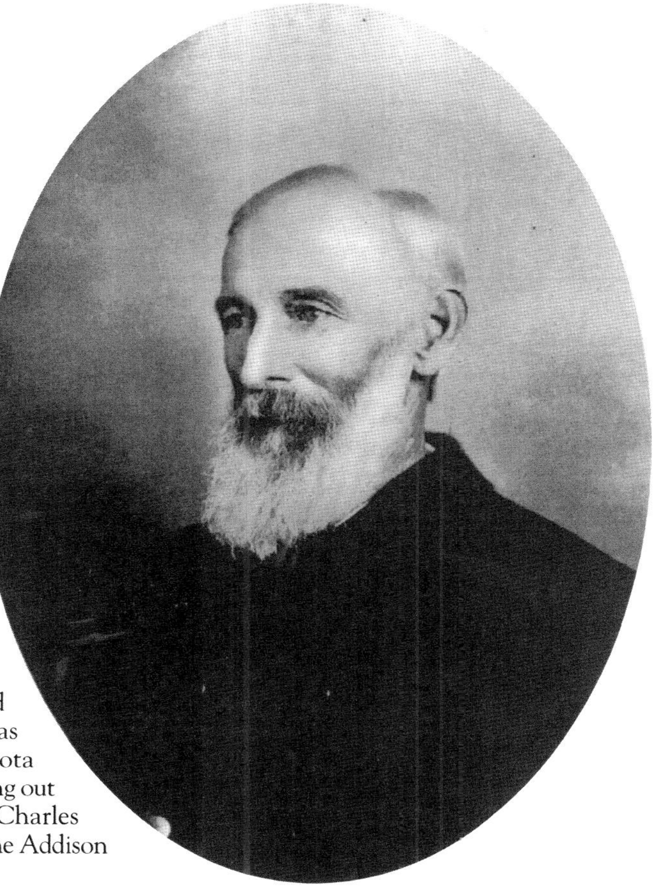

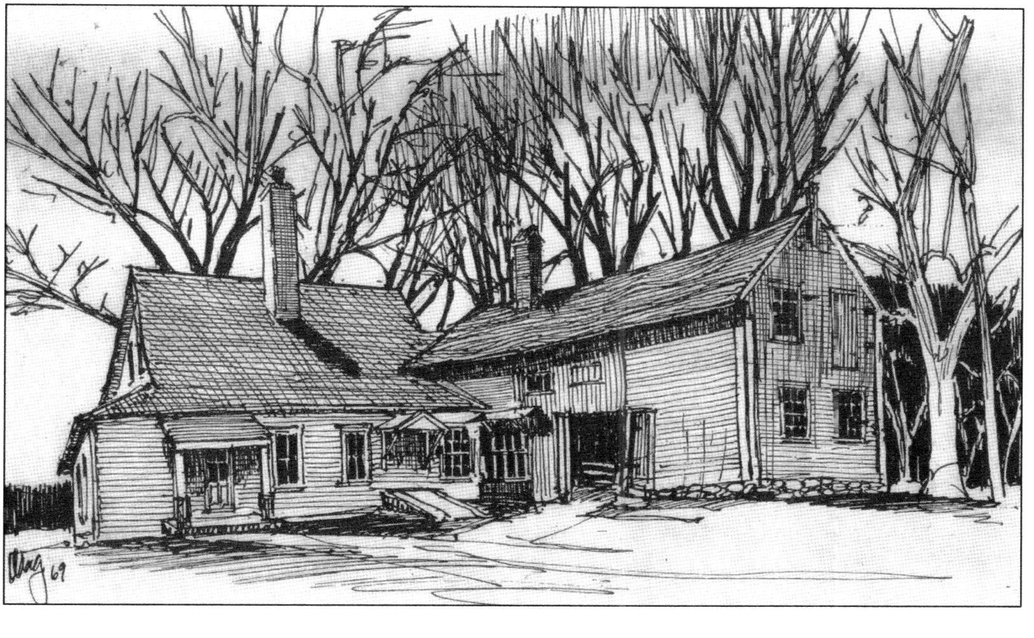

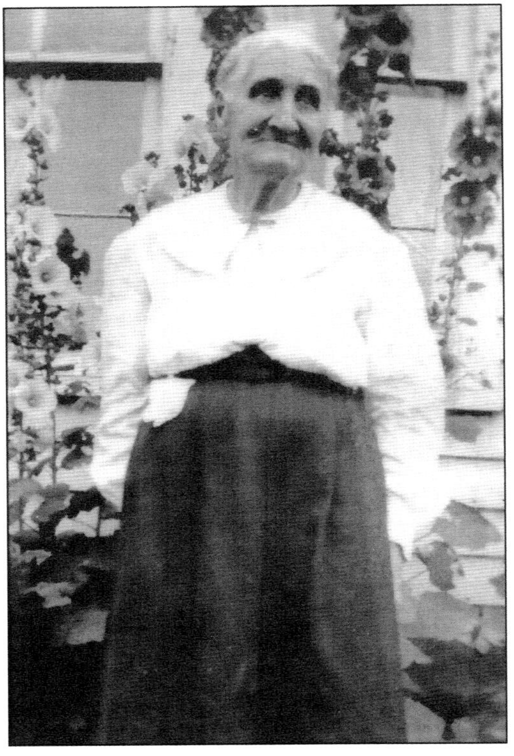

In 1856, Patrick Sheridan settled on Section 20 of Rutland Township, a flat, treeless section of prairie. His brothers and sister visited him as did Jacob and William Murray from his hometown in Ireland. He and Margaret Barton Sheridan (pictured) raised a large family. The town of Rutland grew up around them. Another settler in Rutland Township was Nathanial S. Ames, who served as county judge and supervisor.

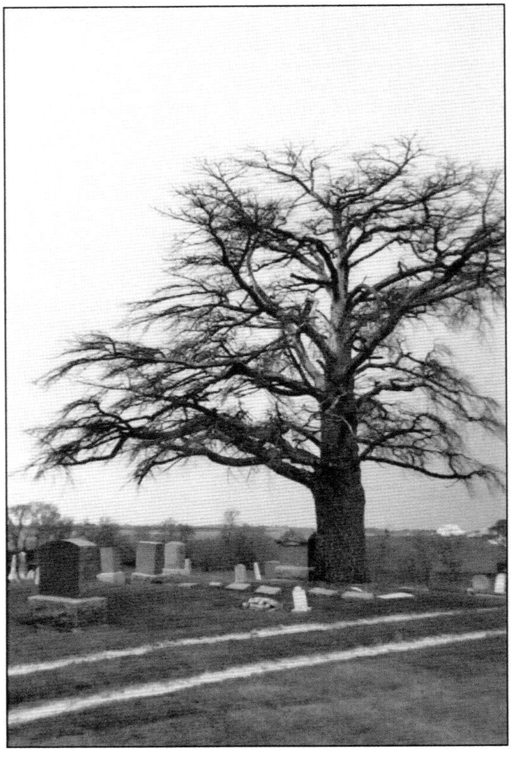

In the winter of 1855–1856, Quaker merchant Peter Collins, his children, and their families immigrated to a new region around Lott's Creek. Sons T. Elwood and Mahlon Collins laid out a town called Sumner. The Dr. Dearman Williams family and others of the Quaker faith joined them. The lovely Sumner Cemetery is now known as Livermore's Union Cemetery.

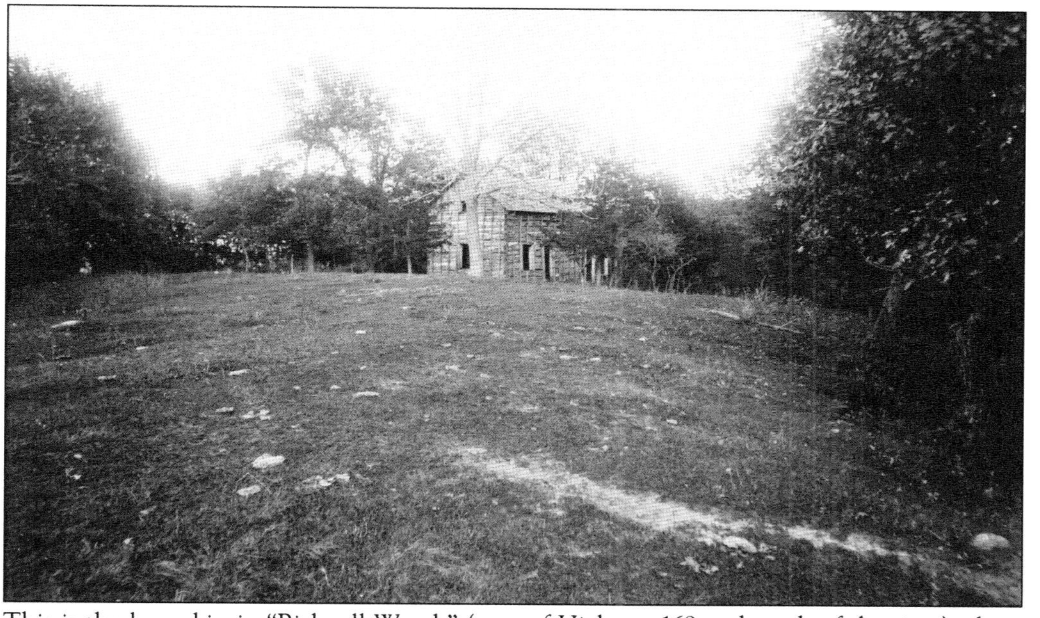

This is the log cabin in "Bicknell Woods" (west of Highway 169 and south of the river) where John Means arrived in the spring of 1856. Built with the help of Indians, this cabin was the first one in the area that later became the city of Humboldt. Eventually, John Johnston and his family arrived and lived in this cabin with Means. Maggie Johnston Duncan was born there in May 1859, the first child born in what was to become the city of Humboldt.

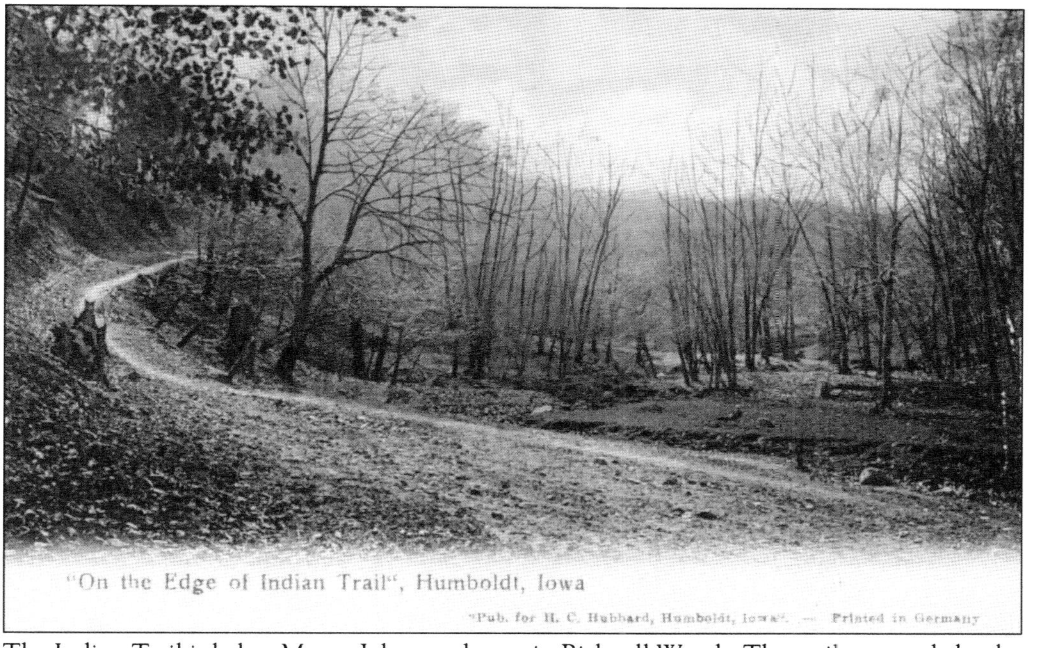

The Indian Trail is below Means-Johnston house in Bicknell Woods. The trail was made by the Native Americans and served as a popular hiking place for generations of Humboldt citizens until it was washed out in the 1970s. These photographs of Bicknell Woods were taken by Frank Bicknell in 1903 and made into postcards by H.C. Hubbard.

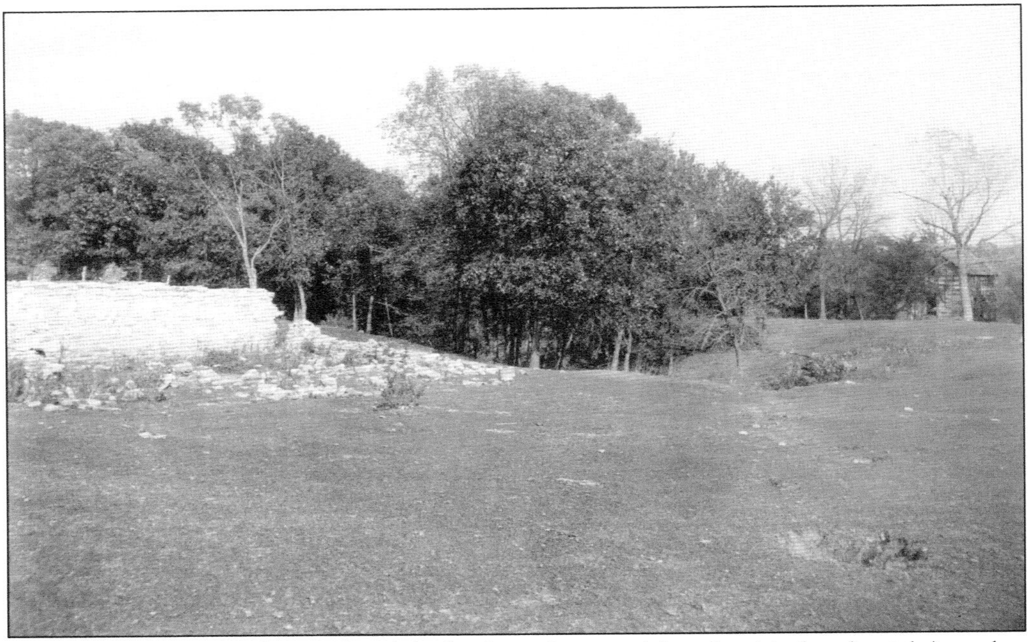

In the spring of 1856, John McKitrick built a log cabin near Means's cabin (on the right) at what was later called "ruin ridge" (pictured). McKitrick's family of five children joined him in July. John Farney lived with the McKitricks until he died in 1857. McKitrick tilled the soil and died in 1872. His widow, Margaret, married Robert Henderson, and together they raised three more children.

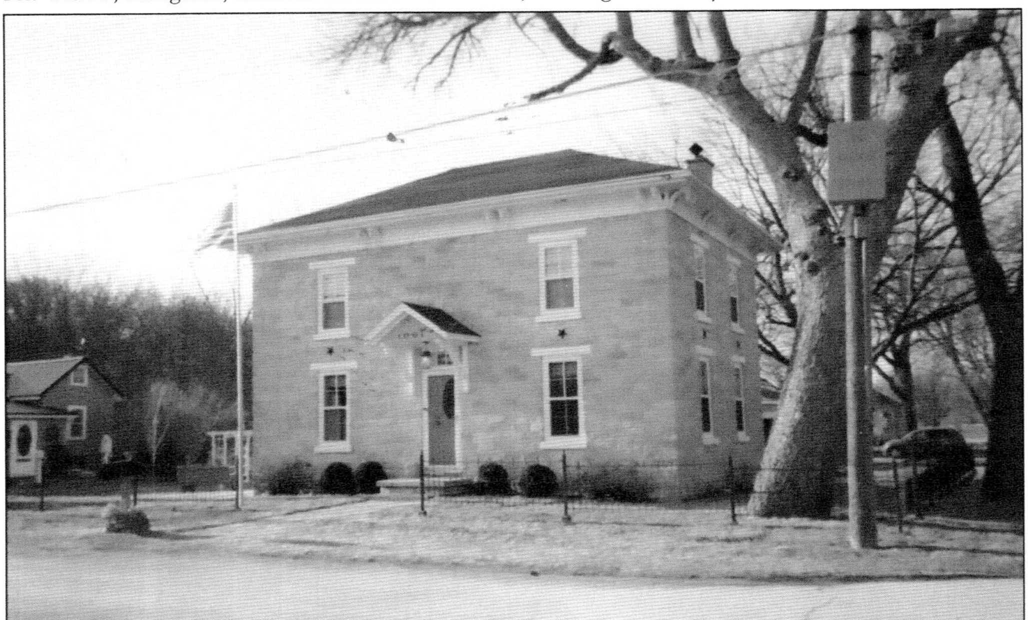

John Means moved from Bicknell Woods to the area known as "Brooklyn," located on the west side of the river and across from Taft's settlement of Springvale. Here, he built a limestone, two-story house in 1875 at 1001 Lewis Street, which was later restored by Ray Lindhart. During the 1881 flood, the water was up to the second-floor windows.

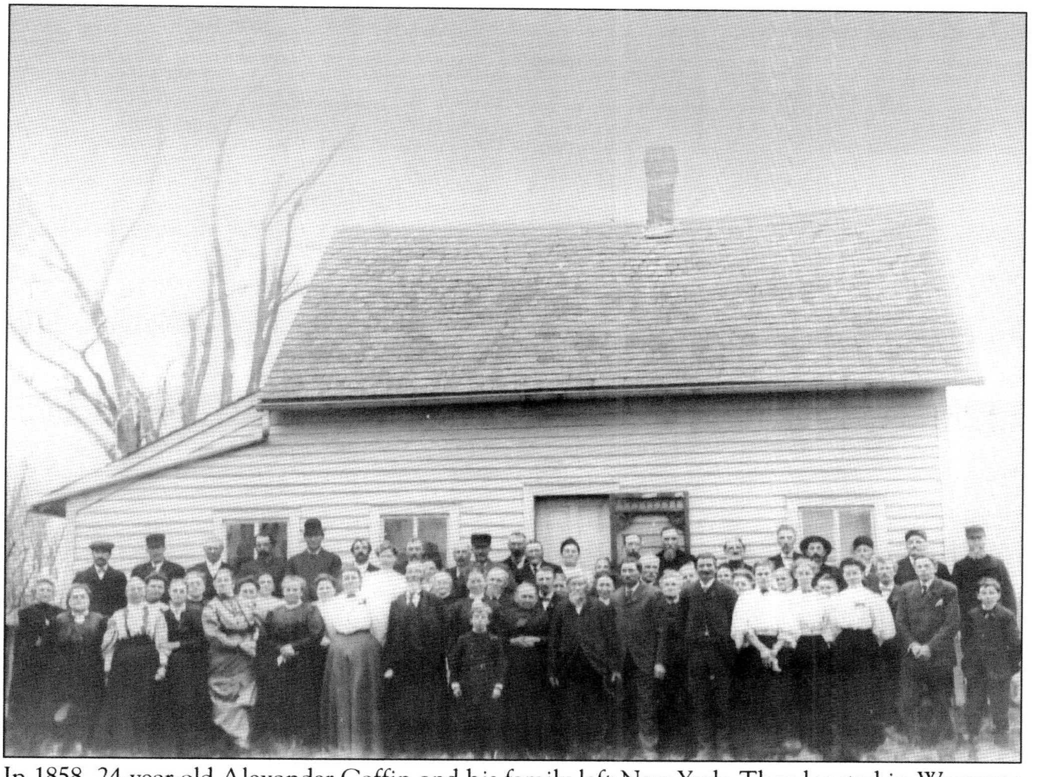

In 1858, 24-year-old Alexander Coffin and his family left New York. They located in Wacousta Township and built a wood-frame house, which was called the "white swan on a sea of grass" by early travelers. The Coffins celebrated their golden anniversary with 63 descendants in 1907. Other early settlers in Wacousta Township were Hiram Evans, Seth Sharpe, Abial Hoag, Ed Hammond, James Dean, John McNally, and James Struthers.

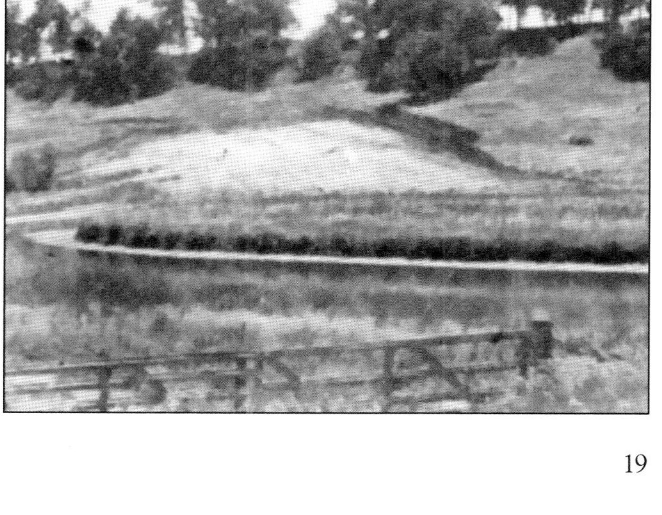

O.F. Avery settled on Avery Hill, located on the bluff west of Bradgate, in 1858. He not only served his community as a postmaster but also farmed, cut lumber for himself, built the first bridge in 1861, and erected the first schoolhouse in 1864. Albert M. Adams was the first teacher. Other early settlers were Peter McClellan, Charles Jarvis, Charles Sherman, and D.W. Rider. (Photograph from *Bradgate Centennial Book*.)

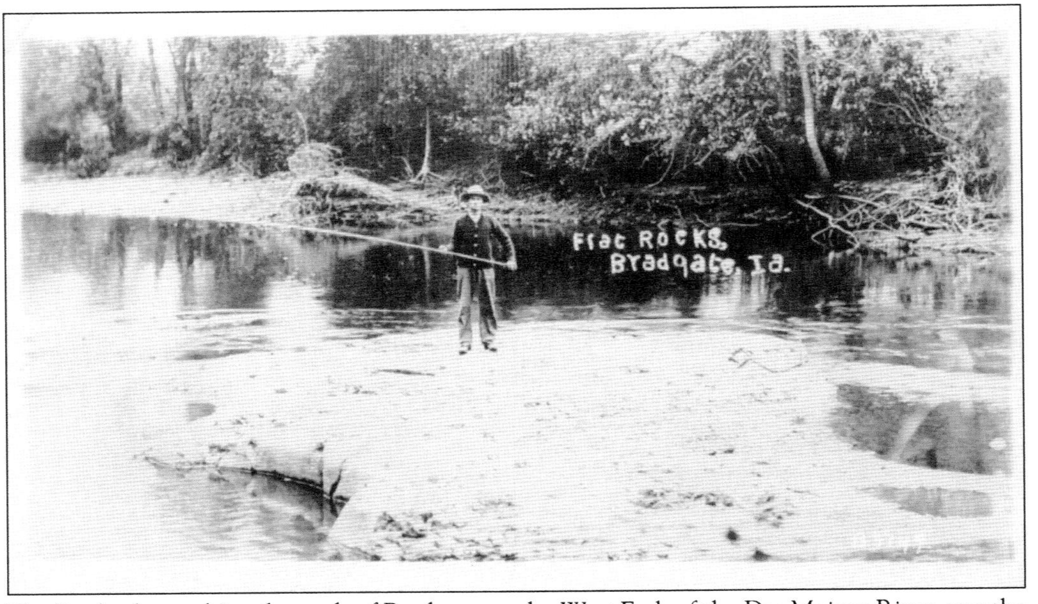

Flat Rocks, located 1 mile south of Bradgate on the West Fork of the Des Moines River, was the site of baptisms as circuit-riding preachers conducted worship services for early settlers. Humboldt County, which had at one time a total of 81 churches, now has 18 as congregations merged.

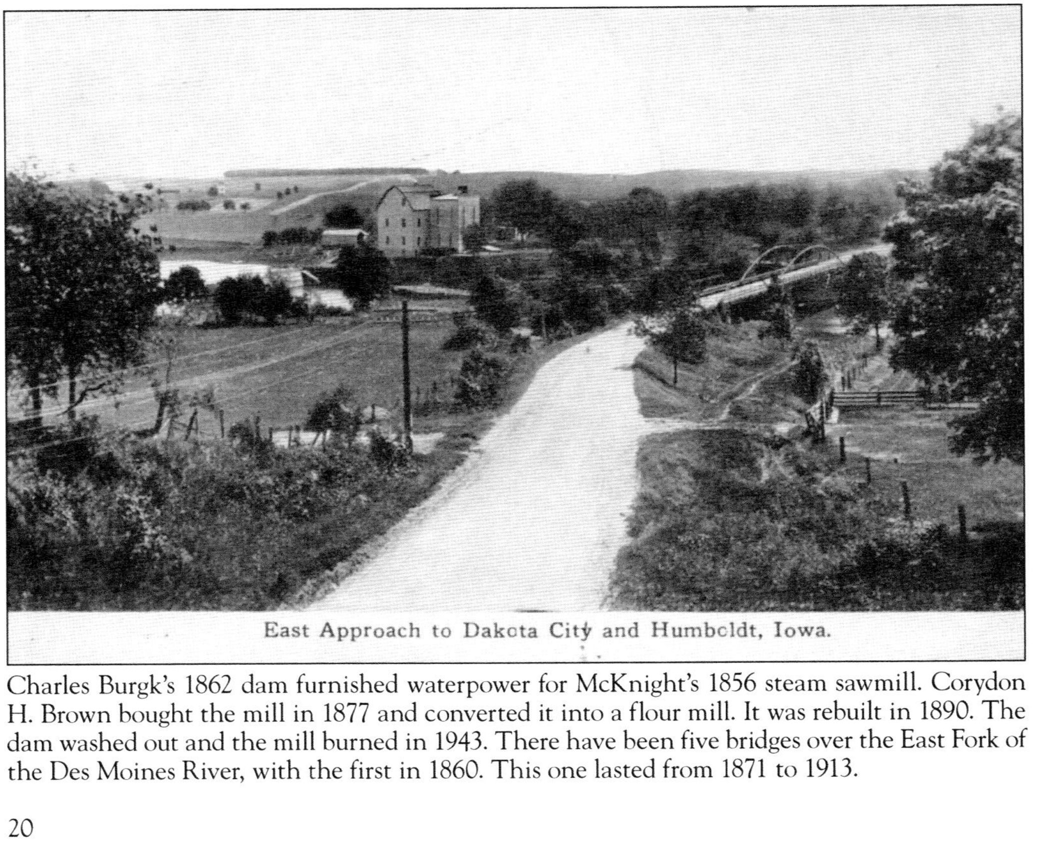

East Approach to Dakota City and Humboldt, Iowa.

Charles Burgk's 1862 dam furnished waterpower for McKnight's 1856 steam sawmill. Corydon H. Brown bought the mill in 1877 and converted it into a flour mill. It was rebuilt in 1890. The dam washed out and the mill burned in 1943. There have been five bridges over the East Fork of the Des Moines River, with the first in 1860. This one lasted from 1871 to 1913.

Two

Dakota City, County Seat

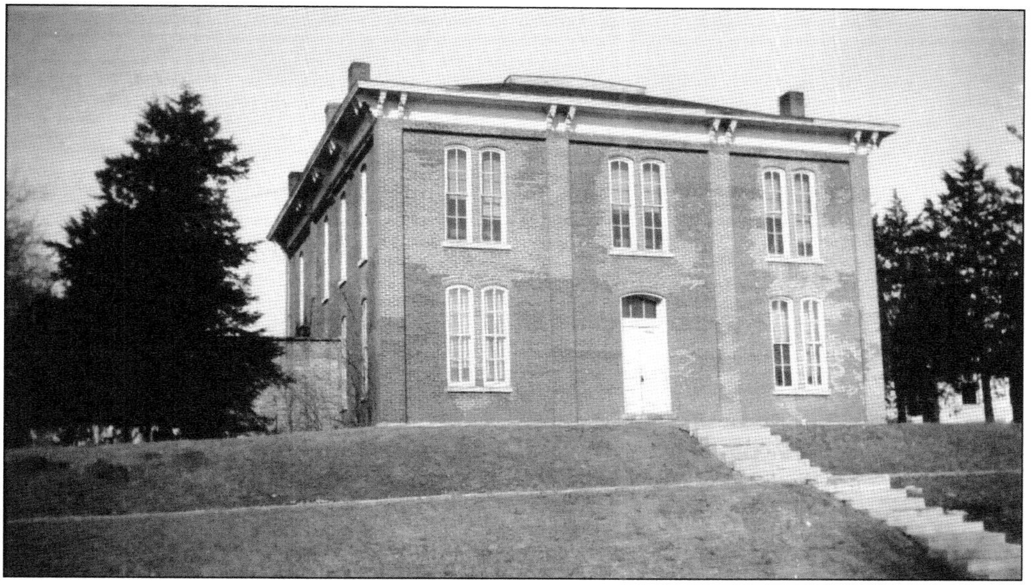

The first Humboldt County Courthouse was built of red brick in 1873 by William Thompson on the hill in Dakota City, overlooking Humboldt. Dakota City was settled in 1854 and became the county seat. In 1868, Taft's new colony in Springvale thought its town was a better county seat location because it was larger and did not sell intoxicating beverages. Several elections were held, and Dakota City won each time.

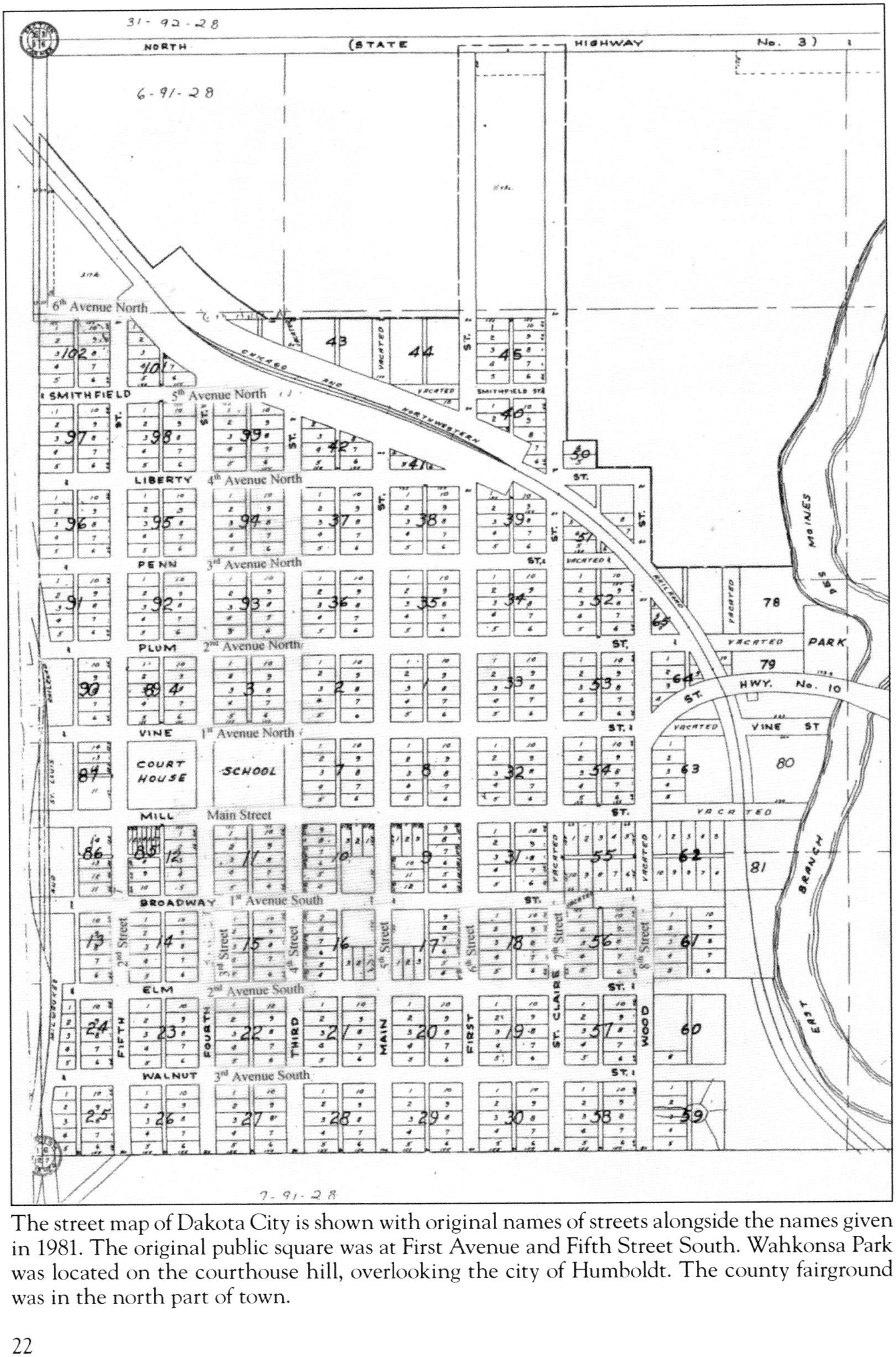

The street map of Dakota City is shown with original names of streets alongside the names given in 1981. The original public square was at First Avenue and Fifth Street South. Wahkonsa Park was located on the courthouse hill, overlooking the city of Humboldt. The county fairground was in the north part of town.

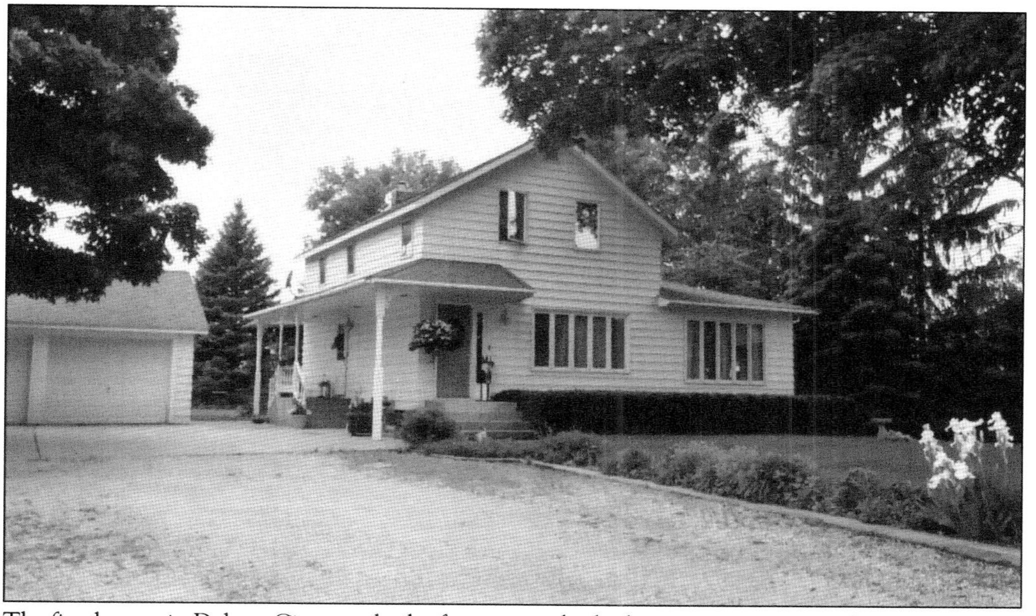

The first houses in Dakota City were built of green wood, which was sawn at McKnight's mill. Located at 22 South Sixth Street, the two-story stagecoach stop and hotel, shown as restored by Robert Eckberg, is included amongst some of the first structures in Dakota City. The hotel was operated by Washington and Albert Clark. The first baby born in Dakota City, named Dakota Clark, was born here. Washington Clark fought in the Civil War and was hung by the rebels as a spy.

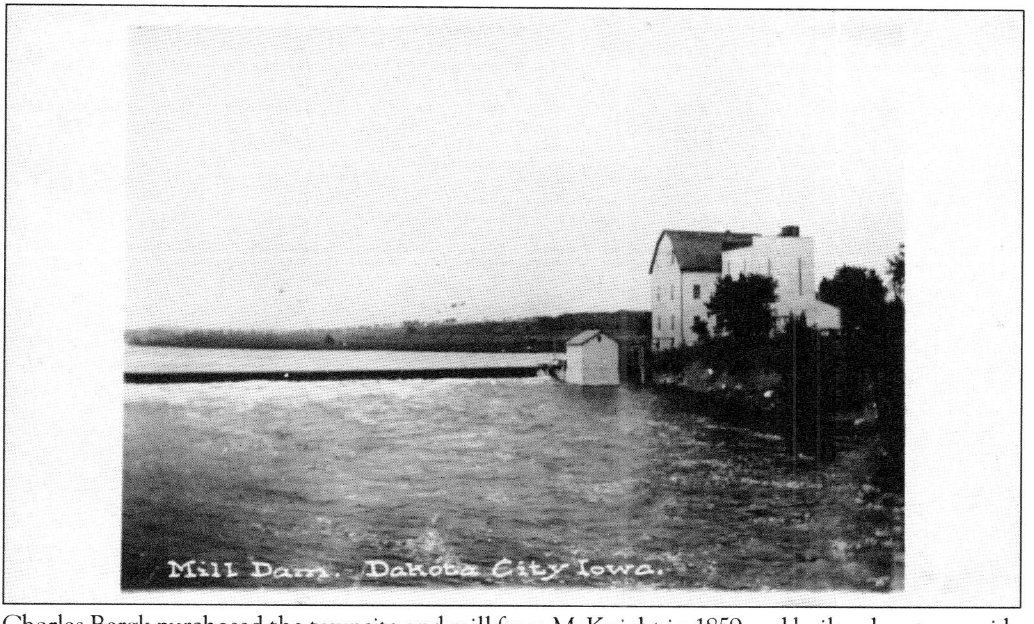

Charles Bergk purchased the townsite and mill from McKnight in 1859 and built a dam to provide waterpower for the mill. Charles and McKnight lived in the hotel while a town hall, stores, and more homes were added. New settlers were William Cragg, Charles Adelsberger, Walter Thomas, G.L. Hess, Henry Foster, Mr. Boswick, Egbert Hulbert, D.F Howell, J.M. Kelly, Alexander McLean, and B. Chauvet.

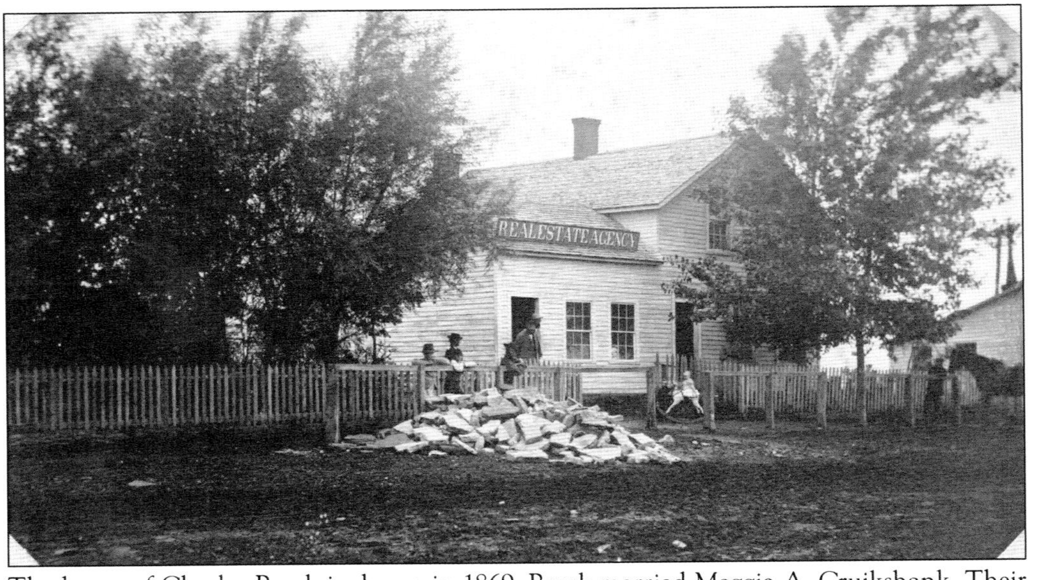

The home of Charles Bergk is shown in 1869. Bergk married Maggie A. Cruikshank. Their children were Kittie (on rocking horse), Carl (at head of horse), and Millie (born in 1870). Bergk was county treasurer and recorder. He owned most of Dakota City and sold lots to settlers. He lost all his holdings in 1874 due to mismanagement, gave everything to the county, and moved to California to start over.

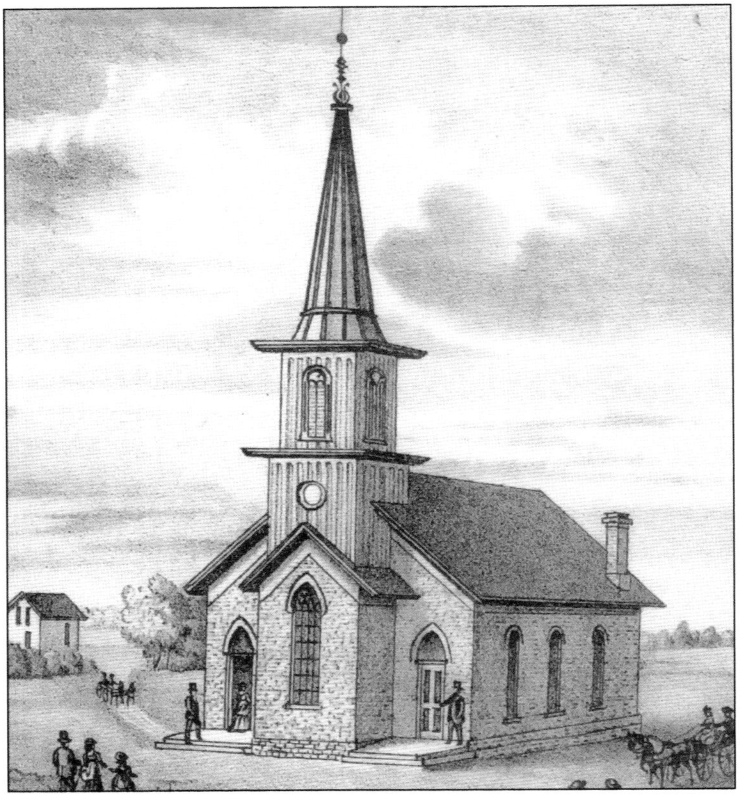

The Dakota Methodist Church was built in 1874. Local citizens donated labor and materials during the hard times. Located on the southwest corner of First Avenue and Fourth Street South, it was served by resident ministers until 1888, when it began sharing pastors with Humboldt. In 1892, the pastor began serving Humboldt only, and the Dakota church closed its doors in 1895. (A.T. Andreas's 1875 *Atlas of Iowa*.)

Albert M. Adams, mayor of Dakota City 1878–1886 and editor of the *Humboldt County Independent*, came to Humboldt County in 1864 with his father's family. During the Civil War, he enlisted twice, was held prisoner at Andersonville, and returned to Humboldt, where he settled on the printer's trade. He married Margaret Cheveaux Little.

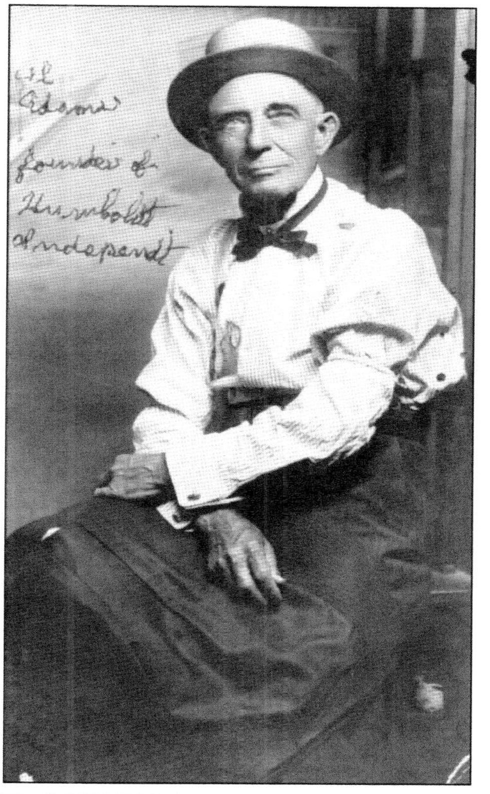

The office of the *Humboldt County Independent*, located at 306 Main Street, Dakota City, was built in 1875. Albert M. Adams bought the weekly newspaper in 1874 from Isaiah Van Metre and continued rivalry "newspaper wars" with the Humboldt newspapers. Adams is shown seated at left. Pictured with him are, from left to right, Will Cheveaux, Verne Baker, and A.E. Minion. In 1892, he relocated to 517 Sumner Avenue in Humboldt.

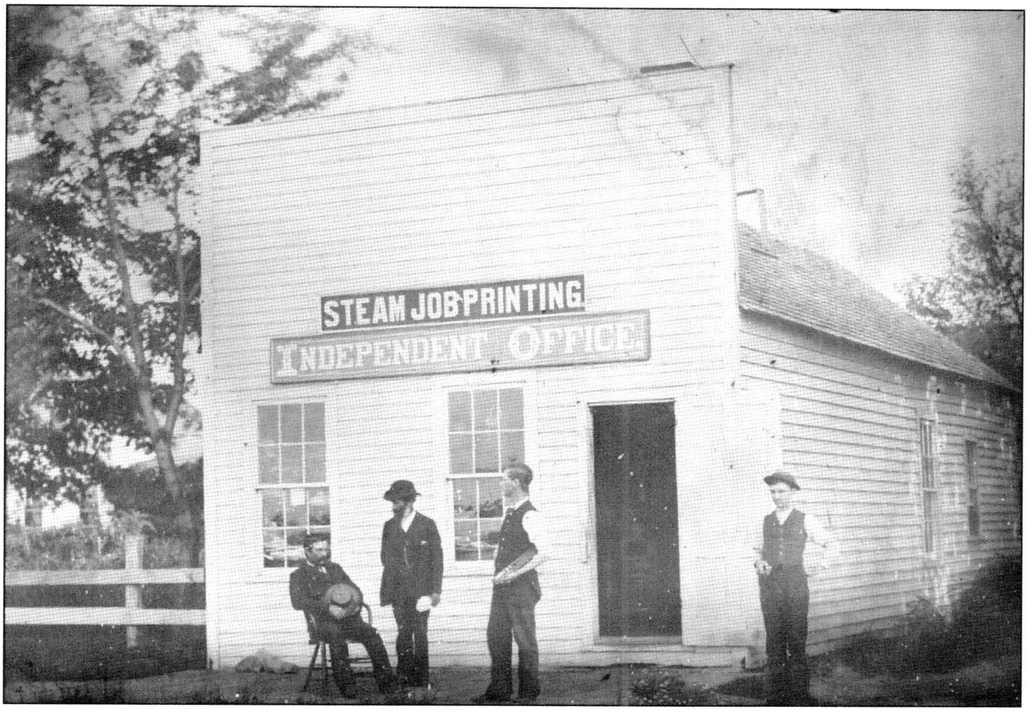

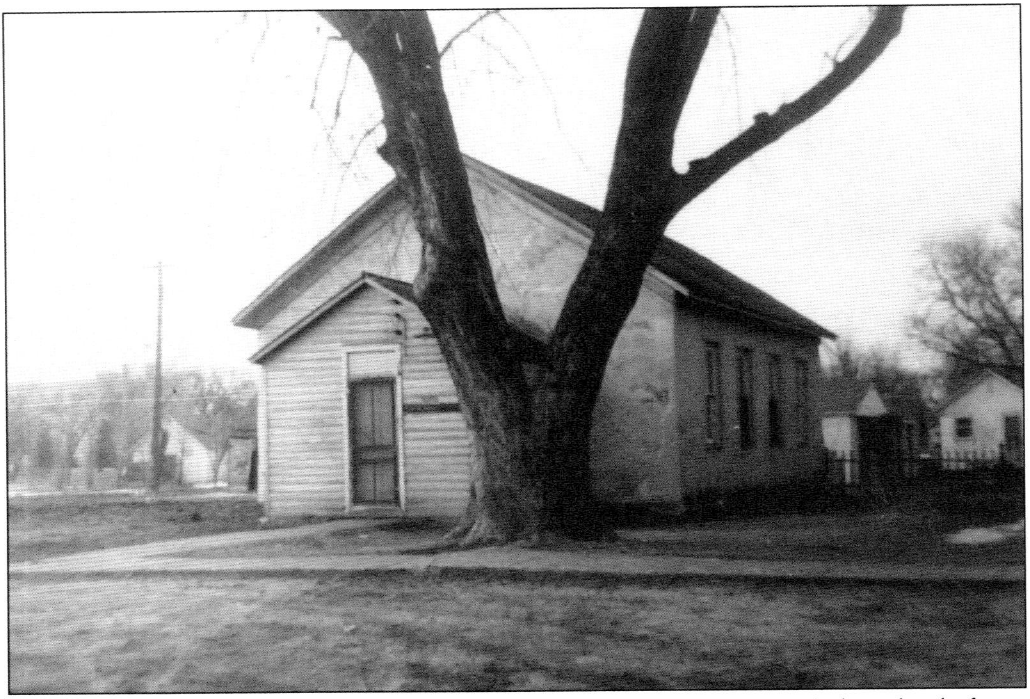

The first school in Dakota City was built of rough planking in 1857. In 1865, this school of pine lumber and brick was constructed on the northwest corner of First Avenue and Fourth Street South. After the red brick school was erected in 1881, this building was used for worship by the Zion Evangelical Church, North America, and was then sold to the Willing Workers. In 1919, it became the town hall.

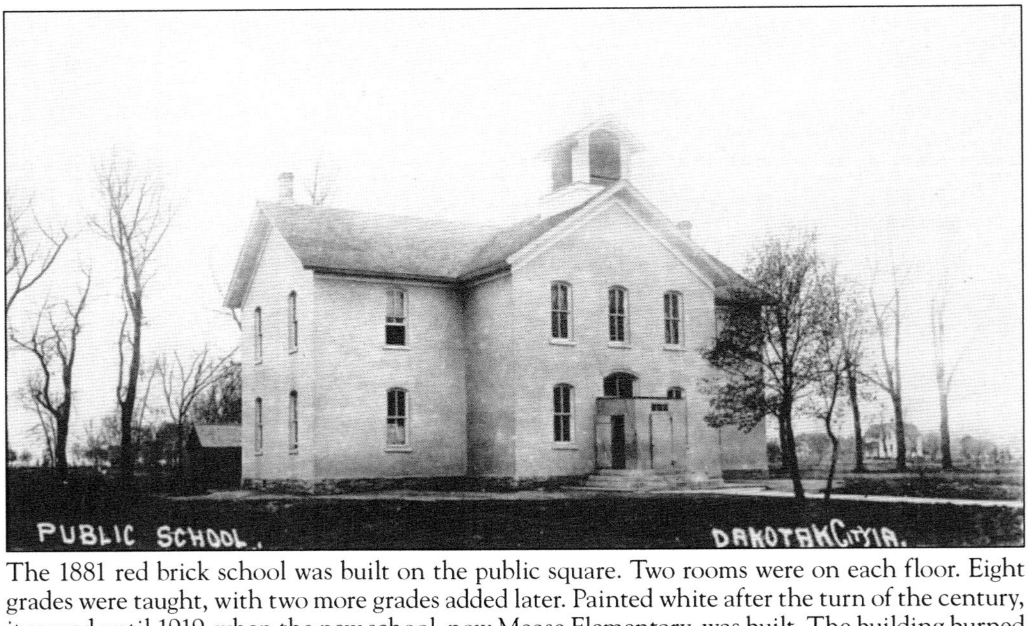

The 1881 red brick school was built on the public square. Two rooms were on each floor. Eight grades were taught, with two more grades added later. Painted white after the turn of the century, it served until 1919, when the new school, now Mease Elementary, was built. The building burned in 1931 with a fire so bright it looked as if all Dakota City was going up in flames.

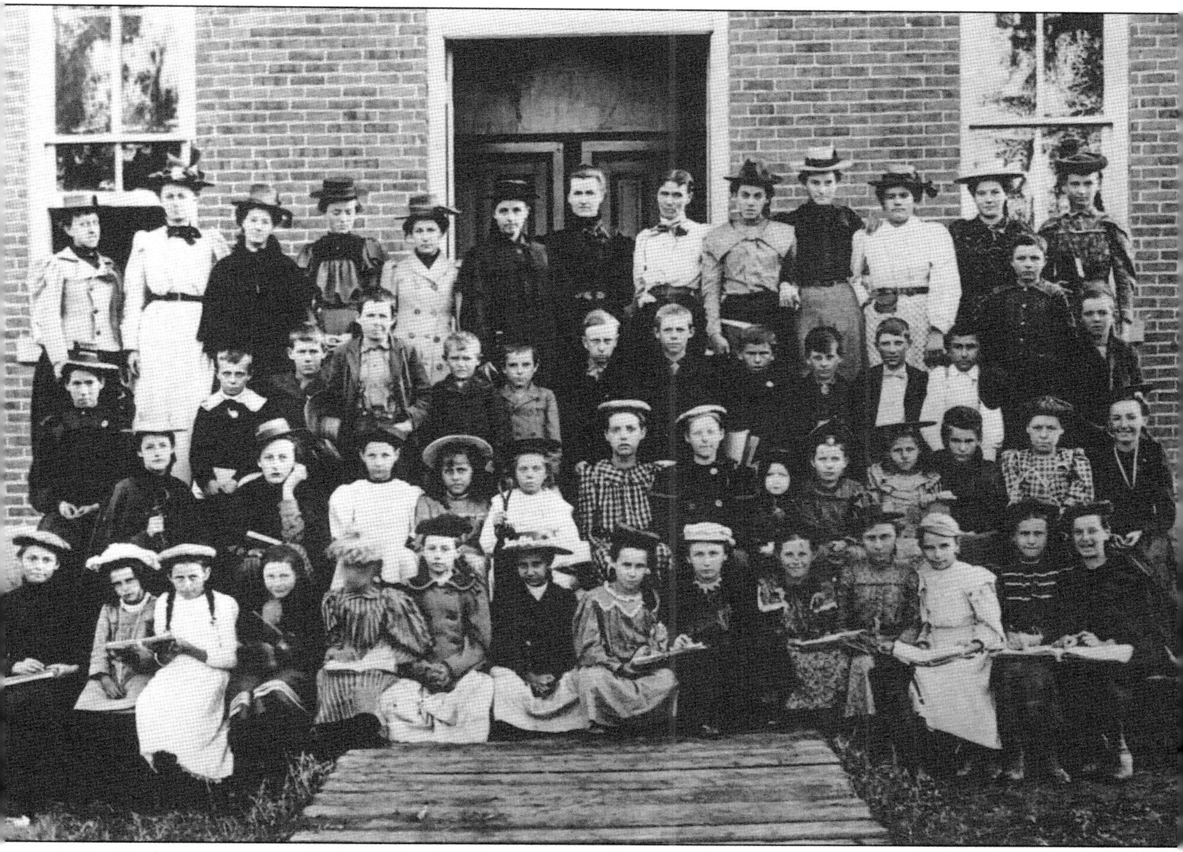

In 1898, the students of Dakota City's red brick school included, from left to right, (first row) Pearl Wagner, Jean Hawkins, Maggie Koob, Fay Clark, Olive Overholt, Frances Ketman, Alice Orvells, Hazel Fairman, Lucy Clark, Annie Volberding, Grace Bunker, Lulu Hawkins, Hannah Brodsack, and Lura Kendall; (second row) Florence Ketman, Juliet Hawkins, Rosa Koob, Alice Holyrod, Tena Torkelson, Ella Matott, Mariah Edge, Gracie Boothroyd, Mamie Volberding, Gertrude Buchholz, Lela Kendall, and Julia Buchholz; (third row) Fanny DeFoe, Roy Buckingham, Lawrence Smith, Stephen Boothroyd, Johnnie Clark, Vinus Kendall, Walter Orvells, George Ketman, Johnnie Brodsack, Lee McCord, Tory Taylor, James Simmons, Willie Edge, and Charley Torkelson; (fourth row) Harriet Orvells, Frances Fleming, Clara Volberding, Dora Buchholz, Ione Lowder, Susie Shaffer, Kate Barrett (teacher), Belle Simmons (teacher), Hattie Sherritt, Lizzie Heatherington, Lenna Kendall, Hannah Heatherington, and May Wagner.

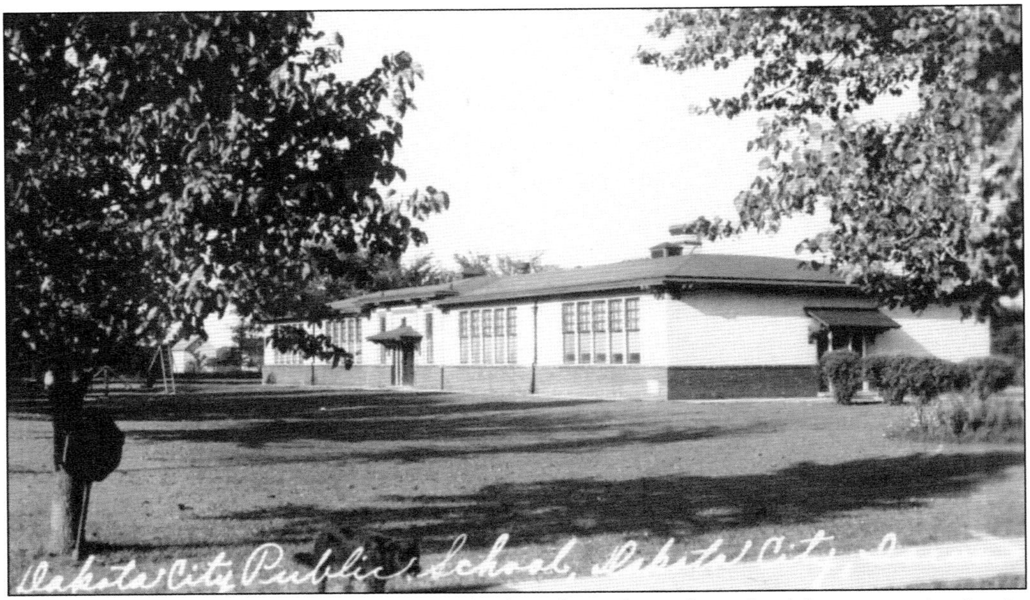

The Dakota City School was built in 1919 for first through tenth grade. After reorganization in 1958–1959, Dakota City became part of the Humboldt Community School District. A new wing was added to the school in 1963. In 1970, it was renamed the Clyde D. Mease Elementary School in honor of the retiring superintendent. Today, it houses preschool through the first grade.

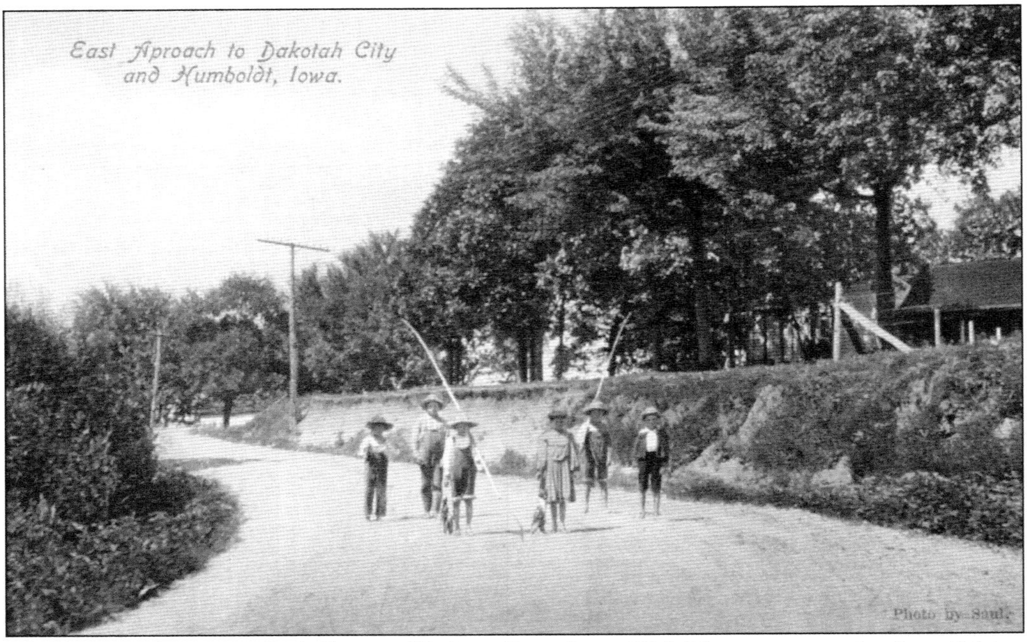

Children are shown on the hill east of Dakota City about 1905. They are returning from fishing in the East Fork of the Des Moines River. The road, named Mill Street in 1857 and renamed Main Street in 1981, was paved in 1920 when both this hill and the courthouse hill were made less steep.

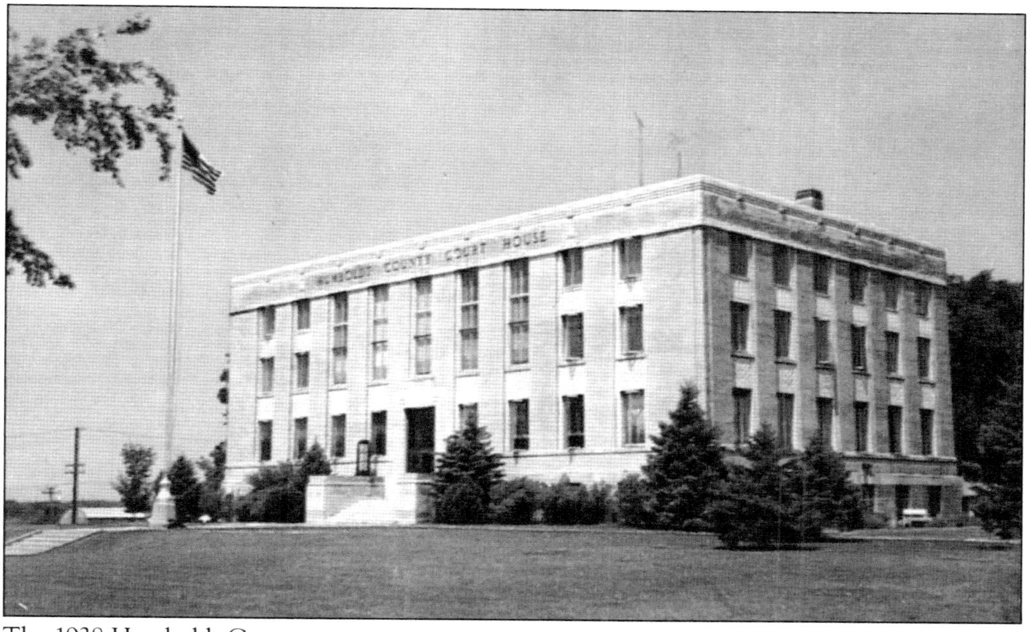

The 1938 Humboldt County Courthouse was erected with the aid of federal funds. It was restored and placed in the National Register of Historic Places in 2003. Today, it houses county offices, courtrooms, rooms for district judge Kurt Stoebe, and human services. A central law enforcement center is shared between the county and city of Humboldt in Humboldt. The county engineer's office and county conservation offices are located on Highway 3.

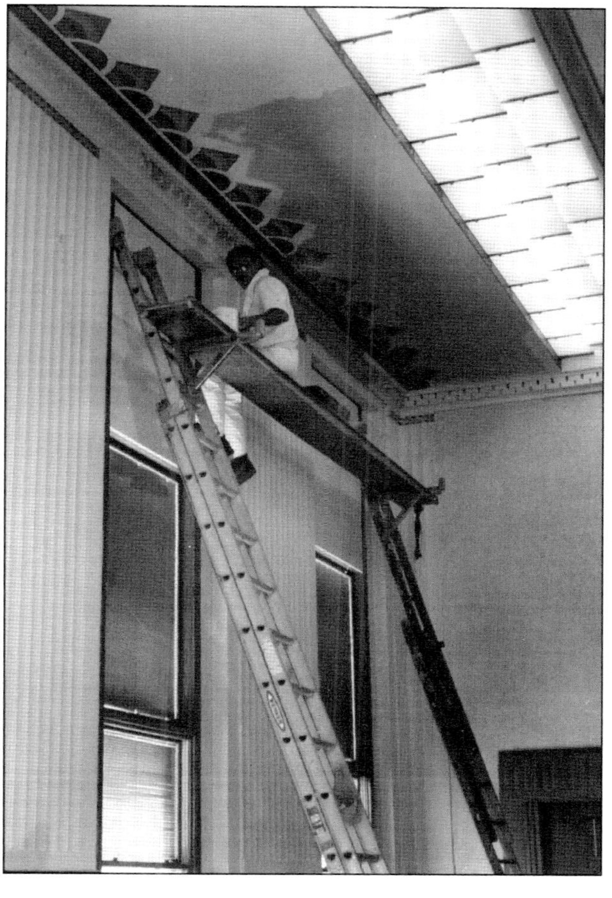

Humboldt County has one of the most beautifully appointed courthouses in Iowa. Painter Mike Opheim is shown restoring the Art Deco paint on the courtroom ceiling during the summer of 1996. Unique solid-bronze light fixtures, once placed on each side of the front door of the courthouse but sold by county officials during earlier redecorating, were found and returned. (Courtesy of Donna Day.)

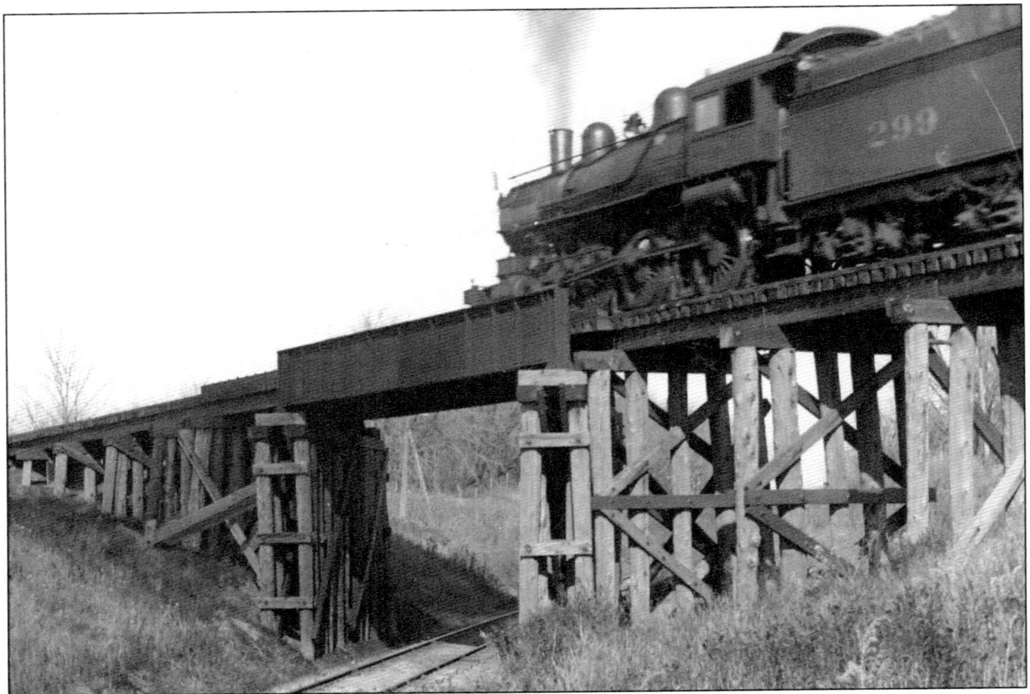

The Chicago & Northwestern train from Dakota City is shown crossing over the Minneapolis & St. Louis railroad tracks in north Humboldt. The Minneapolis & St. Louis railroad came in 1879, after over a decade of efforts to secure it. "Humboldt" signs were posted on both ends of the station, although it was located on the Dakota City side of the line between the towns. It was rebuilt in 1914 for crowds coming to see Frank Gotch wrestle. Pictured below is the Chicago & Northwestern station in Dakota City. The railroad came through Dakota City beginning in 1881. There were four passenger trains per day. Freight trains carried livestock and the catalogue merchandise ordered by Humboldt County citizens. Basil Koob, station agent, took these photographs.

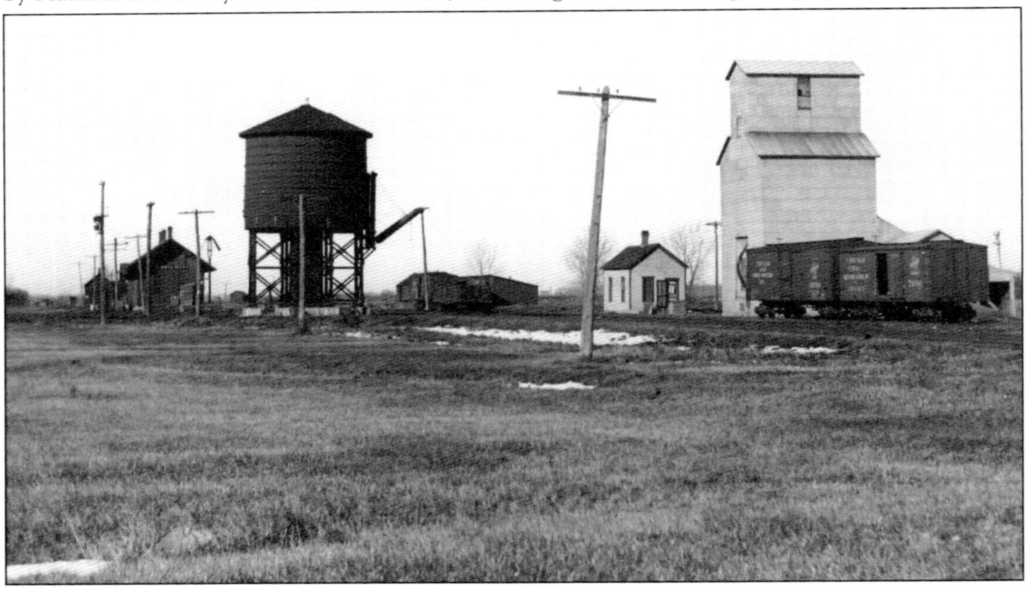

John T. Fockler's Drugstore, 412 Main Street, Dakota City, was built in 1872. Dr. James C. Sprague's office was upstairs. A.W. McFarland bought the building in 1883. His drugstore was downstairs, and his law office was upstairs. In 1930, the post office was moved onto the main floor, with Don Sawyer's law office upstairs. In 1976, the building was torn down. The Veterans of Foreign Wars (VFW) Hall is there now.

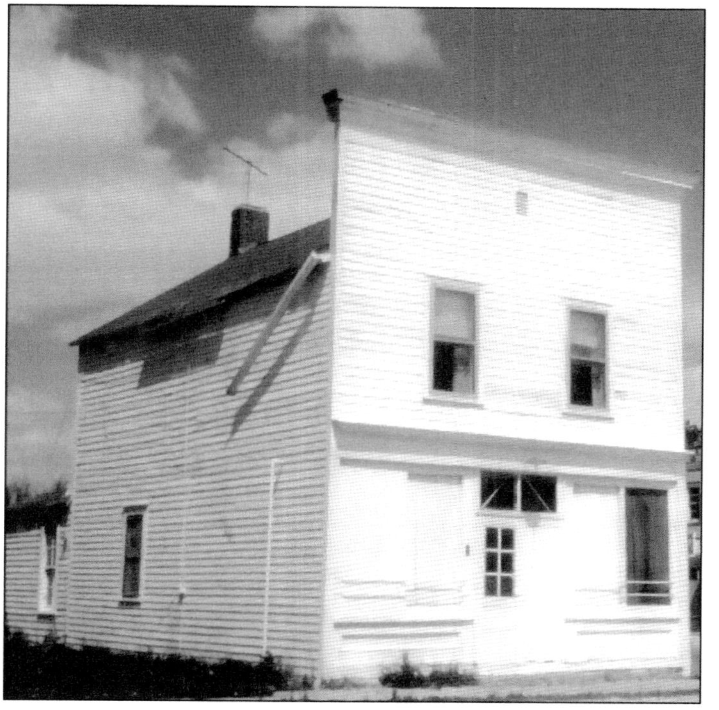

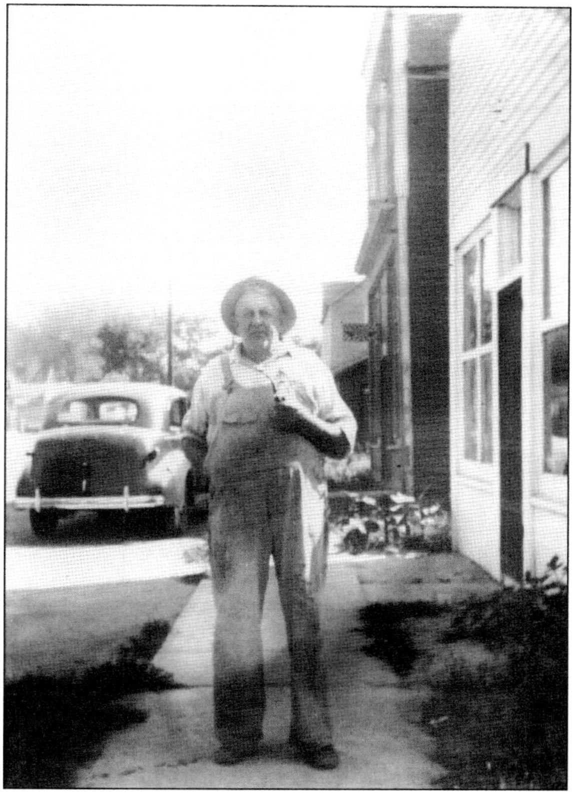

J.D. Craig was the mayor of Dakota City from 1940 to 1943. He oversaw the growth of the town after the highway came through and gas stations and cafés flourished. This snapshot was taken by Don Sawyer on the 400 block of the south side of Main Street, looking east. The man pictured is next to Boothroyd's Meat Market and Brodsack's Barbershop, where kids could get a haircut for 25¢.

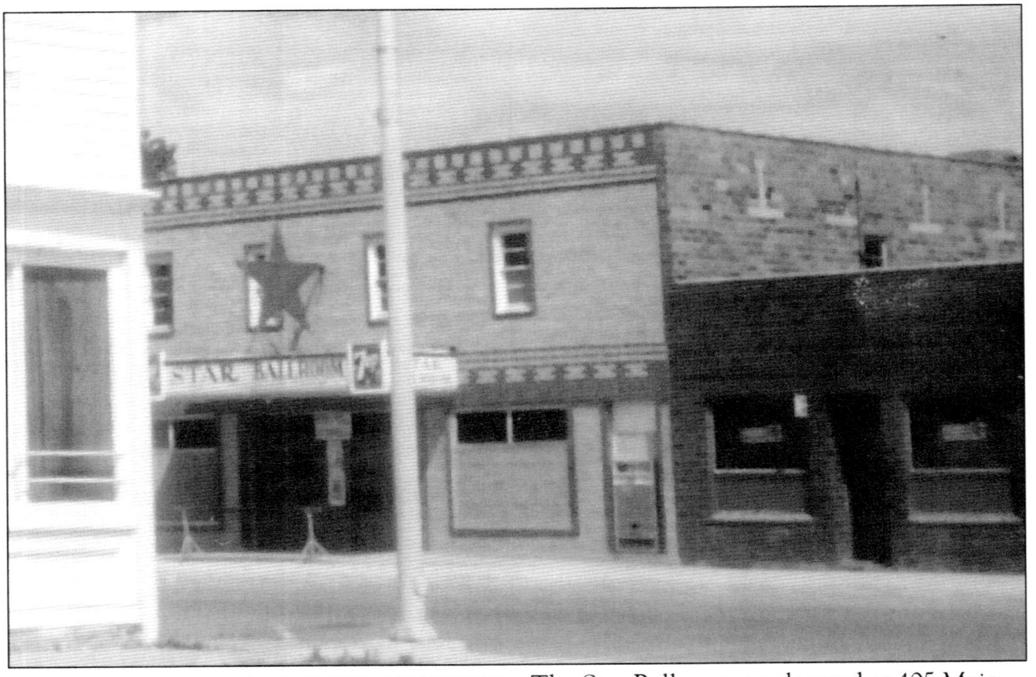

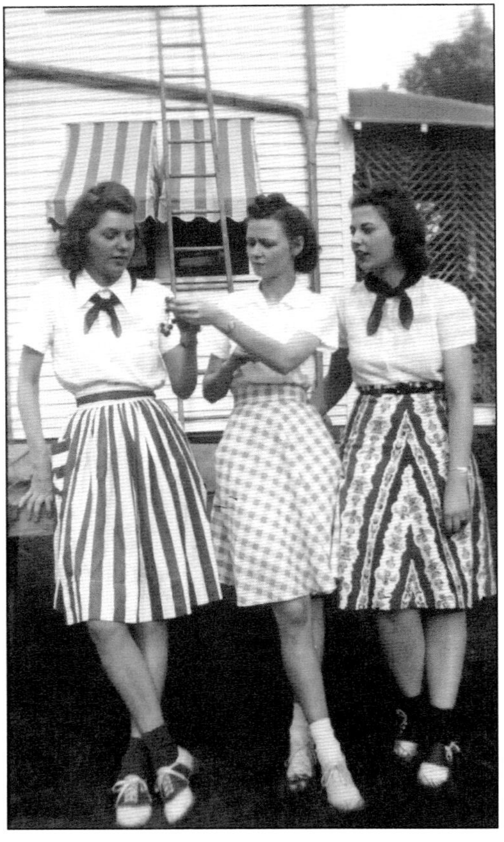

The Star Ballroom was located at 405 Main Street. In 1946, Otto Schultz built what he wanted to be a theater; however, it turned out to be a very popular dance hall. Here, Louis Armstrong, Lawrence Welk, and Stan Kenton played to enthusiastic audiences. In 1975, Al Hadar bought the ballroom. The last dance was in 1992. It currently houses Melinda's School of Dance.

From left to right, Ruth Lindhart, Sonya Sawyer, and Donna Lothian model fashions worn in 1940. Nearly every home had a sewing machine. Girls learned to sew from their mothers at home and Girl Scout troops, 4-H Clubs, and home economics classes in the schools. Fabrics were sold in dry goods stores and at White Department Store.

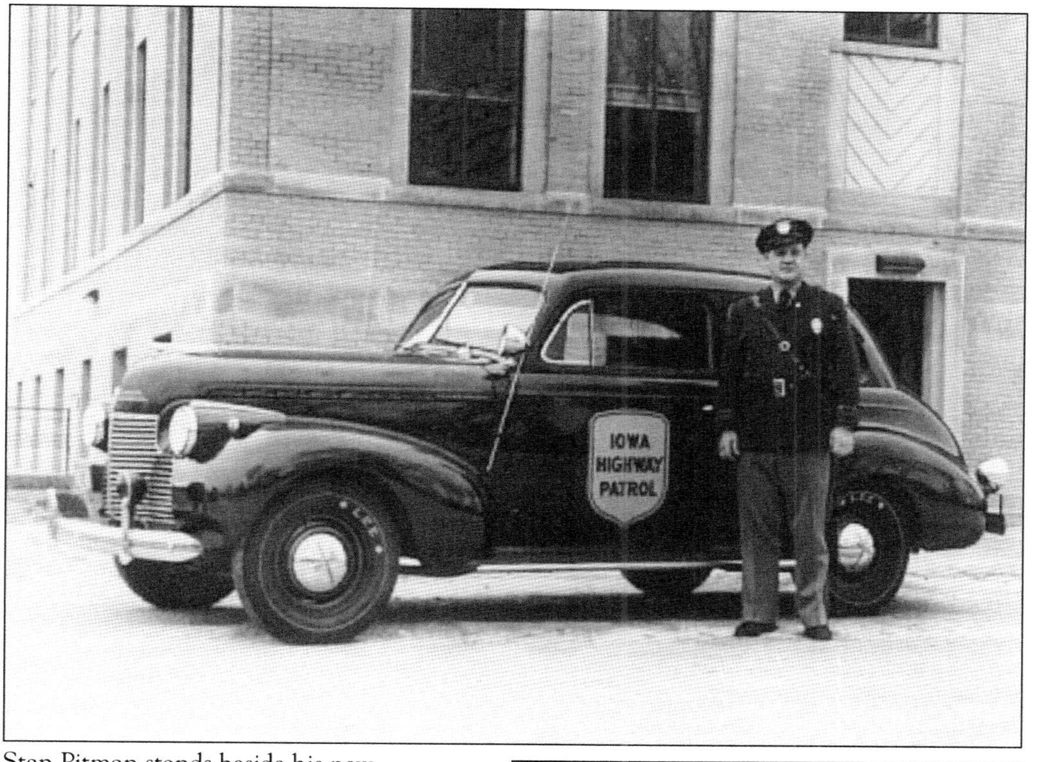

Stan Pitman stands beside his new Iowa Highway Patrol car in 1940. Other Highway Patrol officers at the time included L.W. Dickinson and Hugh Short, who patrolled the roads on his motorcycle. Headquarters for the patrol were located in the new Humboldt County Courthouse in Dakota City.

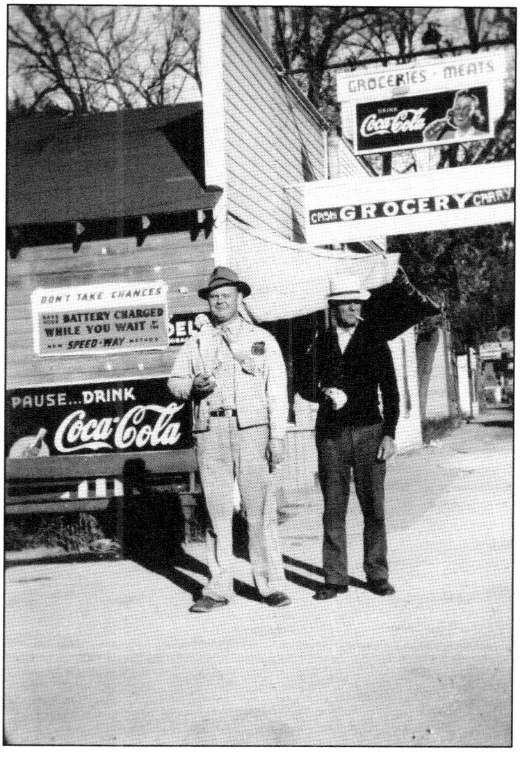

Don Sawyer (left) and Walt Hawkins stand by Ulrich Grocery in Dakota City. Don, a lawyer, had a service station at 501 Main Street. In 1940, gasoline was one-half cent per gallon wholesale. Walt had a bakery and jewelry store. For a few months, Byron Fjetland operated Byron's Blue Front Grocery east of Sawyer's station. During World War II, Elmer and Zula Ulrich had their grocery store in that building.

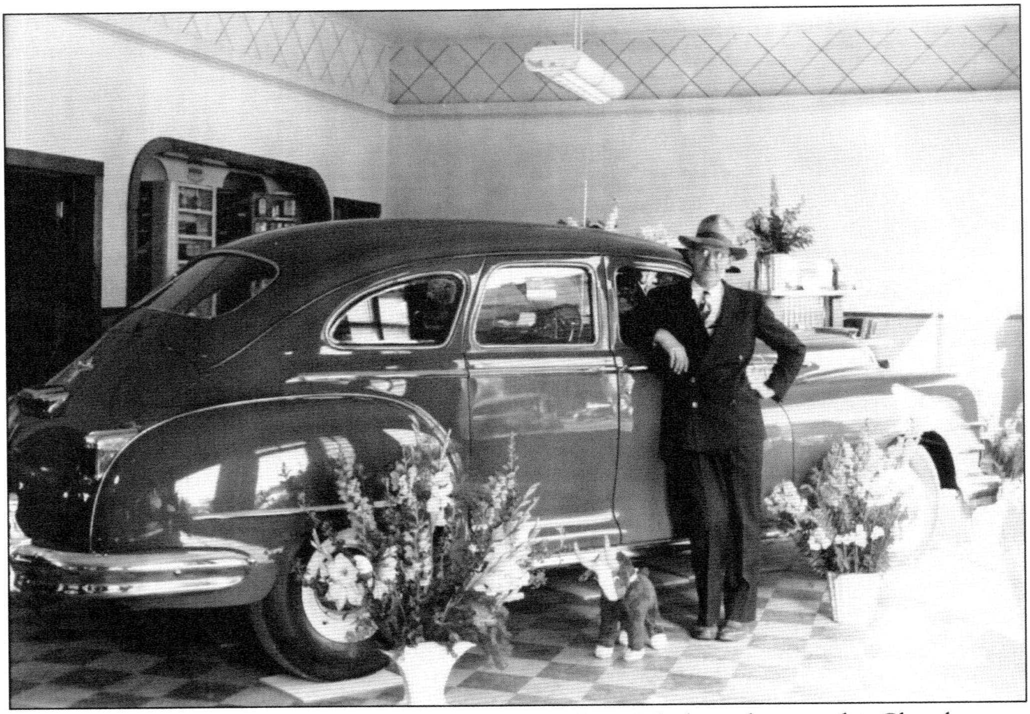

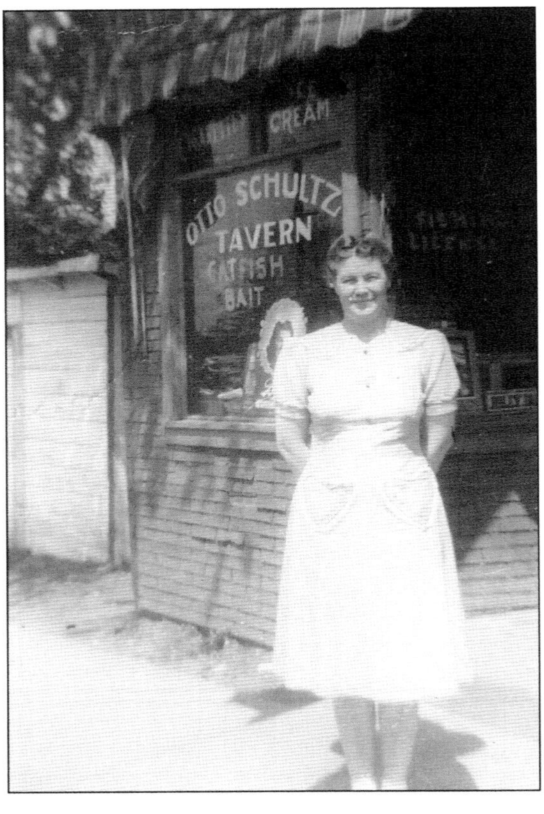

Otto Schultz is shown at his Chrysler-Plymouth dealership at 403 Main Street. In the 1920s, Schultz operated a small food stand in the Dakota City Park and took lunches out to nearby farms to sell. During the 1930s and 1940s, Schultz began buying lots on the north side of Main Street at $100 per lot. He constructed a total of seven brick buildings, thus ensuring the survival of Dakota City

Evelyn Lehman worked at Otto Schultz's Tavern in the late 1930s. One could get a fishing license, catfish bait, ice cream, and cigarettes as well as a beer and a good meal. This is now the center section of Vinny's BBQ. The east part of the restaurant was built in 1936, and the west addition was made in 2008.

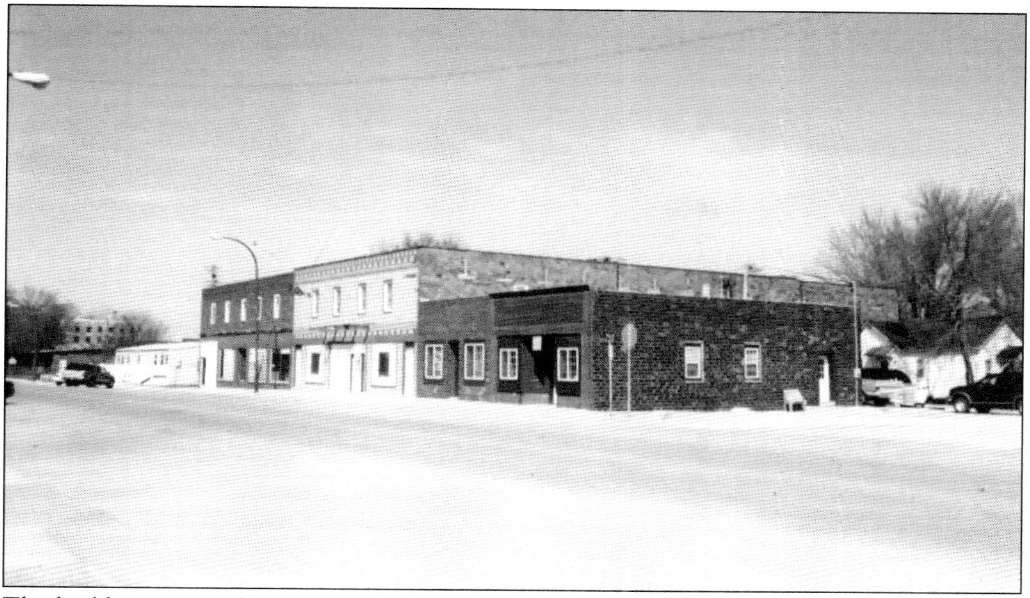

The buildings erected by Otto Schultz in the 400 block, shown in 2008, have housed many businesses. Currently, from left in the distance are the courthouse, Mease School, and Head Start. In Otto's buildings are Roller Country, which was the auto dealership; Melinda's Dance Studio, which was the Star Ballroom; a vacant building, which was a tavern; and Busy Bee Day Care, which was a grocery.

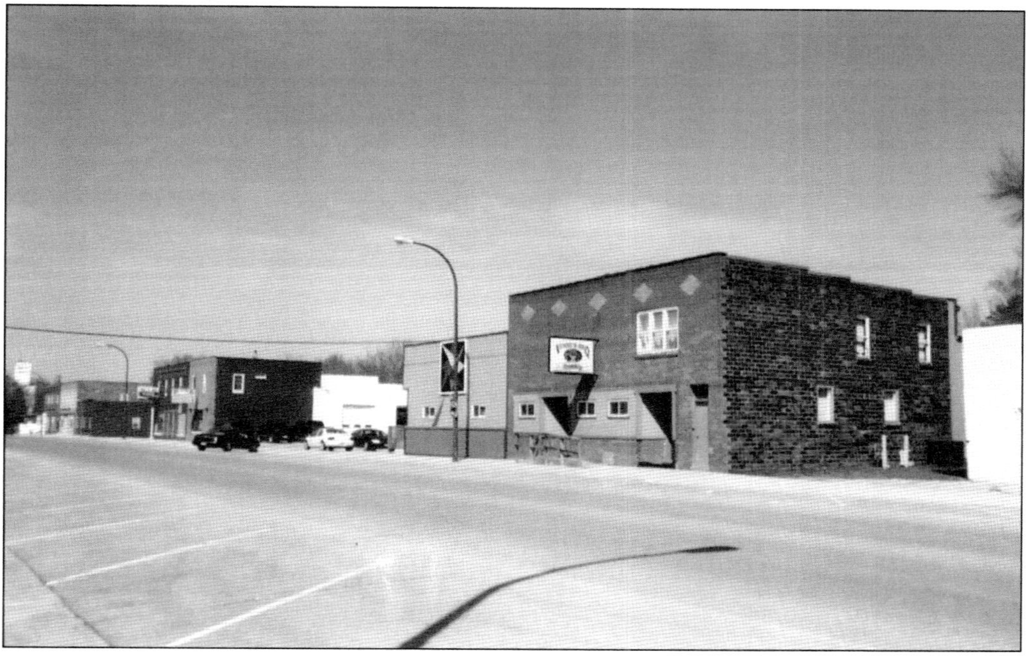

Otto Schultz's buildings in the 500 block are shown in 2008. At left is Treasures and Trinkets Boutique, which used to be a grocery. Next, B and B Sales and Service used to be a hardware store. Right of that is a parking lot, which used to be Vera Miller's Cream Station with the old jail behind it. At far right is Vinny's BBQ, formerly Gordy's, and before that Carl Weigert's Café.

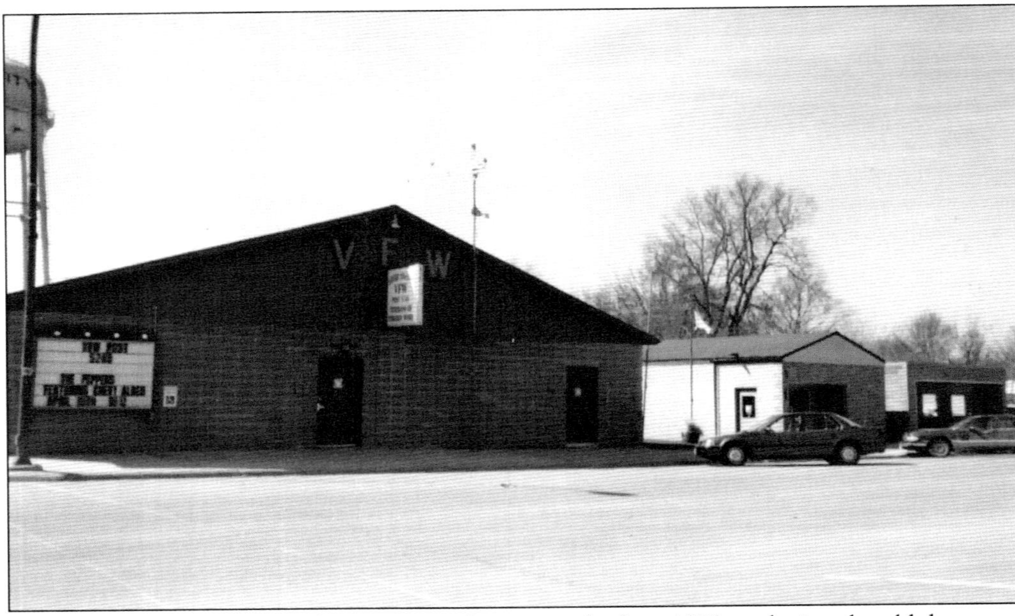

The VFW Hall (left), located at 412 Main Street, was built in 1978, replacing the old drugstore. Also on Main Street were buildings for the post office (408) and Materials Lab (406), both built by the Naeve family. Elwin Hodges had his office for the department of social services there, and later, Yogi's Palace, an antique store, occupied the building. Fancy Pants Women's Clothing Store and then Marso's Ice Cream Store were also located there.

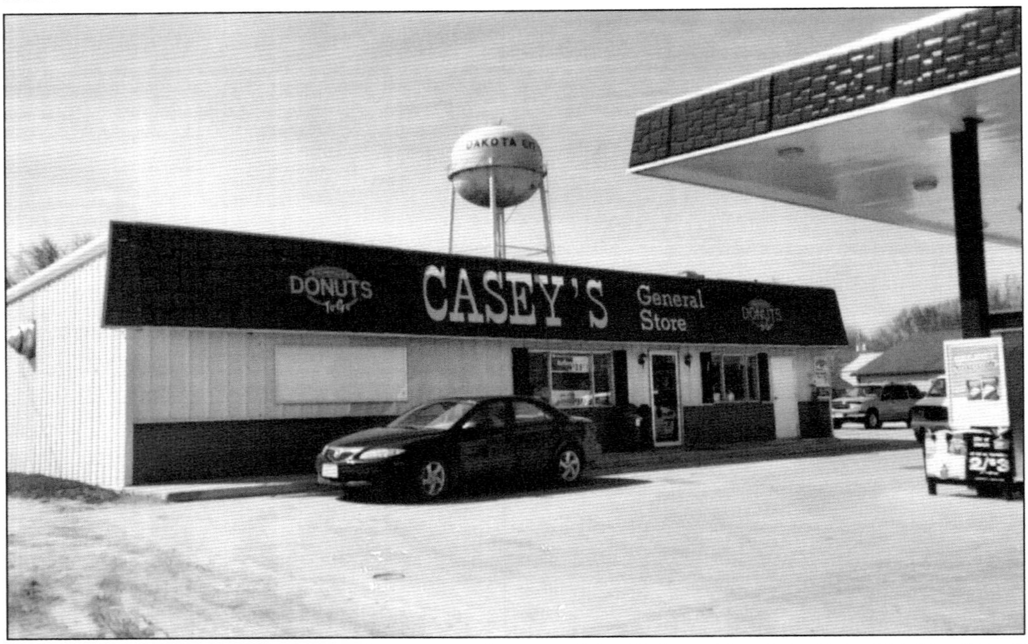

Casey's corner store at 502 Main Street was the site of the Dakota Hotel, built in 1872 by "Doc" Daniel P. Russell. He had trouble finding a manager for the large two-story L-shaped brick hotel that boasted a dining room and stables. In 1876, a fire of questionable origin was put out by the prompt arrival of neighbors; it was the only one of six Russell hotels that did not burn to the ground.

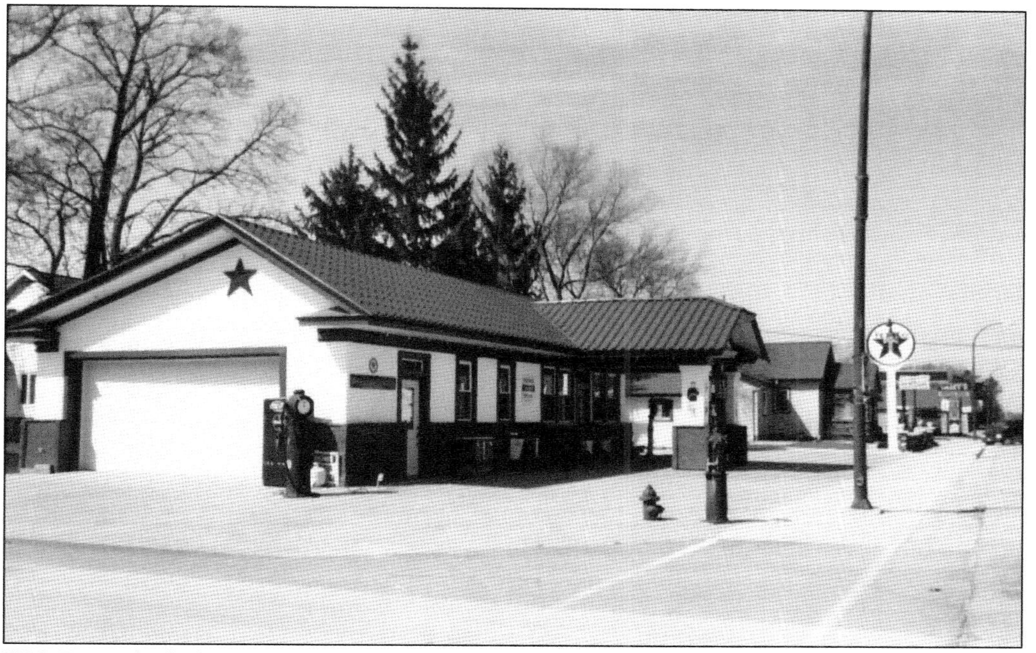

W.O. Brown built the Texaco Station before 1920 for his son Ted. It was one of the first architecturally designed gas stations west of the Mississippi. During Prohibition, there was bootlegging in the basement. Ted died in 1935, and several owners ran the station. After 2000, Pete Holt, who collected gas station memorabilia, restored the station and turned what had been an eyesore into a very popular attraction.

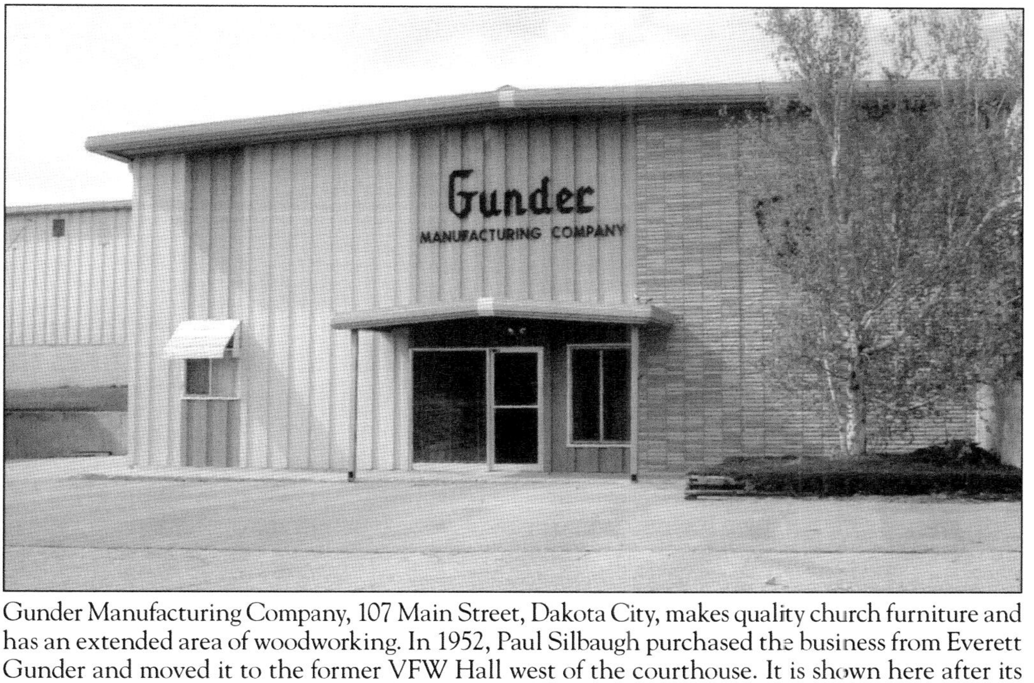

Gunder Manufacturing Company, 107 Main Street, Dakota City, makes quality church furniture and has an extended area of woodworking. In 1952, Paul Silbaugh purchased the business from Everett Gunder and moved it to the former VFW Hall west of the courthouse. It is shown here after its second addition in 1968. The plant employs about 25 workers. (Courtesy of Silbaugh family.)

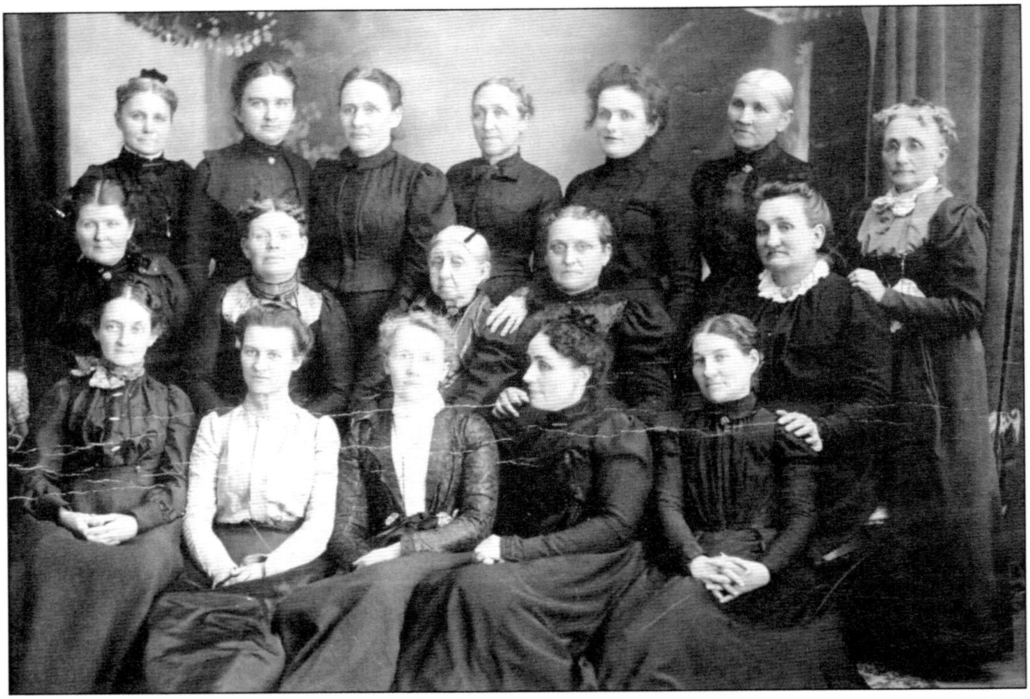

The Willing Workers (later the Worthwhile Club) was organized in 1895 to support any minister and the Union Sunday School. They helped the needy in the community and bought the Zion Evangelical Church, North America, for meetings. The group improved the park and school grounds, supported the wading pool at Taft Park and the hospital fund, and sponsored a Boy Scout troop. The club has 30 members in 2011 and still gives out scholarships.

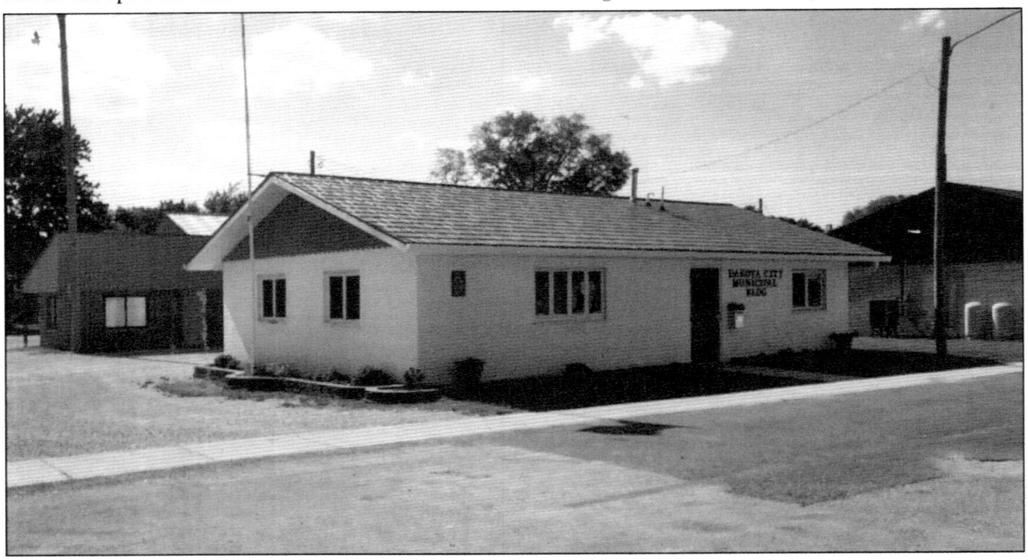

The new Dakota City Municipal Building was erected at 26 Sixth Street South in 1983. It contained city offices and a city council room. In 2009, the building was remodeled and a large community room was added. This room is open for private parties and is where the Worthwhile Club gathers for regular meetings.

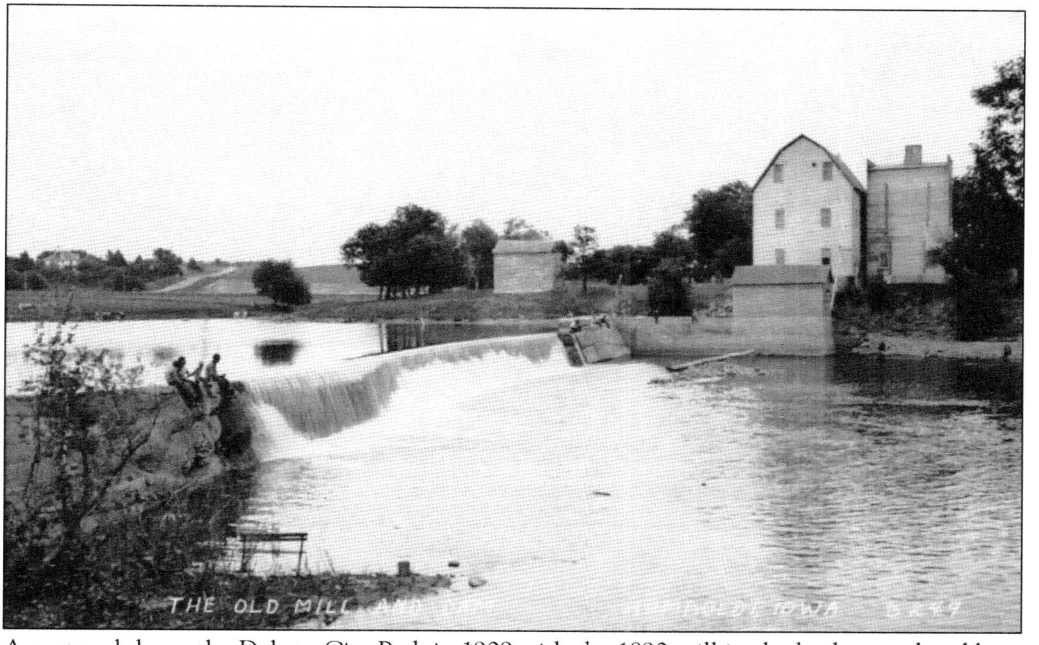

A postcard shows the Dakota City Park in 1909 with the 1890 mill in the background and boys fishing off the dam. The site was often used for swimming and the beach for sunbathing and boating. The dam was the last dam in Iowa to furnish waterpower for a mill in operation.

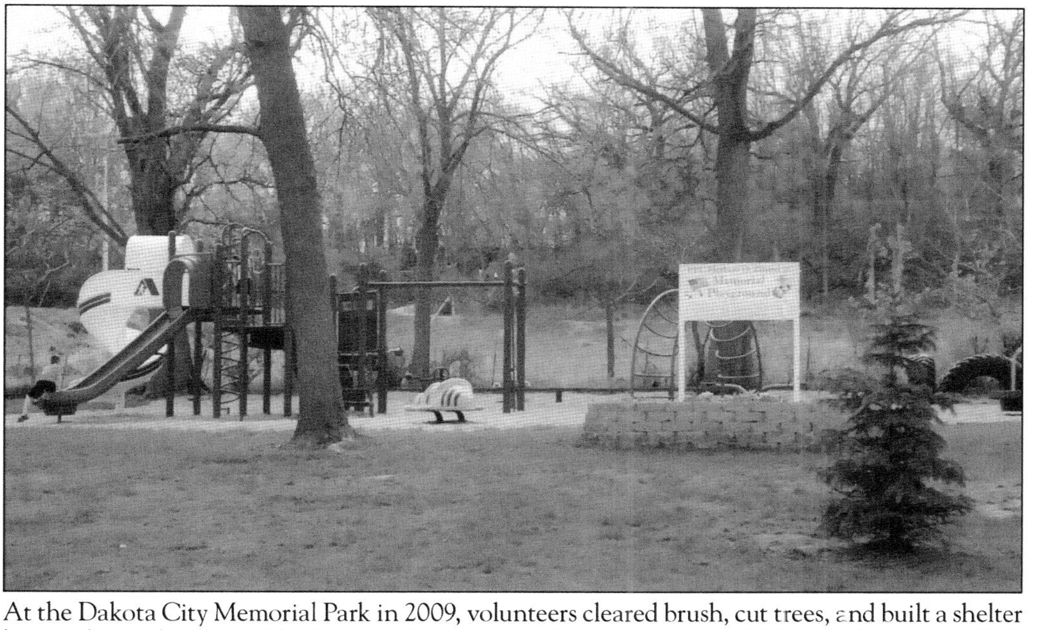

At the Dakota City Memorial Park in 2009, volunteers cleared brush, cut trees, and built a shelter house, shower house, and bathrooms. Boat ramps, picnic benches, and 14 campsites were added. The new playground was dedicated in memory of Pfc. Herbert O. Zinnel, who was killed in the Vietnam War. (Courtesy of Angelique Berry.)

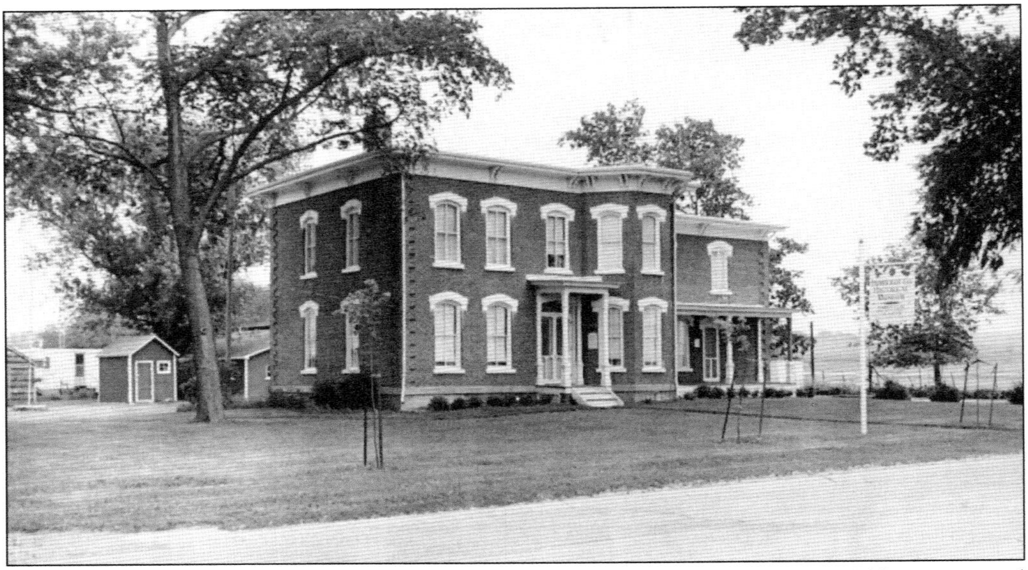

The Mill Farm House, given to the Humboldt County Historical Association in 1966, was restored by volunteers from 1967 to 1974. The two-story Italianate house, built in 1879 of brick quarried nearby, was fashioned after the C.H. Brown family home in Hornel, New York, and included a carriage house. New outbuildings include a log cabin, barn, jail, country church, rural school, post office, and the Clancy Display and Research Building.

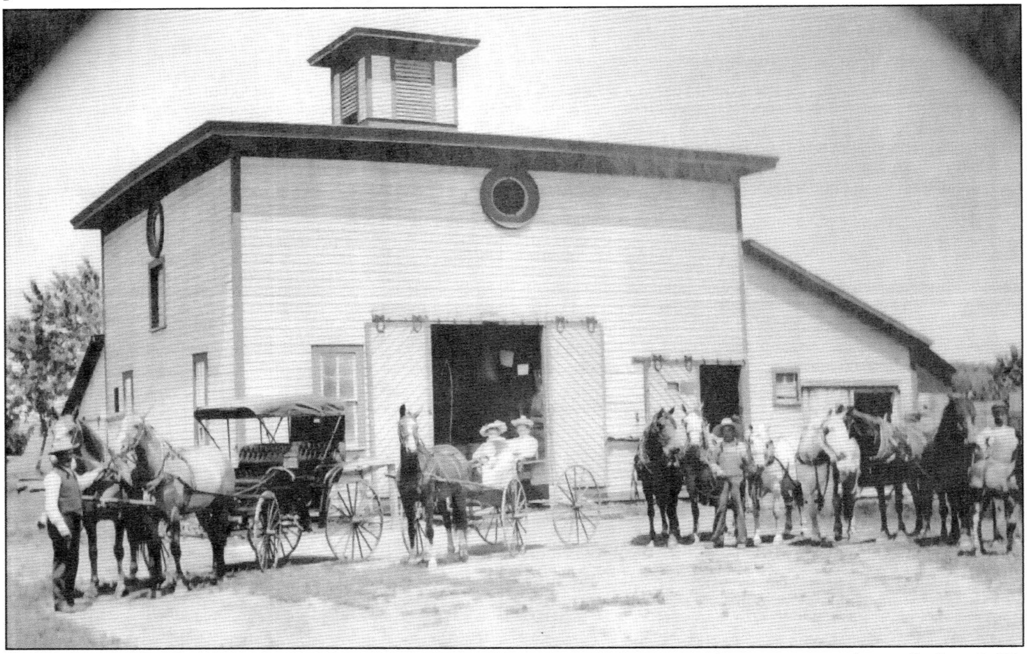

The carriage house was built at the Mill Farm in 1879. During the 1880s and until the C.H. Brown family moved away in 1902, the house was known as "the royal house of entertainment" for the many social events held there. After his parents left, Corydon Brown Jr., his wife, Florence, and daughter Eugenia lived there, followed by Walter and Grace Brown. In 1944, Grace sold the house to the Kunert family.

Three

Reverend Taft's Dream Becomes a Reality

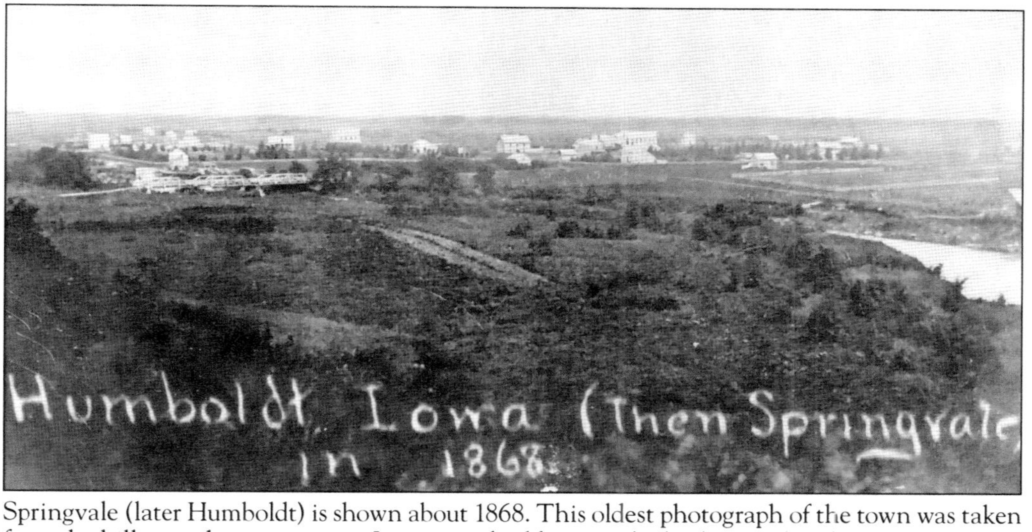

Springvale (later Humboldt) is shown about 1868. This oldest photograph of the town was taken from the hill near the water tower. Limestone buildings in the background include the two-story school and the Russell, Cole, and 1867 blocks. The first Lewis Street Bridge can be seen at left. The Sumner Avenue road bends at the left, turning into Ninth Street North.

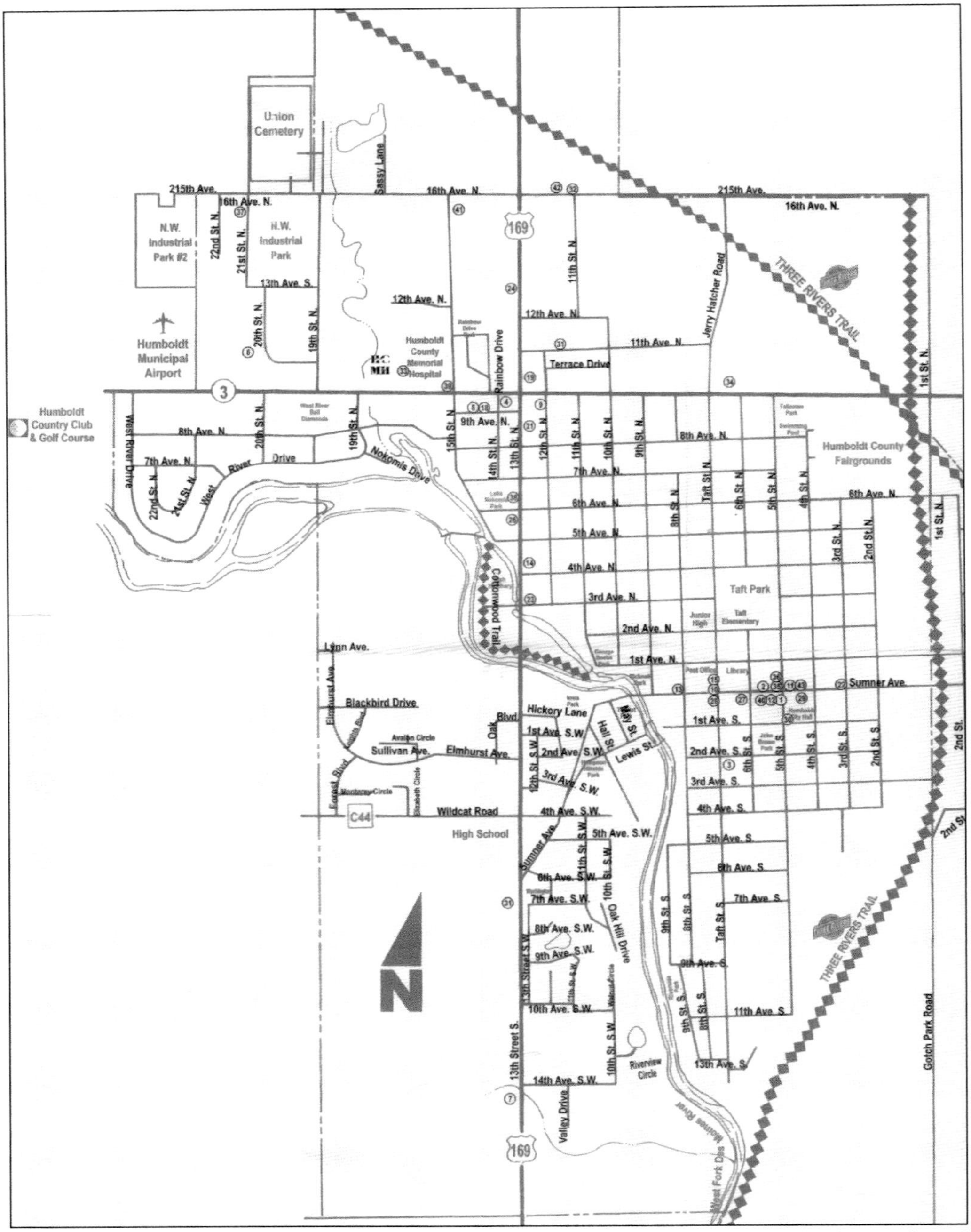

This is a recent map of Humboldt, showing hiking trails where railroad tracks used to be. T. Elwood Collins drew the original town in 1864. It featured two main streets running at right angles to one another: Gerrit Smith Avenue (now Taft Street) and Sumner Avenue. For street names, Taft chose those of distinguished men in the antislavery movement and the Unitarian Church. Names were changed to numbers in 1925.

In 1853, Mary Burnham of Madison Village, New York, married Stephen H. Taft. A devoted wife, she supported her husband's many endeavors. Six children were born to them: George (who died in infancy), William J., Frederick H., Sidney A., Mary V. (who died at the age of 21), and Elwin S. (who died at the age of 38). Mary Burnham Taft lived until 1898.

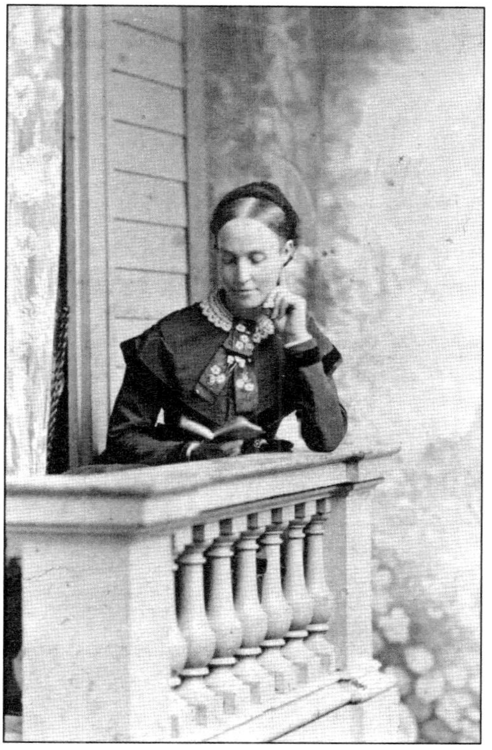

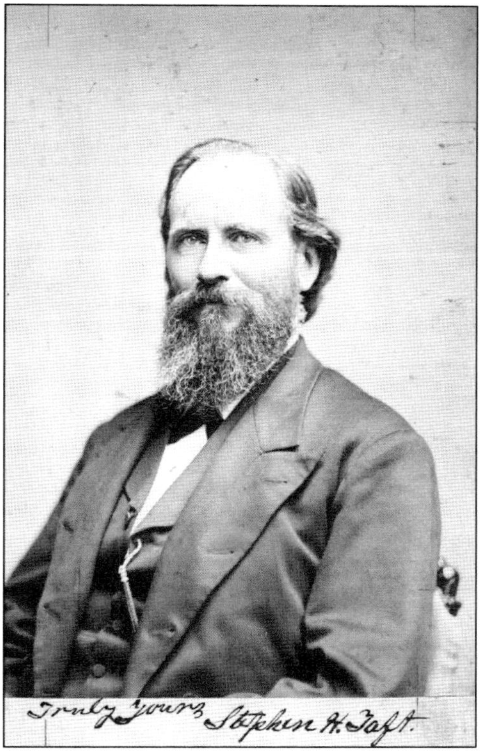

Rev. Stephen H. Taft (1825–1918) was the founder of the city of Humboldt. Largely self-taught, Taft was identified with the independent Christian Union Church. In 1862, he visited the Humboldt area where he led a colony of his church members the following year. A strong advocate for Prohibition and against slavery, he sought to create a wholesome town mirroring his values and founded Humboldt College.

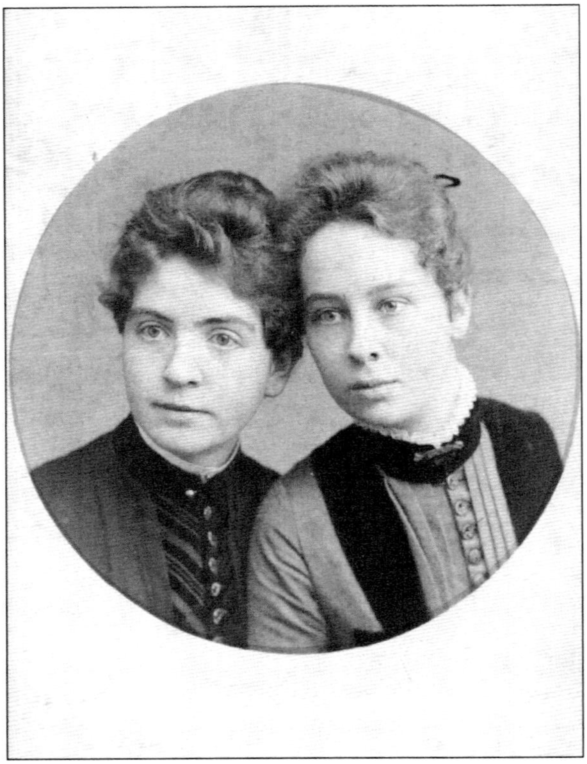

Mary V. Taft (left) and Clara Bicknell were close friends who died as young women. Mary, the only daughter of Reverend Taft, passed away in 1889 at the age of 21. Clara, the daughter of A.D. Bicknell, was one of the first graduates of Humboldt High School. She became the wife of E.E. Hodgin, a prominent Unitarian minister, and died in 1905.

Real estate agents of Taft and Company pose with Reverend Taft (at far left in the first row) around 1904. His son, Judge Frederick Taft of Santa Monica, California, is seated in the center of the first row. Another son, William J. Taft, a local attorney, is standing at far left in the second row. The others are unidentified but may include members of the Taft family.

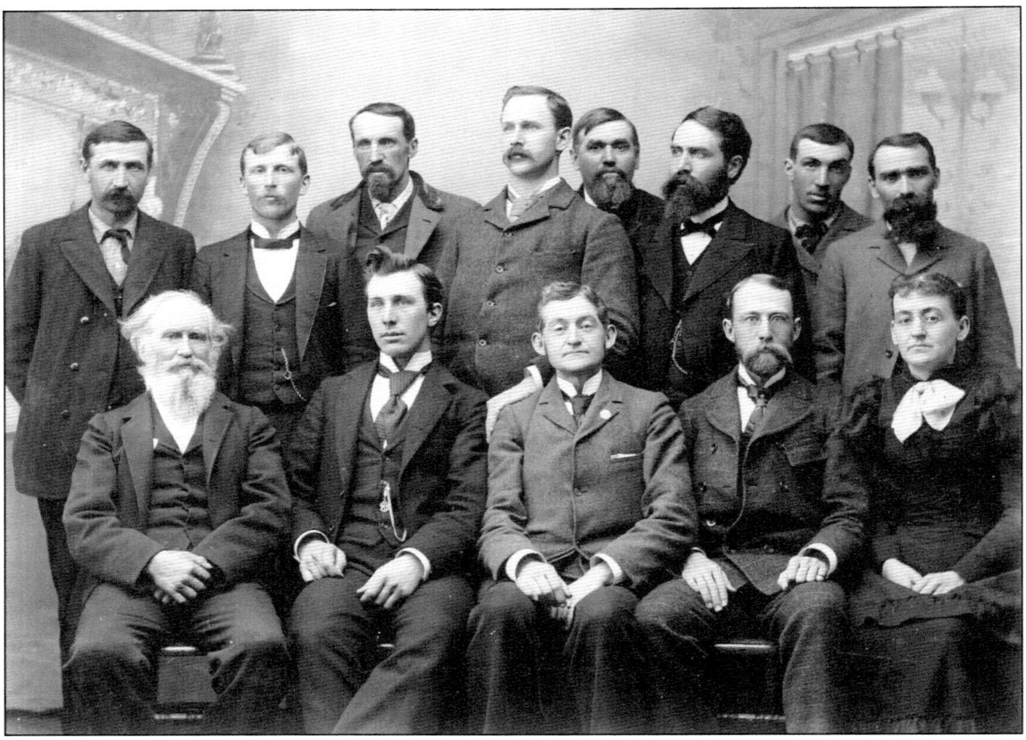

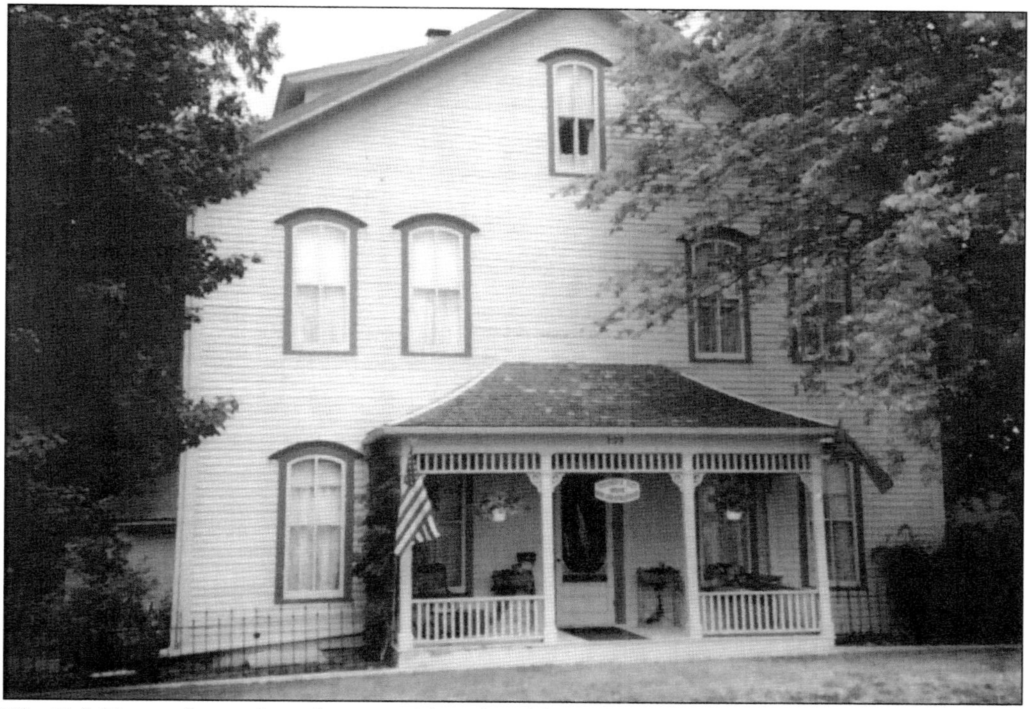

The Taft House, shown from the street (above) and from the back (below), was actually the second house Reverend Taft built. The first, a 16-by-24-foot structure with a cellar beneath it, was one-and-a-half stories high. Built with native lumber sawn at the mill, it was erected in 1864 on the day Abraham Lincoln was chosen president for the second time. The second Taft house was rebuilt or started anew in 1879. It was two full stories, with an attic and cellar, and sided with limestone from the local quarries. After the Taft family moved on, it was occupied by the Earl Butterworth family. Shirley and George Curry ably restored the house and decorated it in Victorian-period decor and used it as a bed and breakfast for a number of years. It is now privately owned.

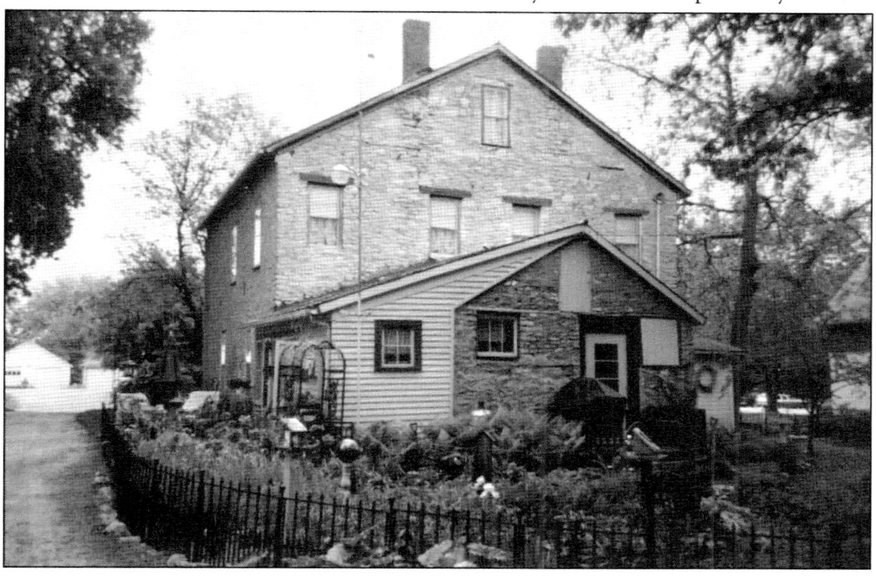

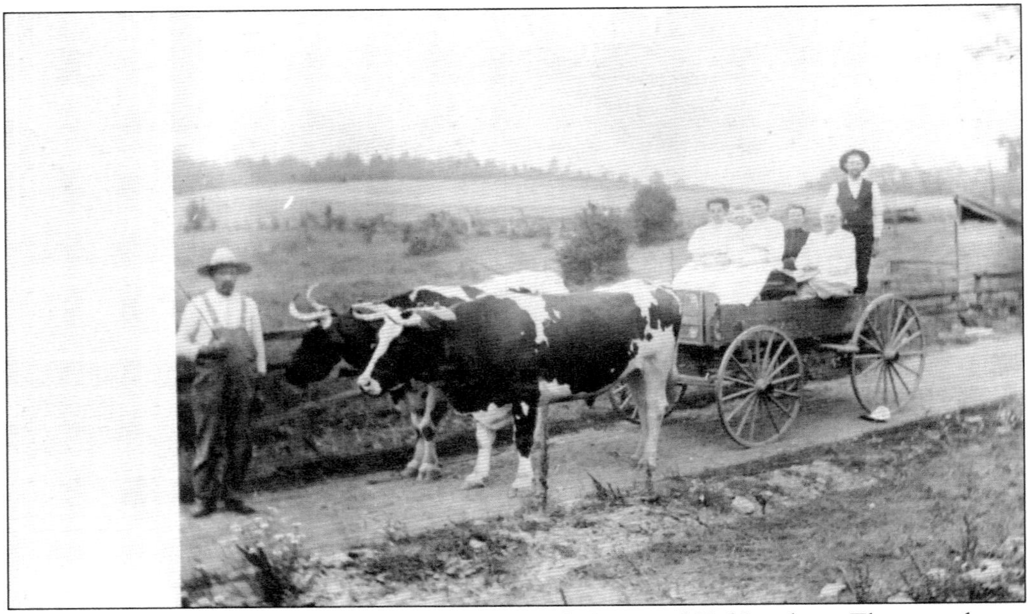

The Lorbeer-Wickes family came to Humboldt with Reverend Taft's colony. They are shown on one of their farms, now the H.E. McBurney place, near Gotch Park. The family consisted of matriarch "Mother" Cynthia Wickes (widow of the evangelical preacher Lewis A. Wickes) and her daughters Aurelia (Mrs. Charles A. Lorbeer), Emma (Mrs. John G. Lorbeer Jr.), and Sarah (Mrs. F.W. Bowen), and Ophelia Joenks (Mrs. Louis K. Lorbeer).

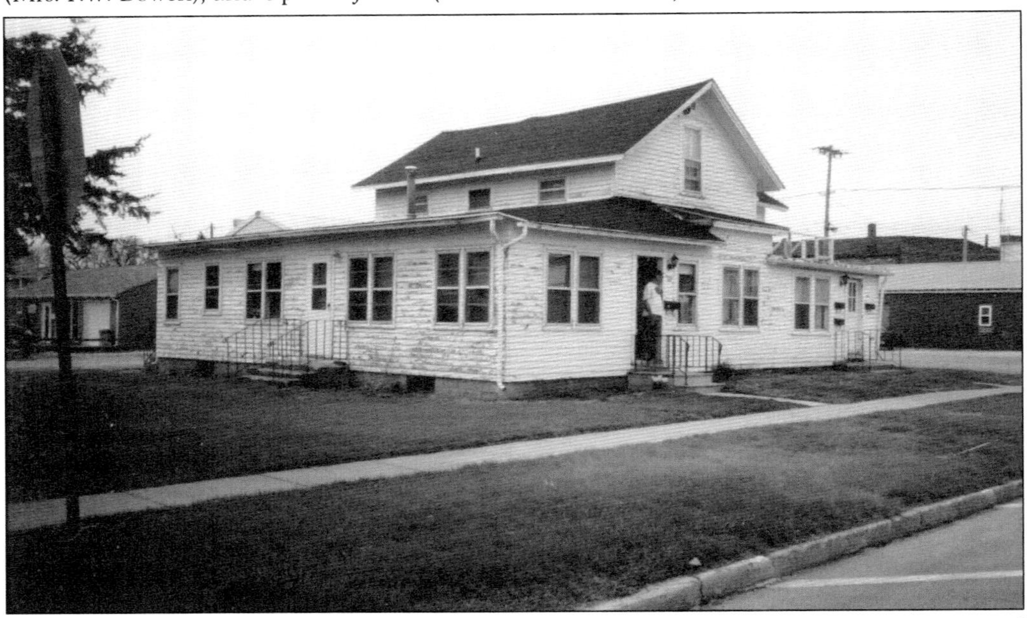

The Charles A. Lorbeer home, 28 South Taft Street, was the first wood-frame house constructed in Humboldt. That it still stands can be attributed to the carpentry skills of Charles, who was apprenticed to learn the cabinet-maker's trade in Germany. His wife, Aurelia, was instrumental in organizing Sunday school teachers in northwestern Iowa, the Women's Christian Temperance Union, Chautauqua, and the Bible Society. They also had 12 children.

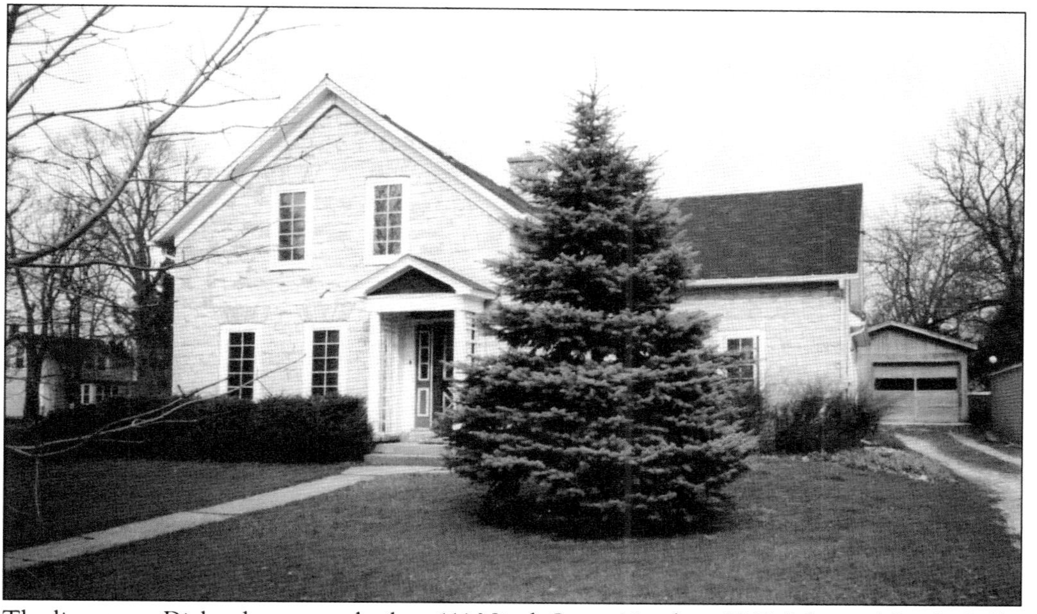

The limestone Dickey house was built at 111 Ninth Street North in 1868. John and Sarah Colby Dickey came from Vermont where he was a stonemason for 30 years prior to becoming a merchant. He was elected county judge and the first mayor of Springvale. In 1872, he became a banker, and his Humboldt State Bank was the first bank in town. John Dickey was instrumental in organizing the Congregational church.

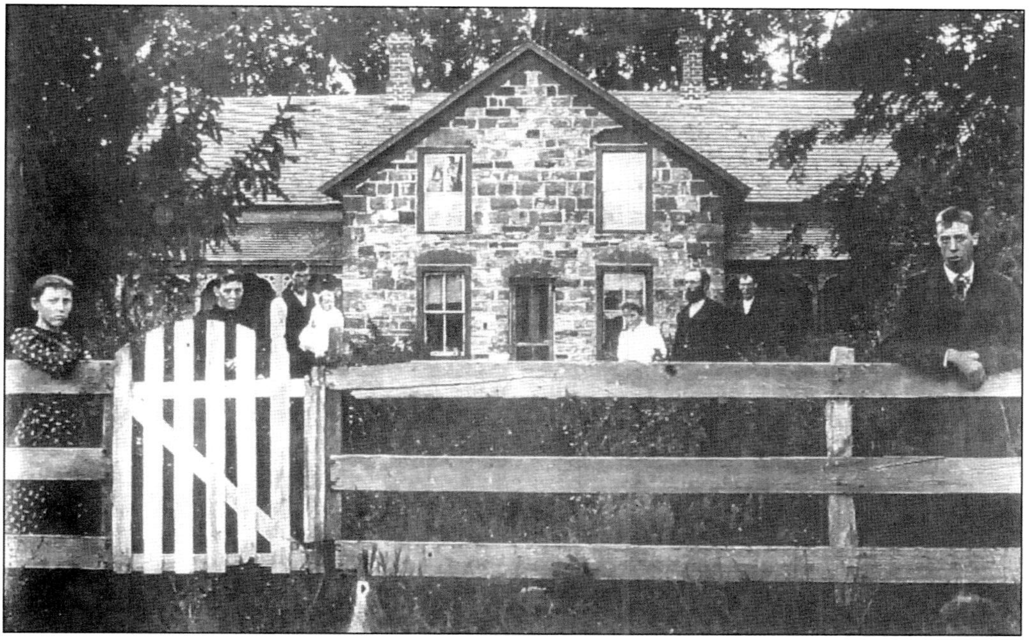

The Mary Jane and Byron Parsons homestead, 2735 Nevada Avenue, was built in 1870 with the help of a relative, William B. Leland. They came to Humboldt from Wisconsin as part of the Taft colony in 1865. Those pictured around 1893 are, from left to right, Maude, Maggie, William with Myrtle, Mary Jane, Byron, George, and Alfred Parsons.

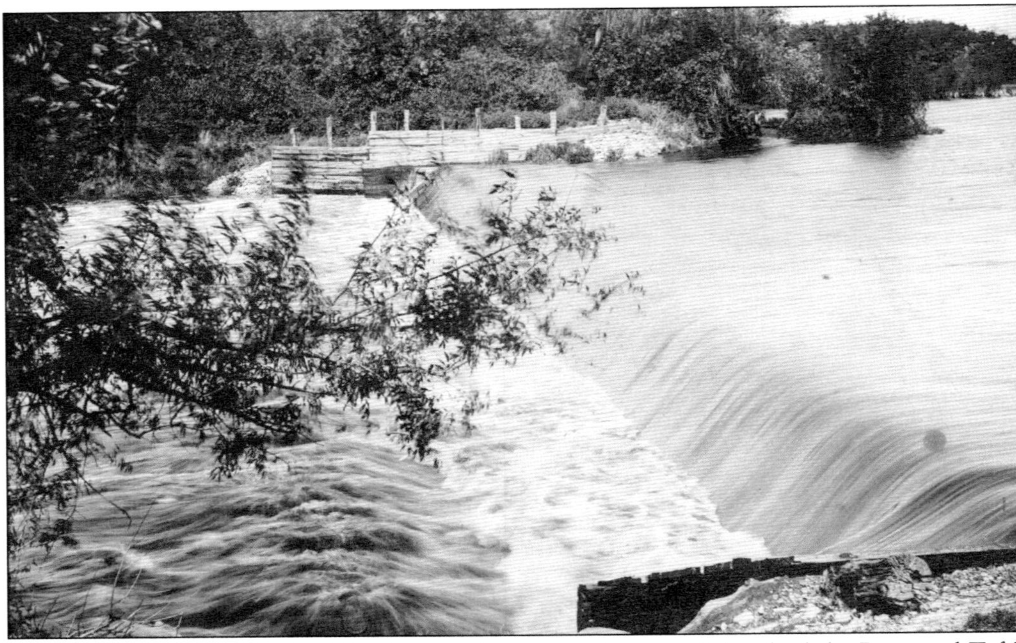

The dam on the West Fork of Des Moines River was the second dam built by Reverend Taft's colony. The first was located a quarter mile downstream and was washed out during the 1867 flood. During the next flood, the new dam forced water to cover part of the west bank of the river. The solution was to create an island in the middle with a dam on both sides.

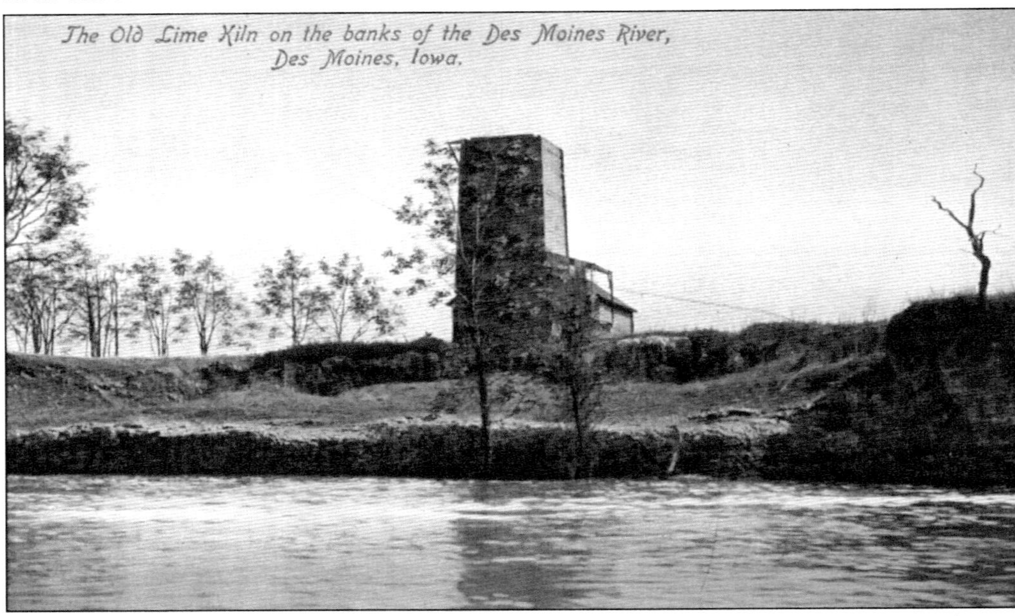

The old limekiln on the east side of the West Fork of the Des Moines River, approximately near Fourth Avenue North, was built in the 1860s. It was used to provide mortar for stonemasons who were building Springvale's limestone structures. Lime was taken from the riverbank and was processed by heating. Wood for the kiln was taken from nearby trees. The kiln was taken down in 1906.

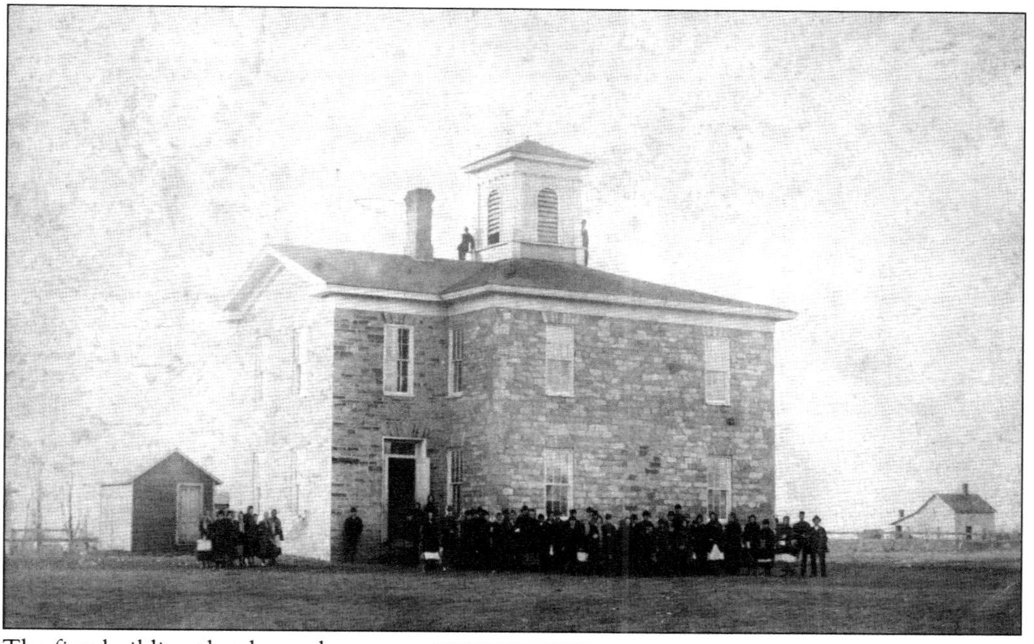

The first building that housed Humboldt School (1870–1893) was constructed of limestone that was quarried nearby. It had two classrooms, one upstairs and one downstairs. Later, these rooms were divided. This was the early meeting place for the Christian Union and Congregational churches. For the first 12 years, the school was a grade school, with from one to five teachers in charge. In 1880, Eleanor Gordon became principal and organized a 10-grade school.

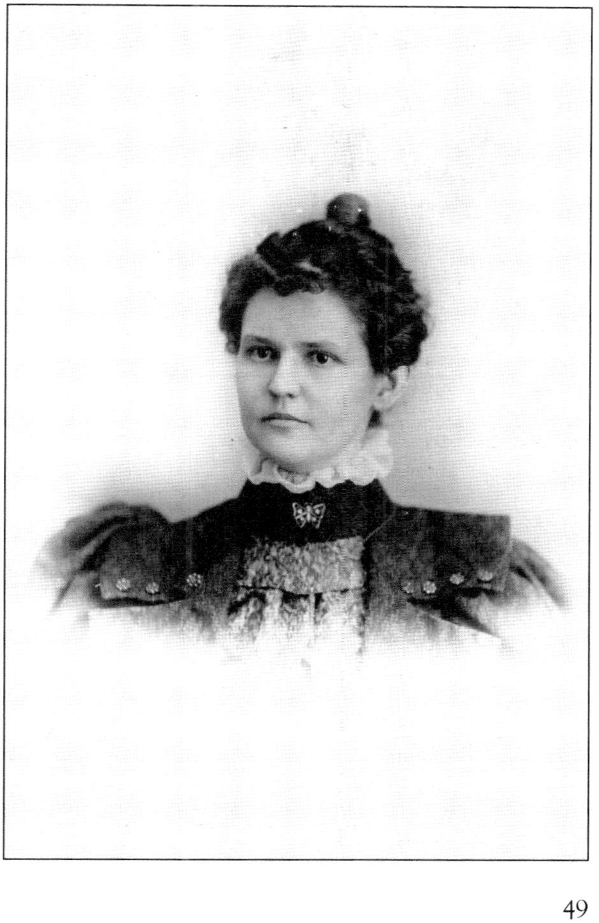

Marian Thomas was one of the town's early teachers. The daughter of David Thomas, who settled here in 1860, and Sarah Rowley Thomas, the widow of Albert Rowley, who was killed in the Civil War, she was educated in rural schools and graduated from the 10th grade in Humboldt's first class in 1888. After taking normal training, she taught in country schools and in the new 1893 schoolhouse in Humboldt.

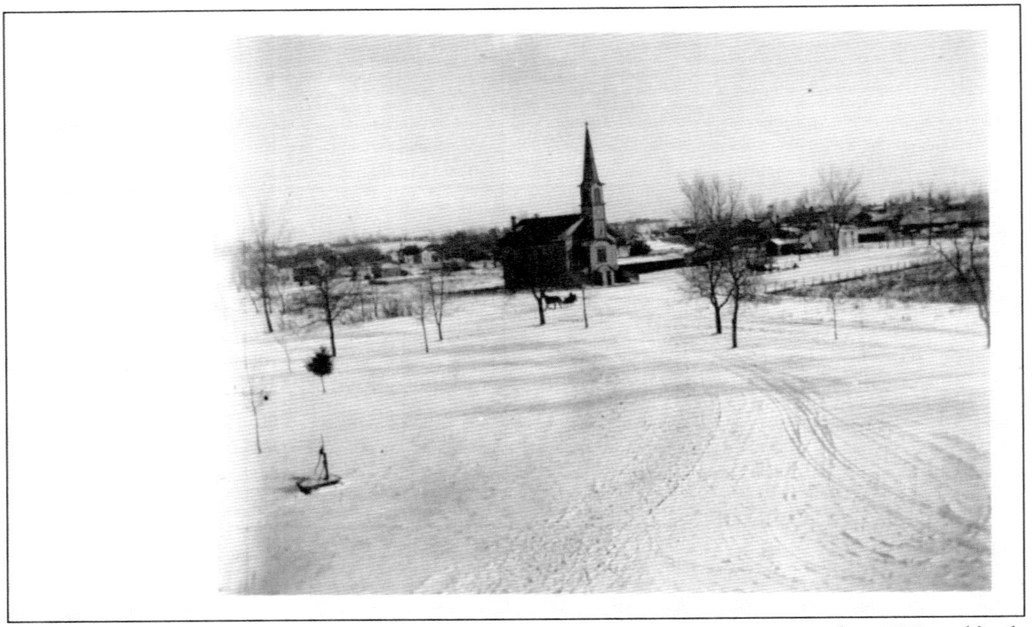

The Congregational Church of Humboldt, 111 North Taft Street, was organized in 1871 and built the first church edifice in Humboldt County in 1873. It followed the traditional evangelical New England Congregational theology, as opposed to the Unitarian liberal thinking of Reverend Taft's church. Taken about 1890, the photograph shows homes and buildings in the area.

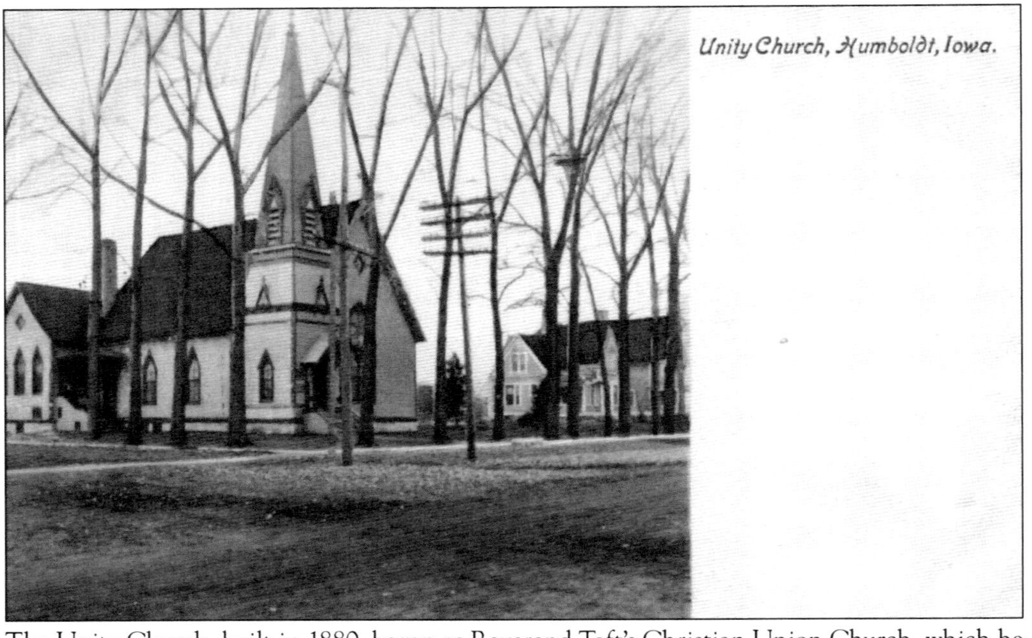

The Unity Church, built in 1880, began as Reverend Taft's Christian Union Church, which he brought with him in 1863. He wanted to do away with sectarian differences and led a church that brought all who professed Christianity into one all-including fellowship. It had no creed or membership requirements. In 1875, he aligned with the Unitarian denomination that he discovered while seeking funds for the college in New England.

The Reverend Mary A. Safford (1851–1927), a Unitarian pastor, was called to the Humboldt Unity Church in 1880. She preached at both Humboldt and Algona on alternating Sundays. A gifted and magnetic speaker, she organized the Unity Club to promote literary, scientific, and cultural education. During her years here, church debt was reduced considerably and 30 new members joined the congregation.

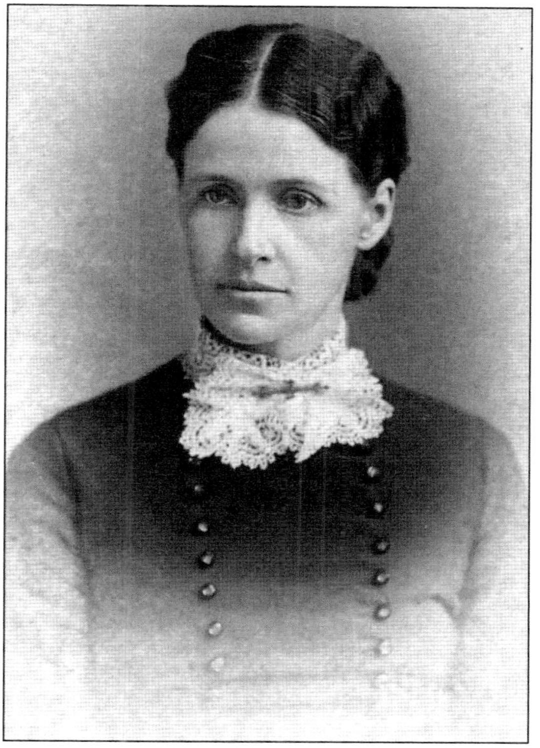

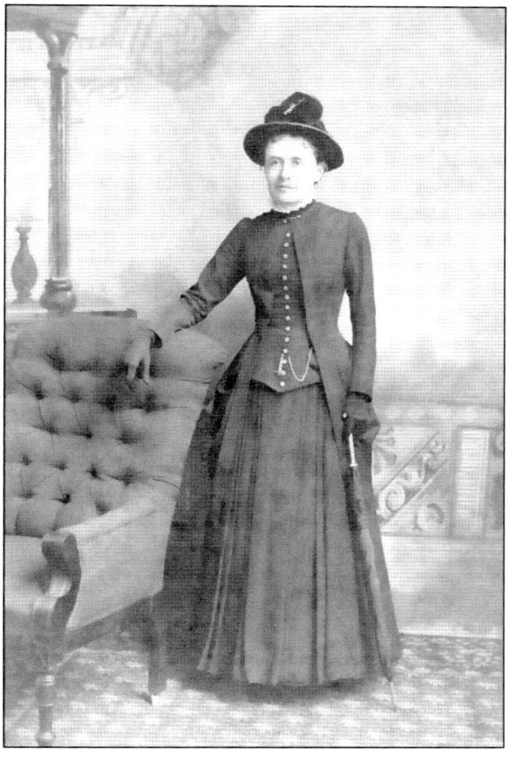

Eleanor E. Gordon (1852–1937) came to Humboldt with Reverend Safford in 1880 and became principal of the Humboldt Schools. The school grew from two to six departments, a course of study was adopted, a two-year high school was added, and a higher course of study was designed so that students could continue their education. She was ordained a minister in the Unitarian denomination in 1889.

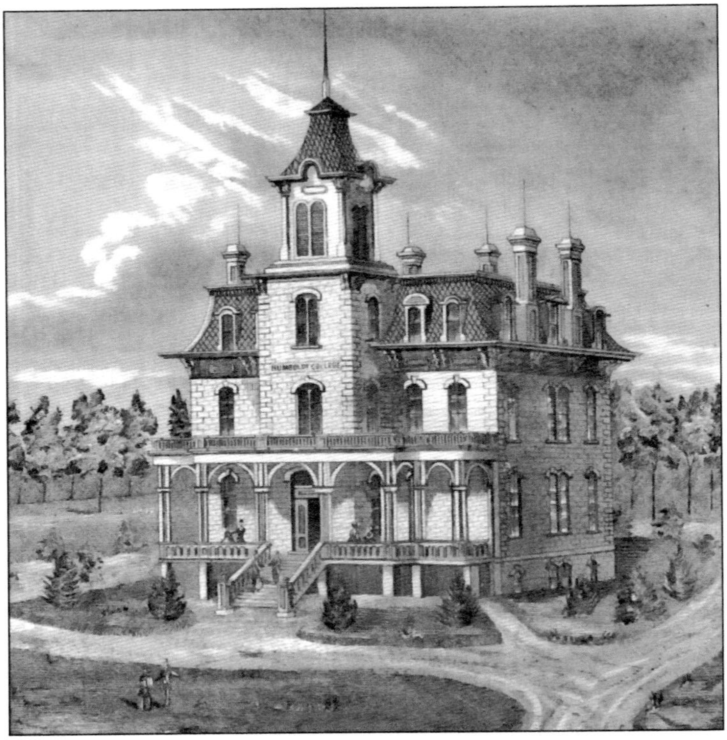

Humboldt College was built in 1871 on a 240-acre tract north of Highway 3. The college was the realization of Reverend Taft's dream of establishing a "Harvard of the West." Each year, about 100 students attended, taking grammar school, high school, college prep, and normal training classes. In 1881, it closed because of debts, but reopened in 1895 under Prof. J.P. Peterson's leadership. (A.T. Andreas's 1875 *Atlas of Iowa*.)

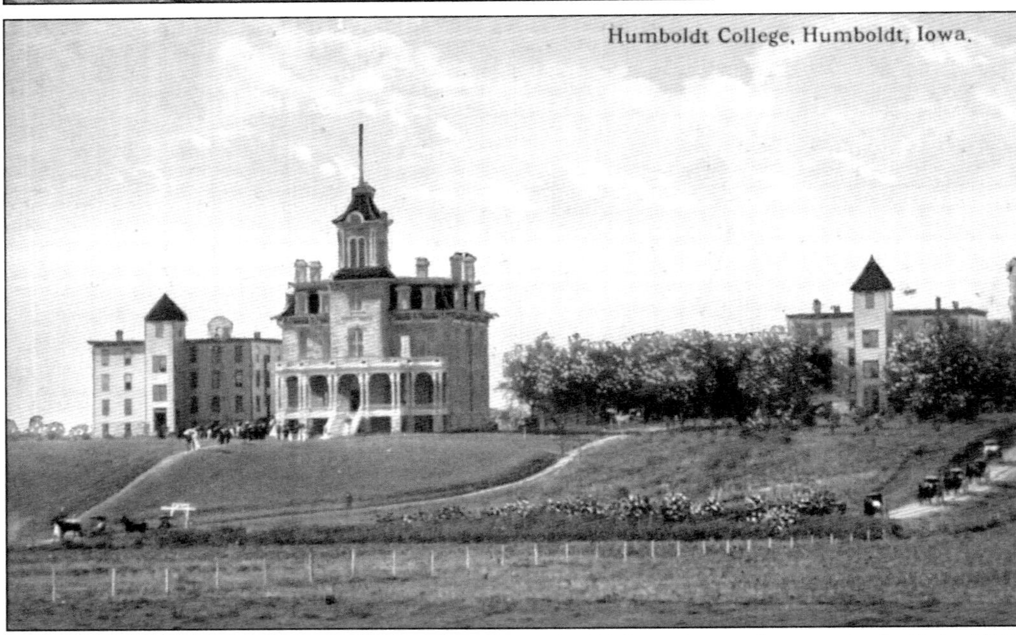

Here is Humboldt College as it appeared in the early 1900s with two dormitories built in 1895. It operated as a high school, an institute for training teachers, and a commercial college. The college could be accessed from town by road. Some students crossed the marshy slough below the buildings on a bridge they made themselves. As high schools began to provide these courses, Humboldt College closed in 1915.

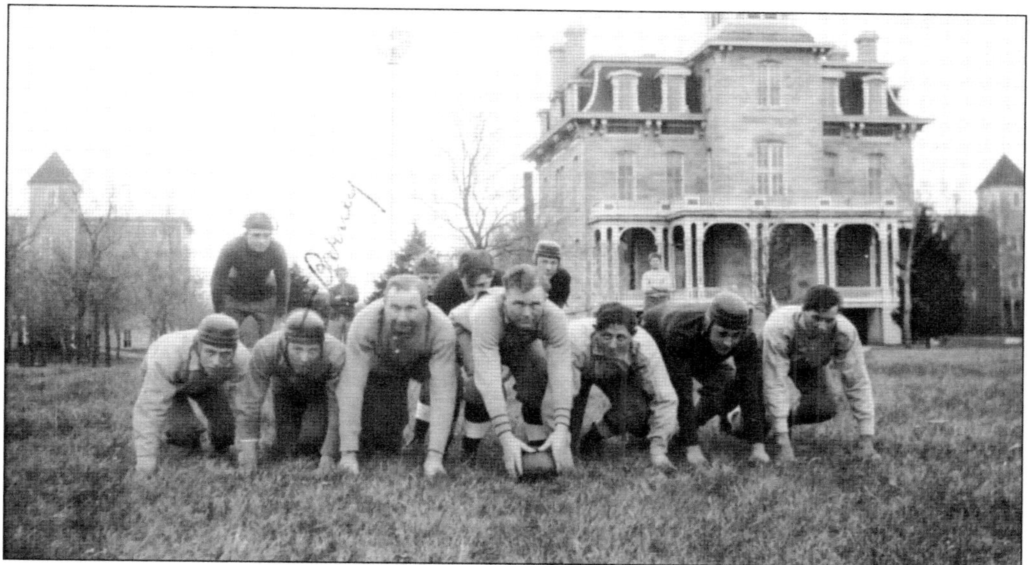

The Humboldt College football team lined up in front of the Old Main building about 1900. The team played two 25-minute halves against teams such as Elmore College in Minnesota. Five points were given for a touchdown, with an extra point for a field goal. Neither side indulged in slugging or improper language, and at the conclusion of the game, there was only the best of feeling between the two teams.

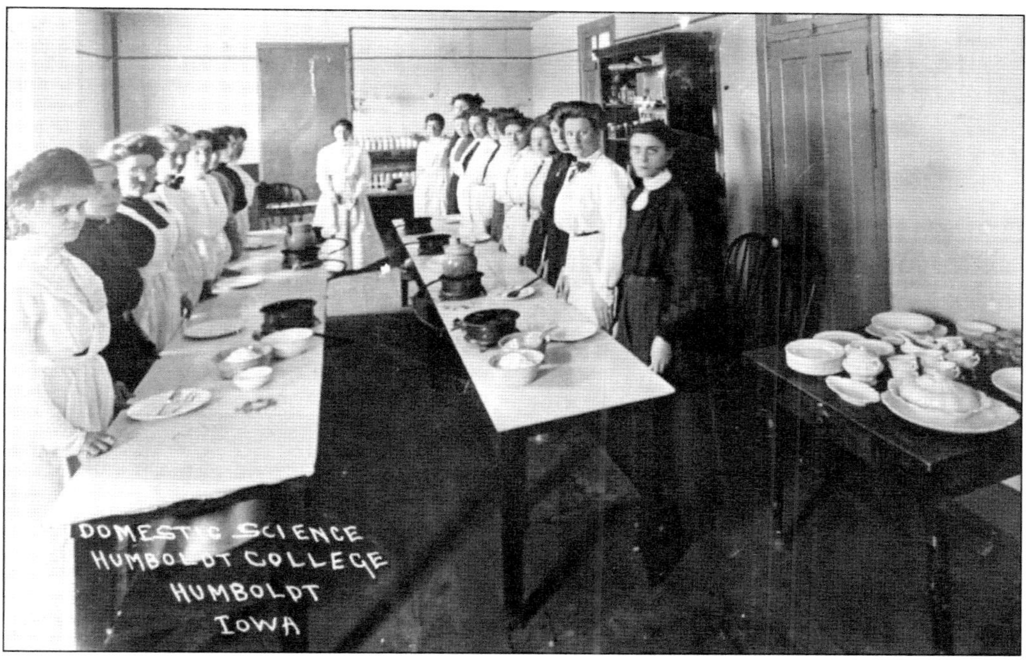

Domestic science was one of the courses offered to women at the second Humboldt College (1895–1915). They learned how to prepare food, construct clothing, sew a French seam, raise healthy children, and keep a proper home. Some graduates became teachers or consultants; most used their skills at home.

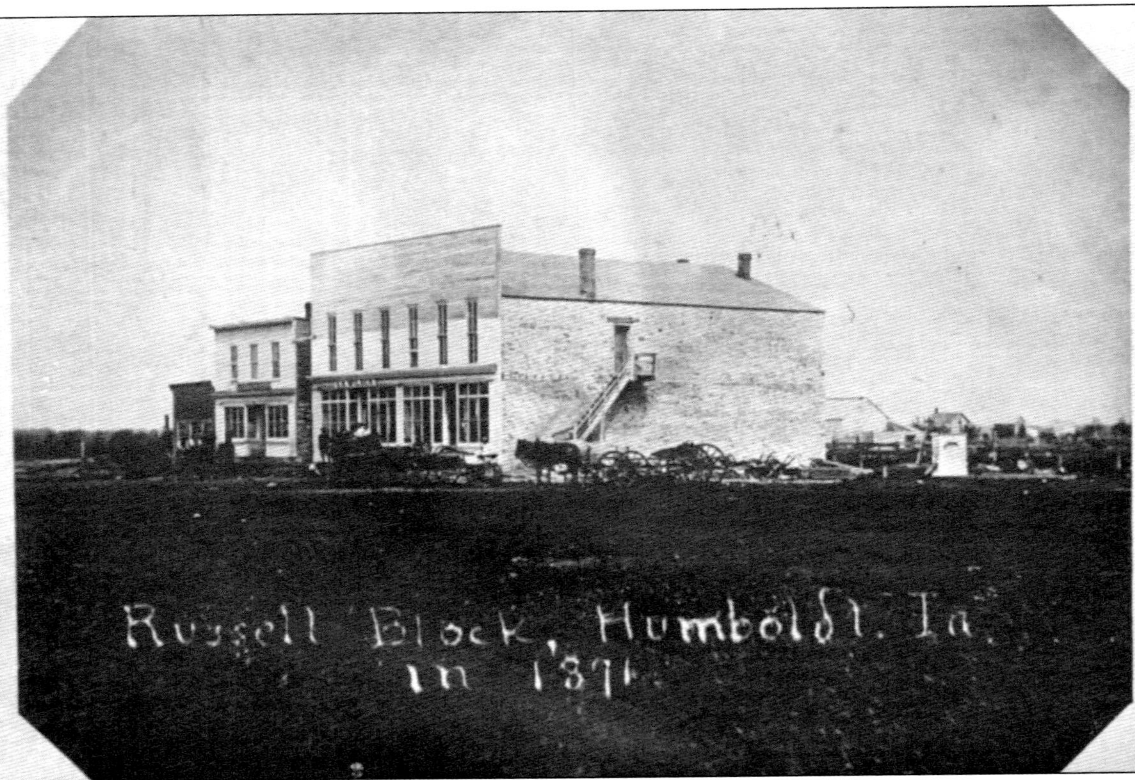

The first stores on Sumner Avenue burned in a fire in 1877. The center building, Union Hall, was a meeting room built by Reverend Taft in 1864, with newspaper offices upstairs. In the fire, Ward's Hardware, occupying the ground level, lost goods and the *Humboldt Kosmos* newspaper lost its press. The larger Russell Block to the right was started in 1865 by Dr. D.P. Russell. The stone building housed several general and hardware stores and pharmacies. During the fire, dry goods and grocery stocks of B.H. Harkness and Wilder and Taylor were partially saved. Upstairs in Parley Finch's law office, only one book was rescued. Russell Hall at the back of the second floor was destroyed. The small building to the left, constructed by Alfred Owens in 1869, was J.B. Simmons Jewelry Store beginning in 1875. His goods were also lost.

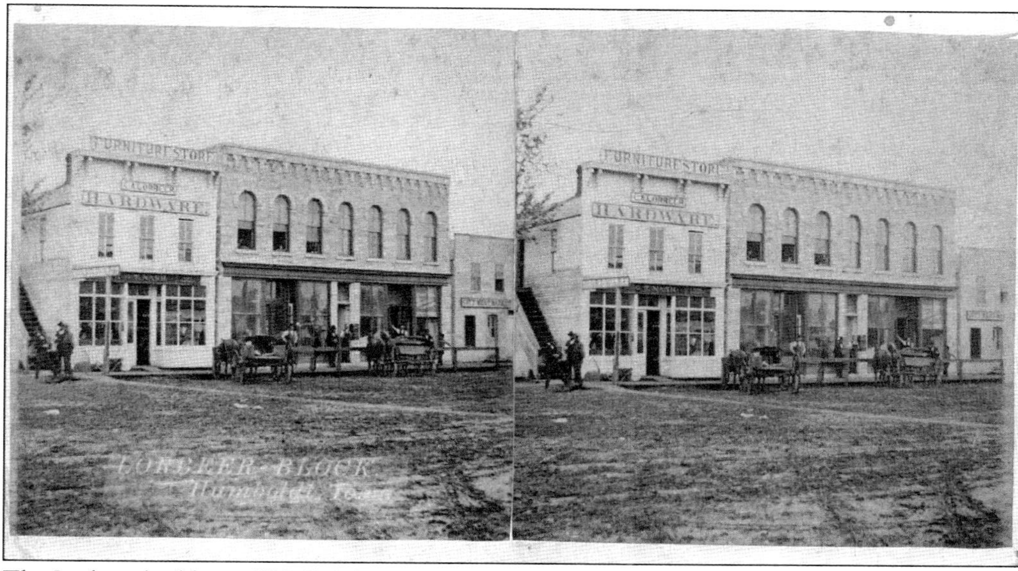

The Lorbeer buildings, 702–710 Sumner Avenue, are shown in 1879. The two-story building on the left was constructed before 1873 and served as the G.T. Nash hardware store downstairs and the Lorbeer furniture store upstairs. The stone, two-story Lorbeer Block was built in 1879 by C.A. and L.K. Lorbeer. McKinstry was the stonemason. D.A. Parker, Lorbeer's son-in-law, took the photograph on this stereoscope slide.

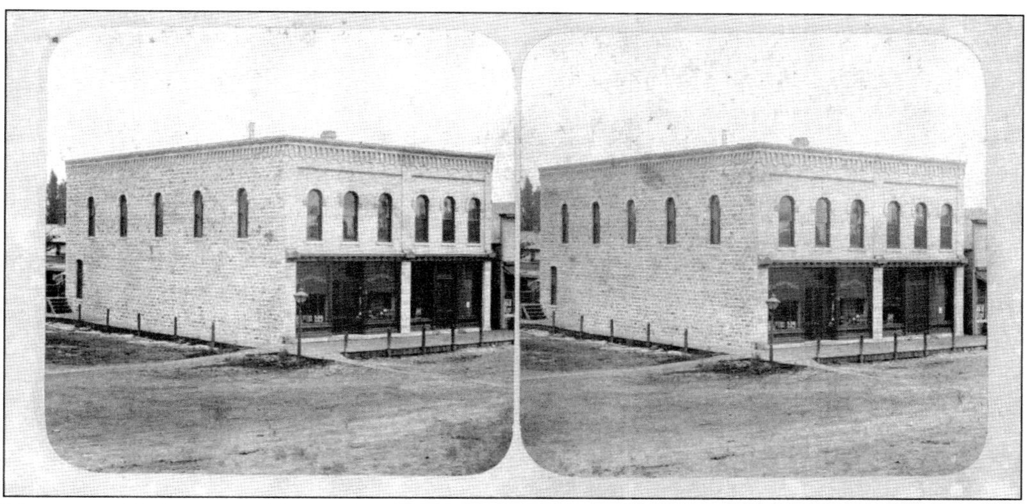

The stone Harkness and Prouty Buildings were constructed 1881 at 625–627 Sumner Avenue. The Harkness Building, to the left, was a dry goods and grocery store with a hall upstairs for meetings. Note the outside stairway. The Prouty Building housed law offices of J.N. Prouty, D.F. Coyle, and Edith Prouty. Dr. Hardy's office was upstairs. D.A. Parker took the photograph on this stereoscope slide.

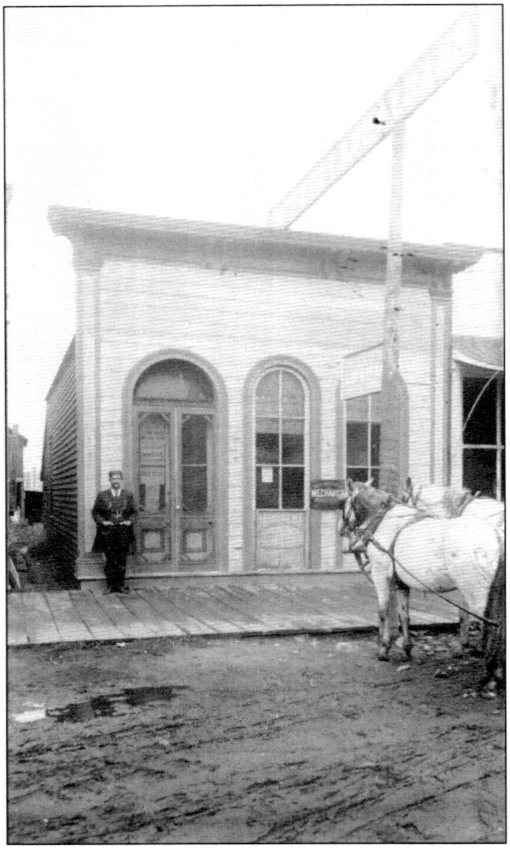

The Humboldt County Bank was built in 1872 on Mill Street across from the courthouse. In 1876, the bank was picked up and moved to 617 Sumner Avenue. In 1880, the building was moved to 603 Sumner Avenue, pictured, where it became the real estate office of Henry Wells. In 1890, it was moved again to 501 Sumner Avenue, where it was Harold's Hair Designs for a time.

Once known as the Soldier Block, the Smith Insurance Building at 514–516 Sumner Avenue is one of the older stone buildings in Humboldt. David Fickes built it in the late 1860s, and Gilbert D. Coyle had his drugstore there in 1869. He sold it to Dr. O. Harron in 1871. Albert M. Adams purchased the building in 1911 for the office of his newspaper, the *Independent*.

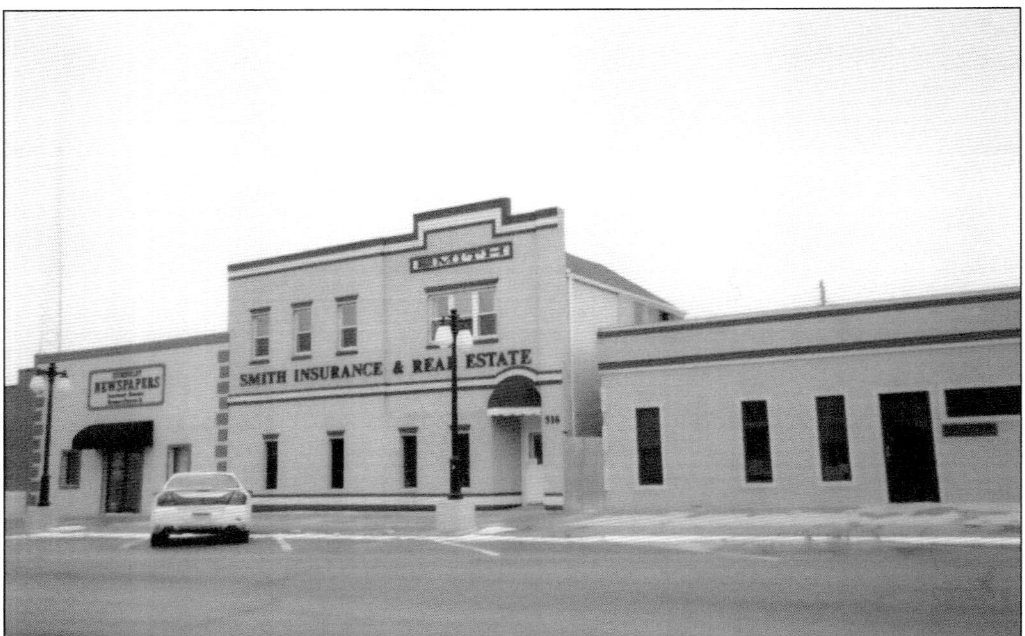

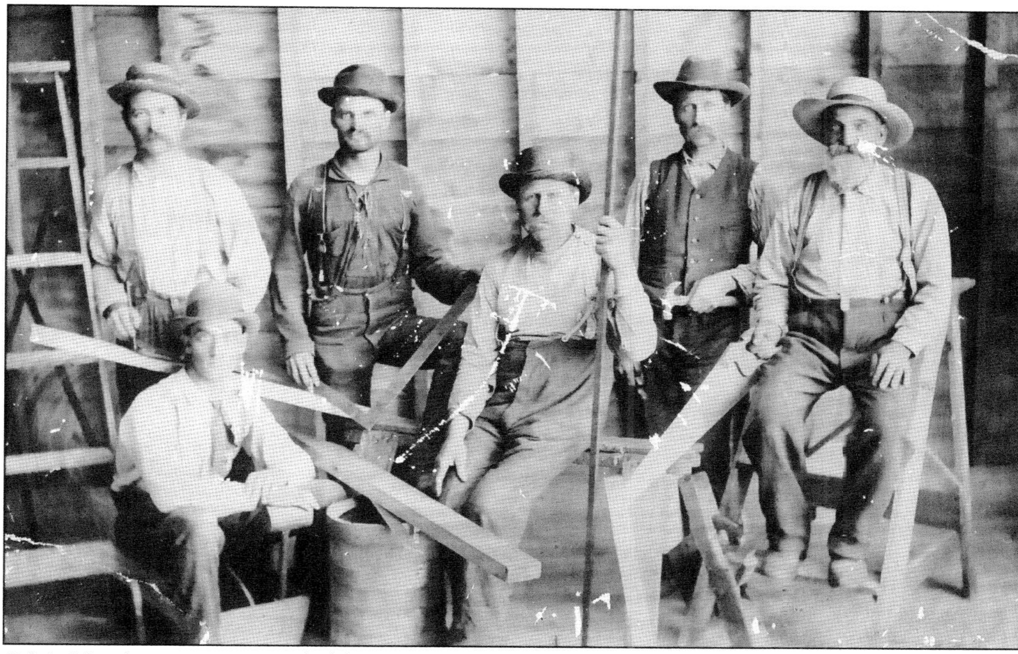

O.M. Marsh came to Humboldt in 1864 and operated the gristmill for Reverend Taft. The miller's stone house, 111 North Eleventh Street, still stands. Marsh was the father of three boys who became skillful carpenters and built many homes and business buildings. Pictured are, from left to right, (sitting) Willie Marsh, Billy Quick, and O.M. Marsh; (standing) Judd Marsh, Fred Marsh, and Bill Pinney.

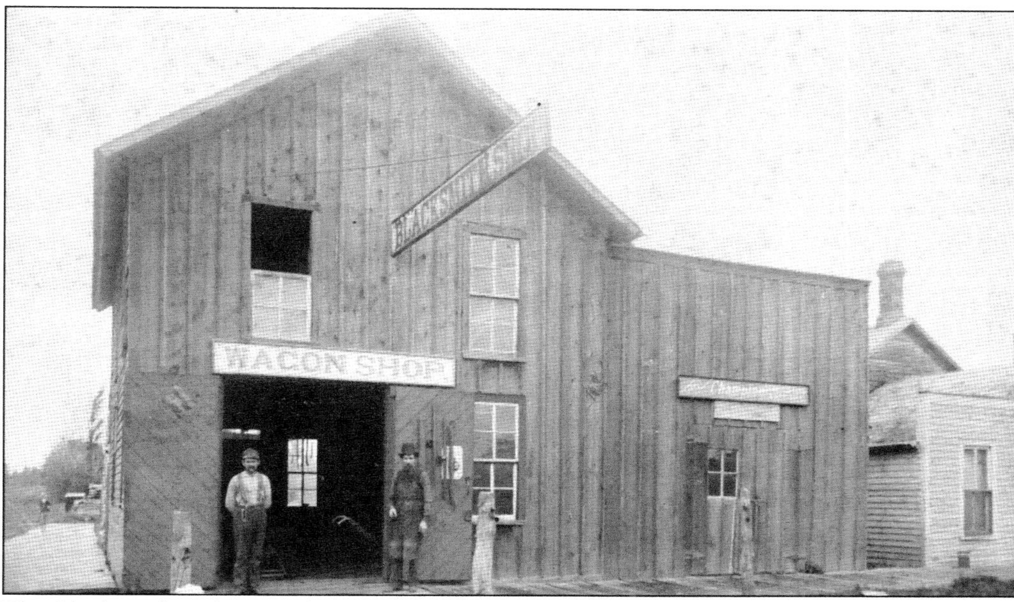

This blacksmith and wagon shop was located at 527 Sumner Avenue in the 1870s. Frank A. Dean is shown on the left. The building was later Sid's Cash Grocery, then White and Bull's, then Rine Grocery, and later Sherwood's Smoke Shop. A new building on the corner became Anthony's; Dollar General is currently located there.

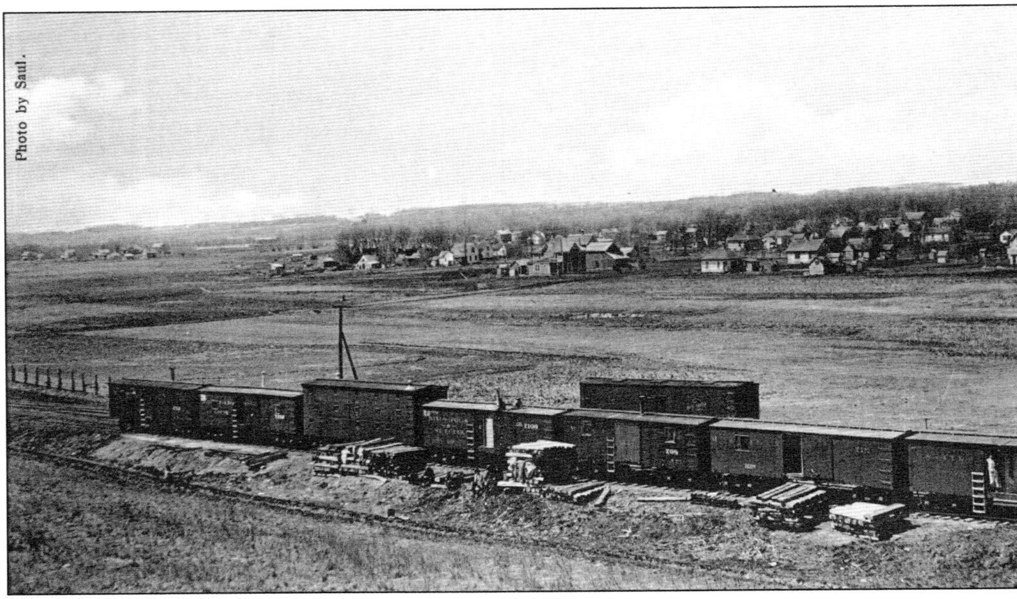

After a long struggle, Humboldt and Dakota City secured the services of the Minneapolis & St. Louis Railway in 1879. The trains brought prosperity. In Humboldt, several large business buildings were erected of native stone, and the new business section moved east along Sumner Avenue. This view of the Minneapolis & St. Louis Railroad with Humboldt in the background was taken about 1901. Humboldt's population at that time was about 1,500. Many homes dotted the south part of Humboldt. The new Lutheran church (below) can be seen at the intersection of Third Street South and Sumner Avenue. There are no homes east of Second Street, and the school's roofline peeks over the trees in the distance.

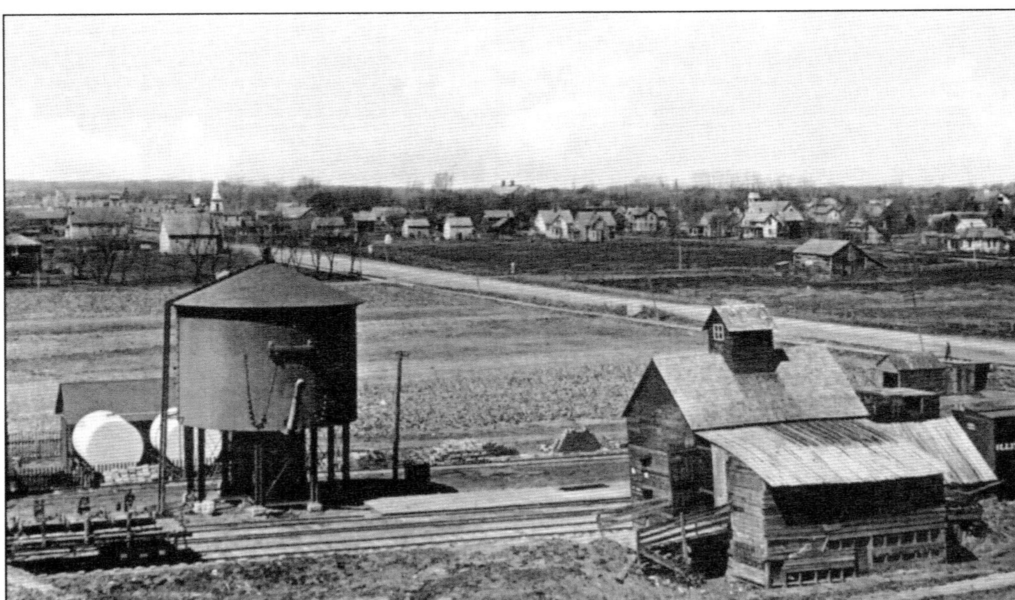

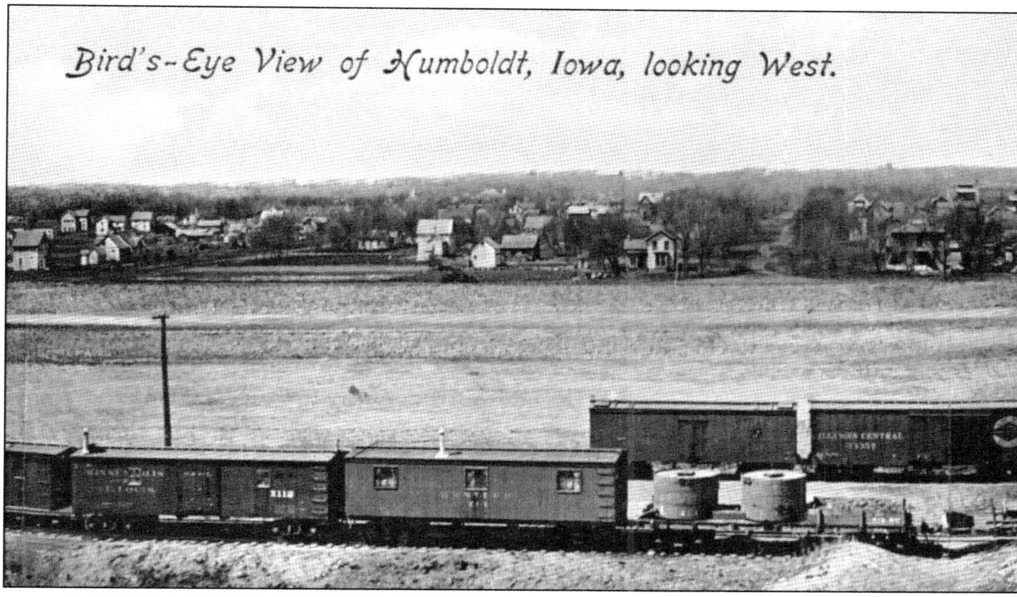

In the period after the railways came from 1880 to 1890, markets were established for crops and Humboldt County rapidly developed. First Avenue South (above) winds its uneven path in front of the Catholic church at the northwest corner of Third Street. In the distance is a building on top of the hill. The impressive Minneapolis & St. Louis Depot with its sign "Humboldt" can be seen next to the tracks (below). Across the road, the grain elevator towers over smaller structures while Humboldt College buildings can be seen behind it in the distance. The undrained wet spot identifies an ancient creek bed, which still floods on occasion.

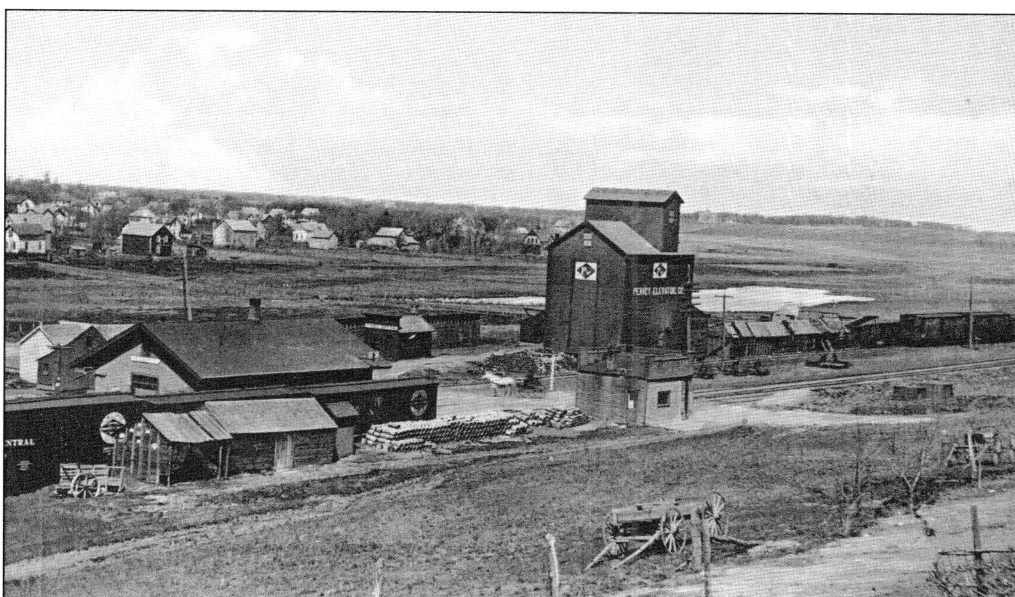

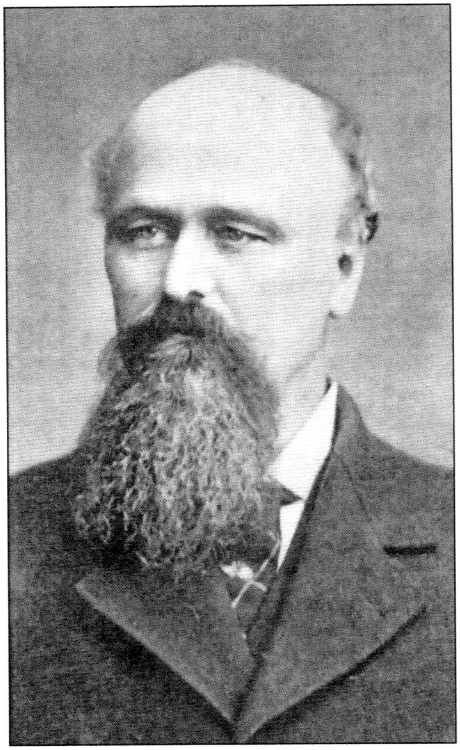

Anson Dodge Bicknell (1838–1918) came to Humboldt County in 1862 and then practiced law in Fort Dodge for five years. He moved to Rutland in 1868 and, in 1877, built a large home at 1005 Third Avenue North in Humboldt. He owned a half mile on the west side of the river, known as Bicknell Woods, and Bicknell Park on the east side, which was given to the city of Humboldt.

The Rev. Julius Stevens taught Latin at Humboldt College, edited the *Humboldt Kosmos* newspaper, and preached at the Christian Union Church until it became Unitarian. From left to right are (first row) Angie Stevens Gardner; (second row) Adell Stevens Welch, Roma Stevens Huntington, Rev. Julius Stevens, and Morda Stevens Van Patten; (third row) Gazelle Stevens Sharp, Rev. Julius Merle Stevens, and Nora Stevens Huntington.

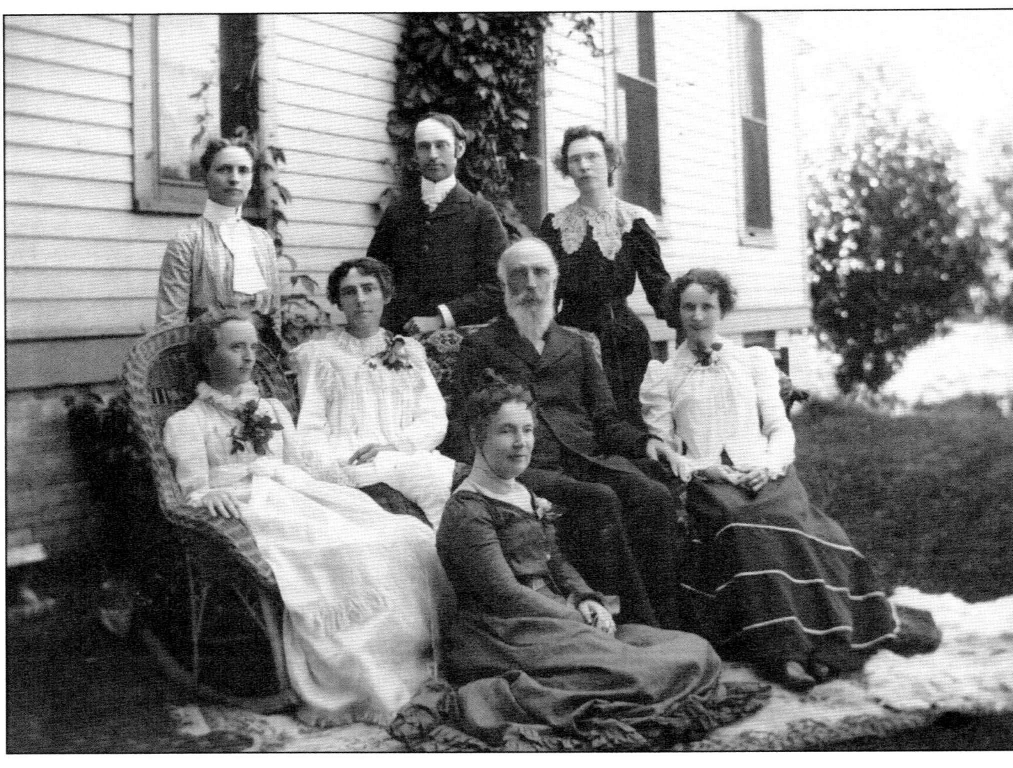

Four

Railroad Brings Prosperity to Humboldt County

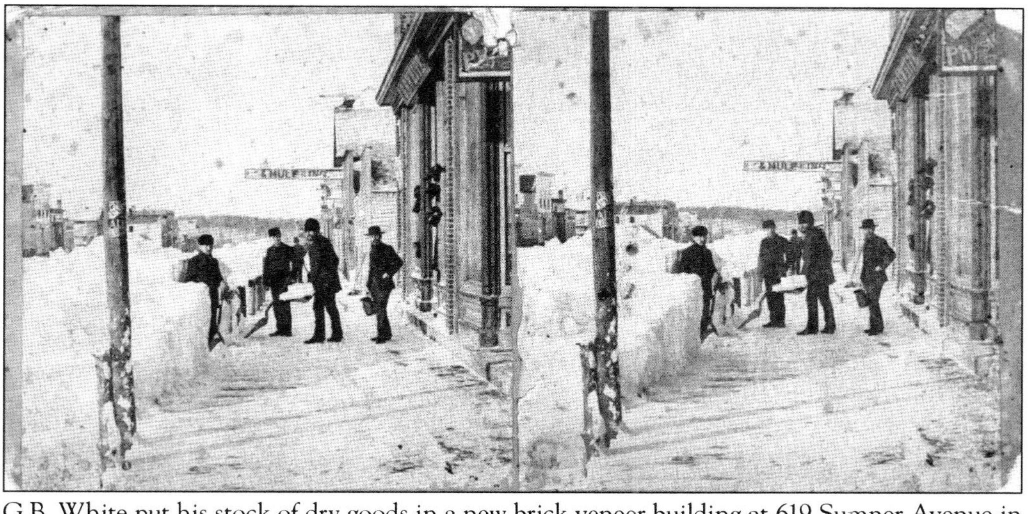

G.B. White put his stock of dry goods in a new brick veneer building at 619 Sumner Avenue in 1881. From left to right, his son Charles A. White, Milford Lyons, Dr. E.H. Kinney, and H.J. Preble are shown clearing snow from the board sidewalk in front of White's store in 1886. Behind them, Tom Nickson stands with a shovel in front of his blacksmith shop.

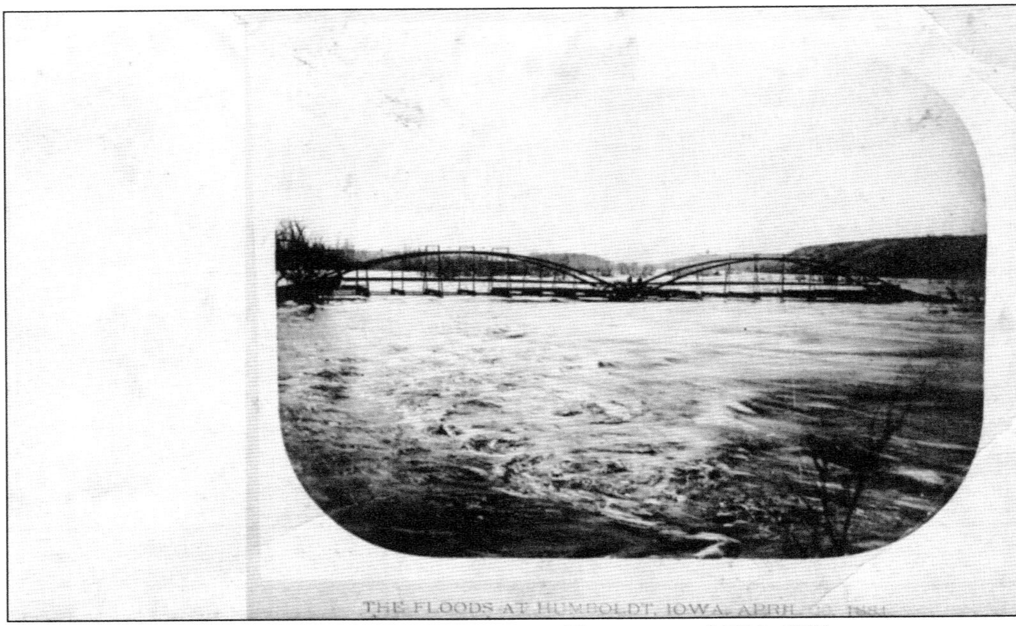

The winter of 1880–1881 was severe with deep snow on the ground from early October to April. In 1881, melting snows brought to Humboldt the highest water level that was ever recorded, covering the floor of the Lewis Street Bridge and washing out its footings. Part of the Humboldt Dam and the whole Rutland Dam washed out. The mill was damaged, and many homes were flooded.

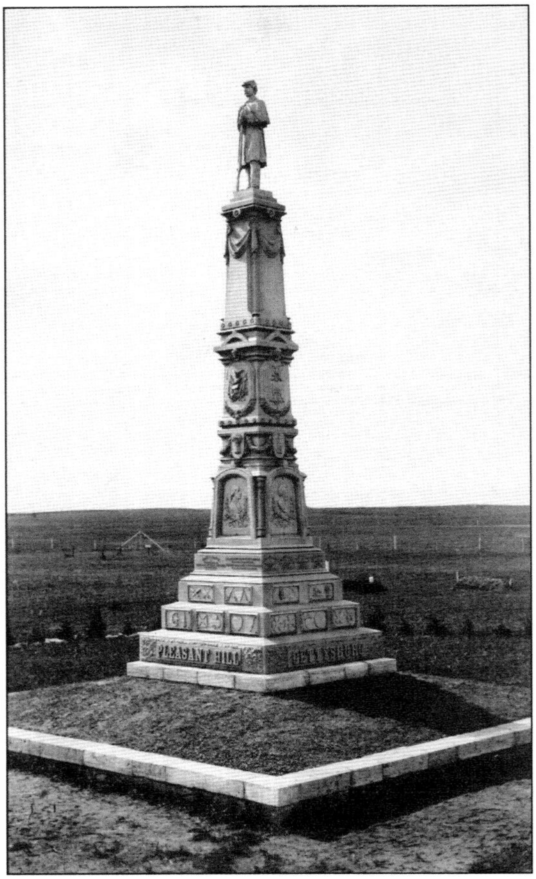

The Civil War monument in Union Cemetery was unveiled in 1885. On the four plinths are names of the battles in which Humboldt County soldiers fought, their 24 corps badges, assorted war emblems, and the engraved names of the dead from Humboldt County. On top is a statue of a soldier standing at parade rest. The monument is 36 feet tall from base to the top of the soldier's cap.

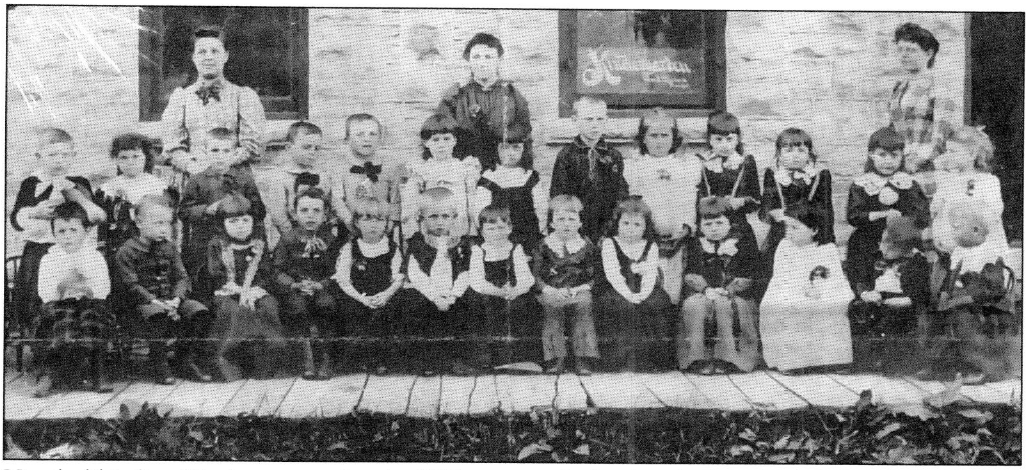

Humboldt's first Kindergarten class in 1891 was taught by Amelia Murdock Wing (center, third row). Assistants were Faith Jones West (left) and Myra Sterns (right). Harry Strong is in the second row on the far left, and George J. Bicknell is right of Amelia. Other children include Kate Preble Lane, Helen Harkness McGee, Bertha Harkness Shepard, Olive Shellenberger, Genevieve Hubbard, Dwight Spayde, Hugh Kinney, the Herrick brothers, Florence Weist, Forrest Avery, and Leta Russell.

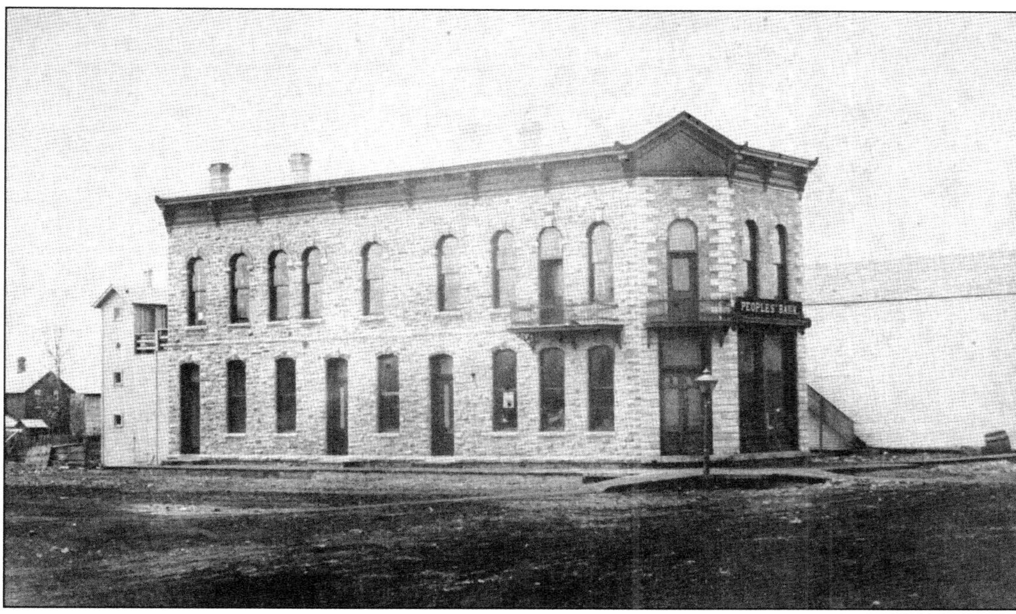

The People's Bank was built in 1882, as the Humboldt County Bank was erecting a stone building across Sumner Avenue. At first, a kindergarten class met in a room behind the bank. The second floor held apartments and offices. The small wooden structure attached to the rear was a two-story toilet. The building was remodeled extensively in 1915, and a bank occupied the front of the first floor until 1963.

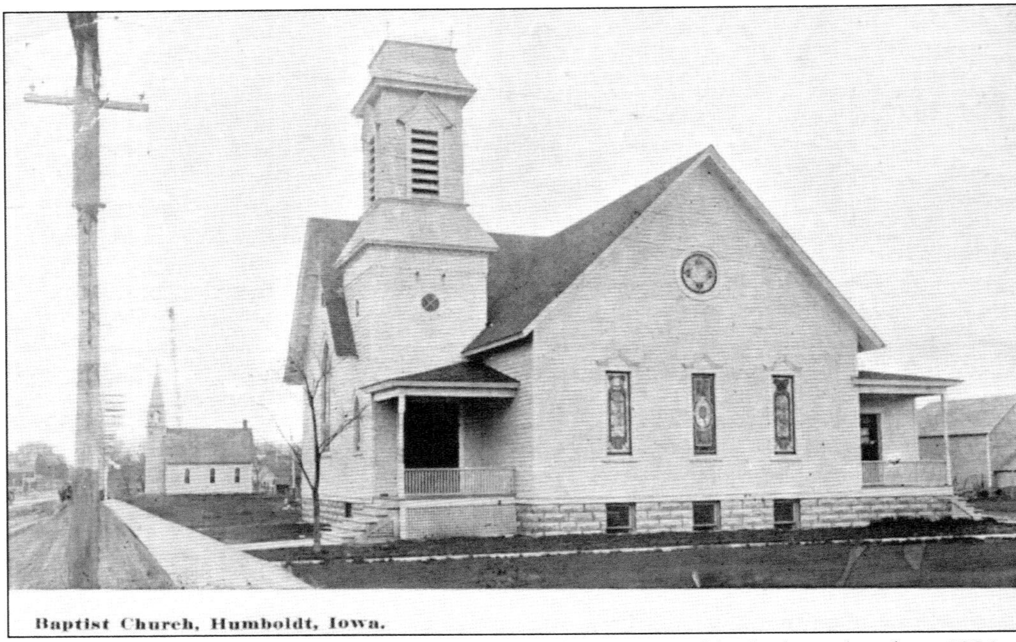

The Humboldt Baptists first met in 1881, organized in 1883, and built their church in 1884 at 332 Sumner Avenue. In 1933, they merged with the Danish Baptists as the Fifth Avenue Baptist Church. In 1972, the Oak Hill Baptist Church was built on Highway 169. The First Lutheran Church, built in 1898, can be seen in the distance one block east.

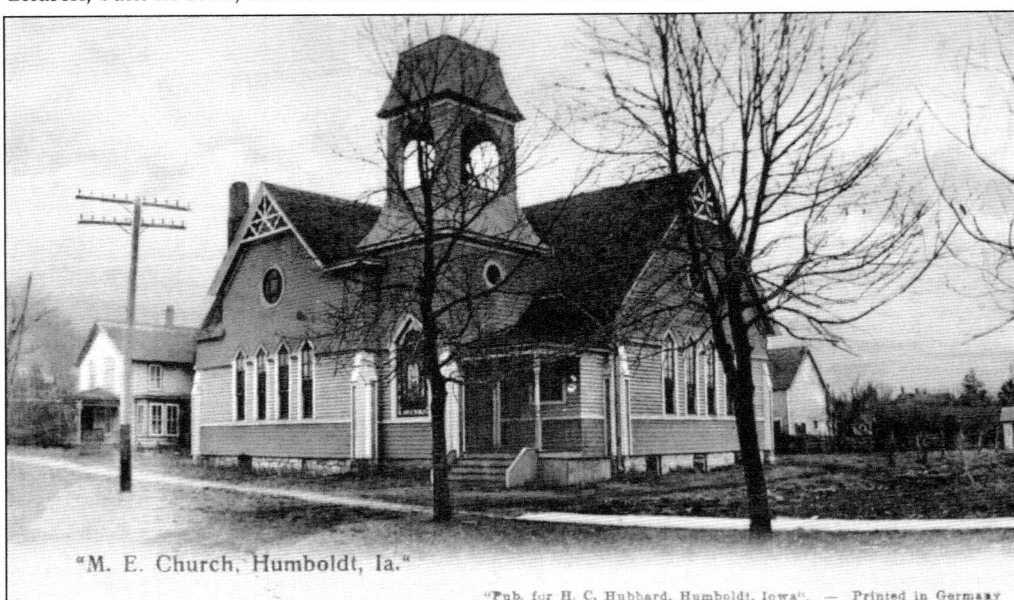

The Humboldt Methodist Episcopal Church was organized in 1882 and met upstairs in rooms in the Harkness Building, after which they met in the Baptist church on Sunday afternoons. The first Humboldt Methodist Church was erected in 1888 and cost $2,500. They shared a pastor with Dakota City until 1892. The parsonage was built in 1896, and in 1919 and 1981, new churches were built.

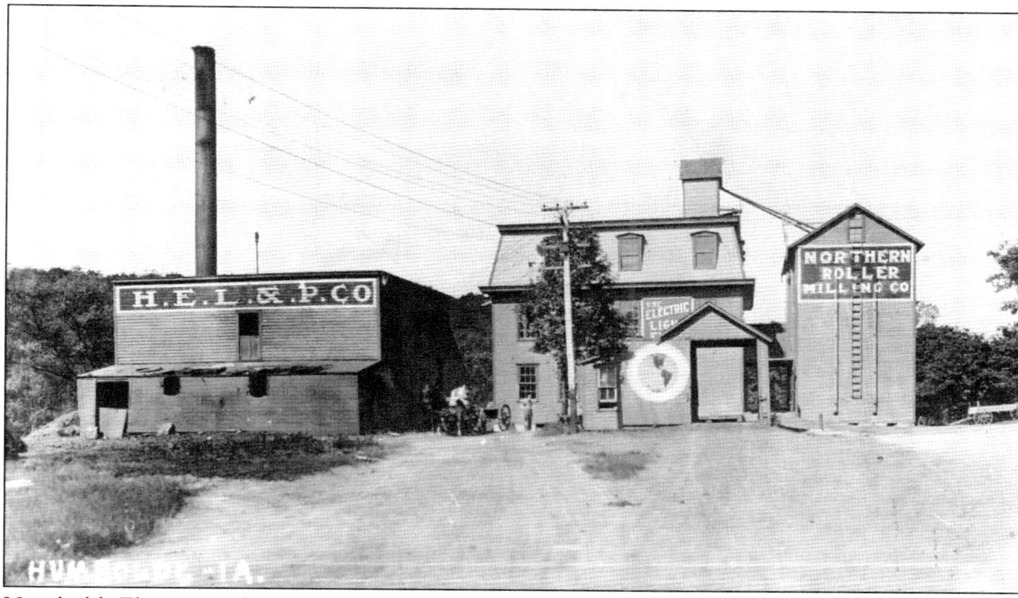

Humboldt Electric Light and Power Company was formed in 1898 by local men who produced electricity by a waterwheel connected to an electric generator at the old mill. In 1911, the Northern Iowa Power Company built the hydroelectric power plant and concrete dam. Shown above are the first power plant, the old gristmill erected by Taft in 1865, and the tower of the Northern Roller Milling Company.

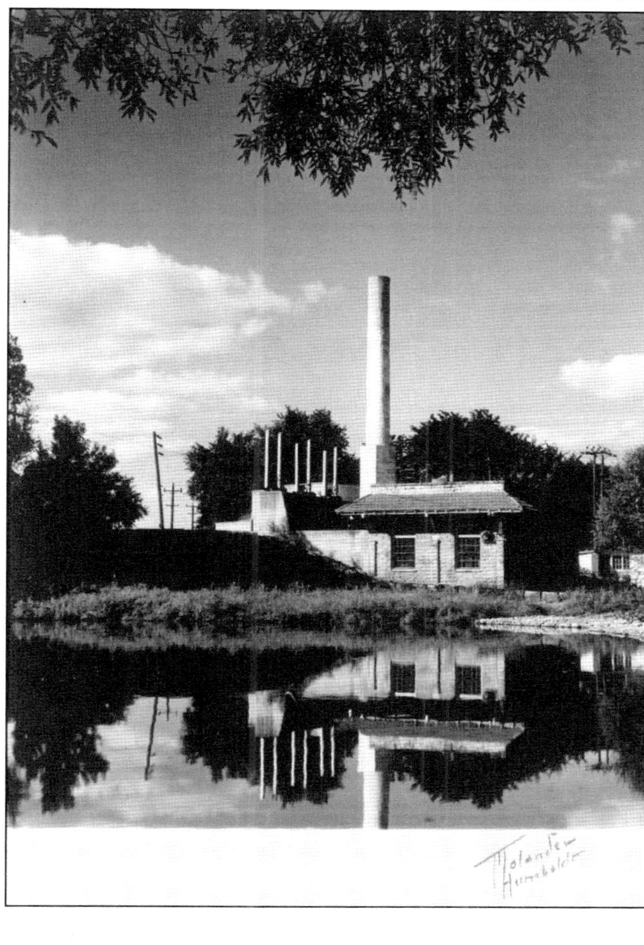

The hydroelectric power plant, built in 1911 by the Northern Iowa Power Company, is shown in this photograph taken by Ben Molander from across the river. In 1915, it was sold to the Northern Iowa Gas and Electric Company. This company made further extension of lines and, in 1923, built the Rutland Hydroelectric plant.

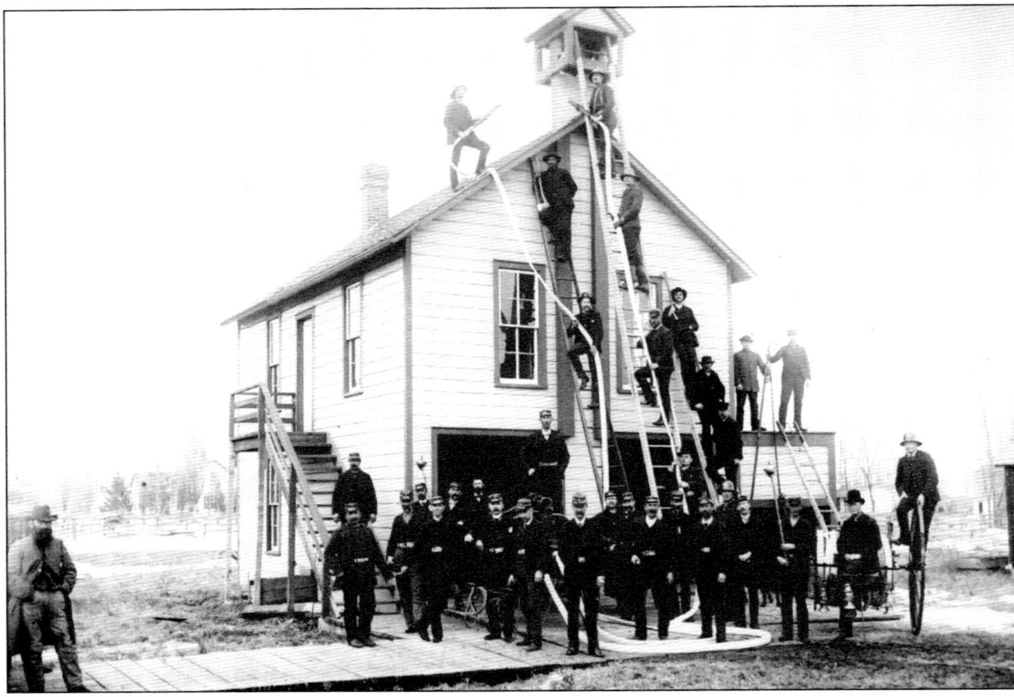

Firemen display their equipment at the town hall in 1893. City offices were upstairs, and fire trucks were below. The jail is to the right. The volunteer company was founded in 1884 with 34 men. The first piece of equipment was a hand pump. Three huge cisterns were dug on Sumner Avenue to provide water. A suction hose was dropped into the nearest cistern, and the hose was carried to the flames.

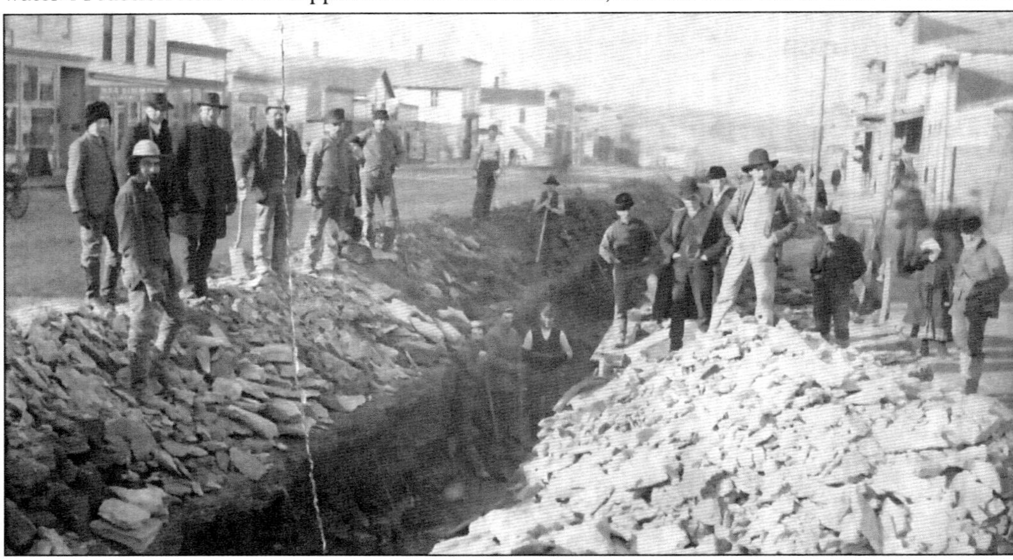

In 1898, the Humboldt City Council granted a group of downtown businessmen the right to construct a sewer. Workmen are shown digging through the limestone on Sumner Avenue to install the line, which went south at Sixth Street to Second Avenue South, where it turned west and emptied into the river. A number of Humboldt's early business buildings can be seen in this photograph. Many workmen were Danish immigrants.

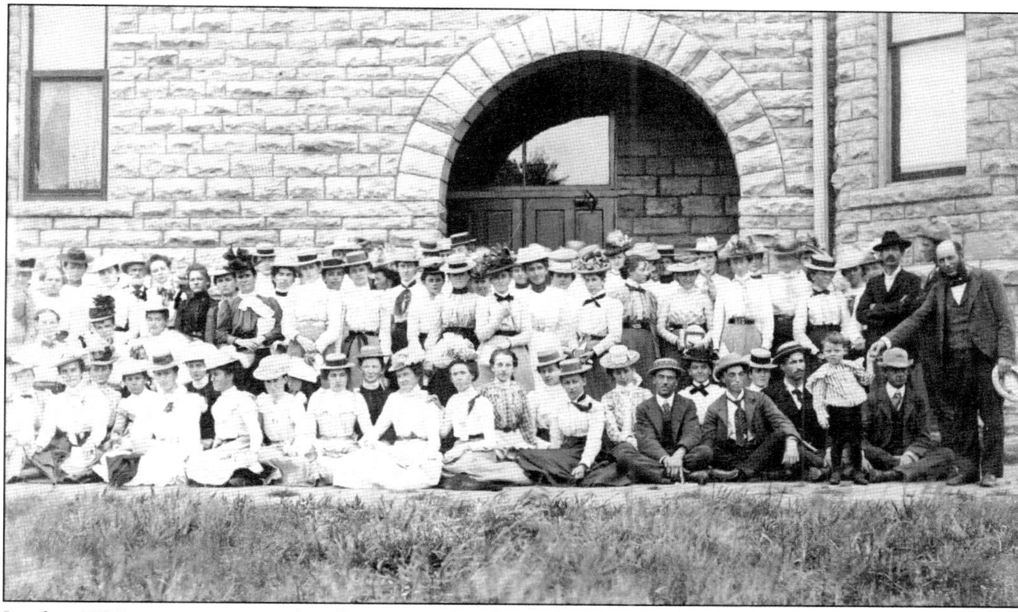

In the 1890s, a county teachers' institute was held every summer for all teachers who taught in the rural and town schools. This group is shown posing by the door of the new Humboldt School. Superintendent Clarence Messer is shown at the right holding the hand of his son Angus.

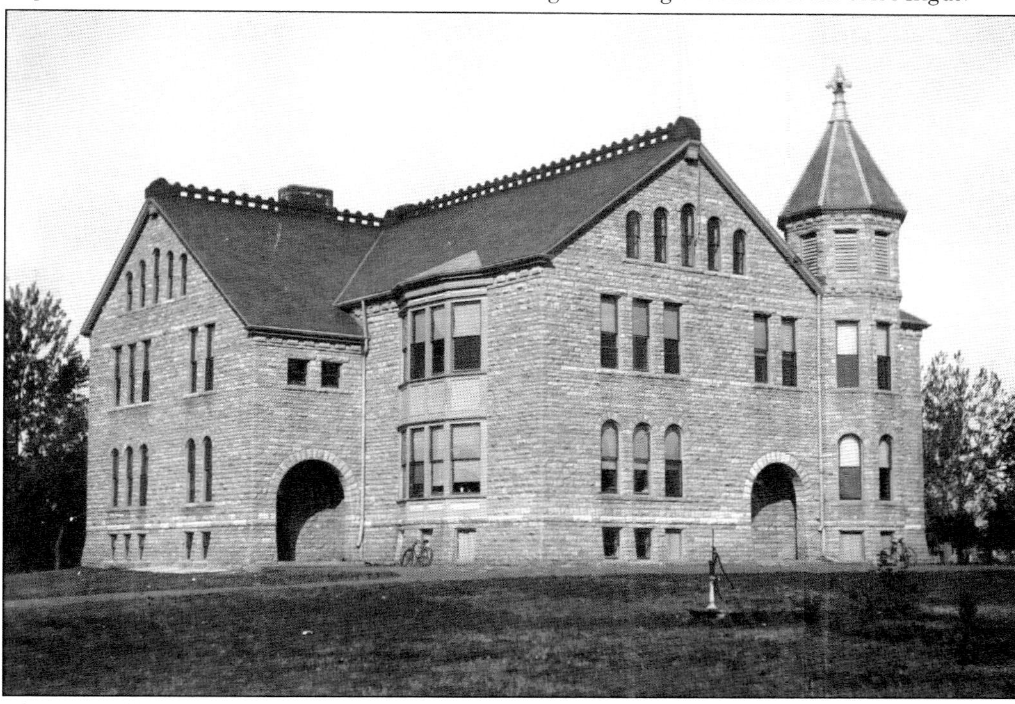

The second building for Humboldt School served from 1894 to 1918. A majestic stone building, it set the tone for a prosperous town. The first floor provided four large classrooms and the superintendent's office. The second floor had a large study hall, four recitation rooms, and a library. Large corridors were found on each floor. Students slid down the stair rail whenever possible.

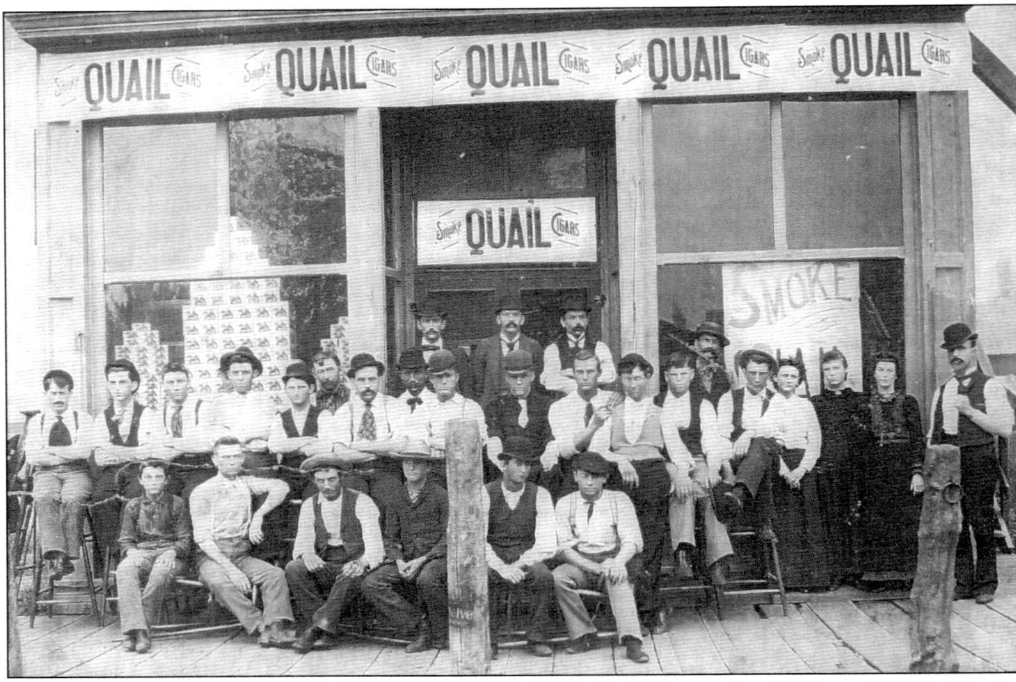

Humboldt had four cigar factories that produced many cigars during the 1890s and 1900s. Modoc cigars were manufactured at 506 Sumner Avenue. The Quail Cigar Factory, located at 710 Sumner, employed 27 people and had a good baseball team. The Hilsenoff Cigar Factory was at 619 Sumner. Another made Koepe's Speckled Trout cigars, which sold for a nickel.

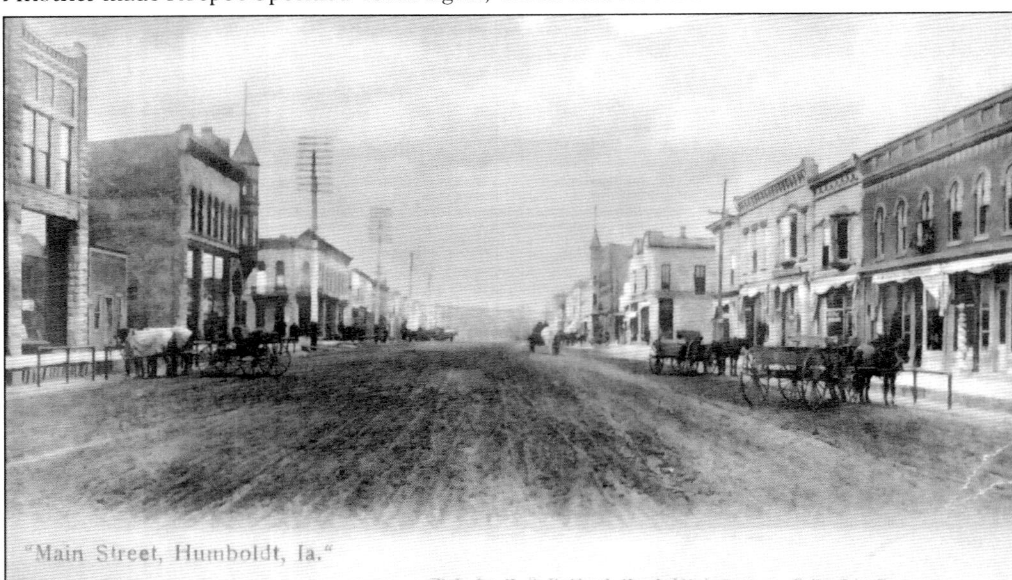

Sumner Avenue in Humboldt is shown looking west from the 500 block. Telephone poles on the left (south) side of the street reveal this photograph was taken about 1905. Electric lines were strung along the right (north) side of the street. Prominent buildings were the White Department Store on the left corner and the Finch Buildings at center right.

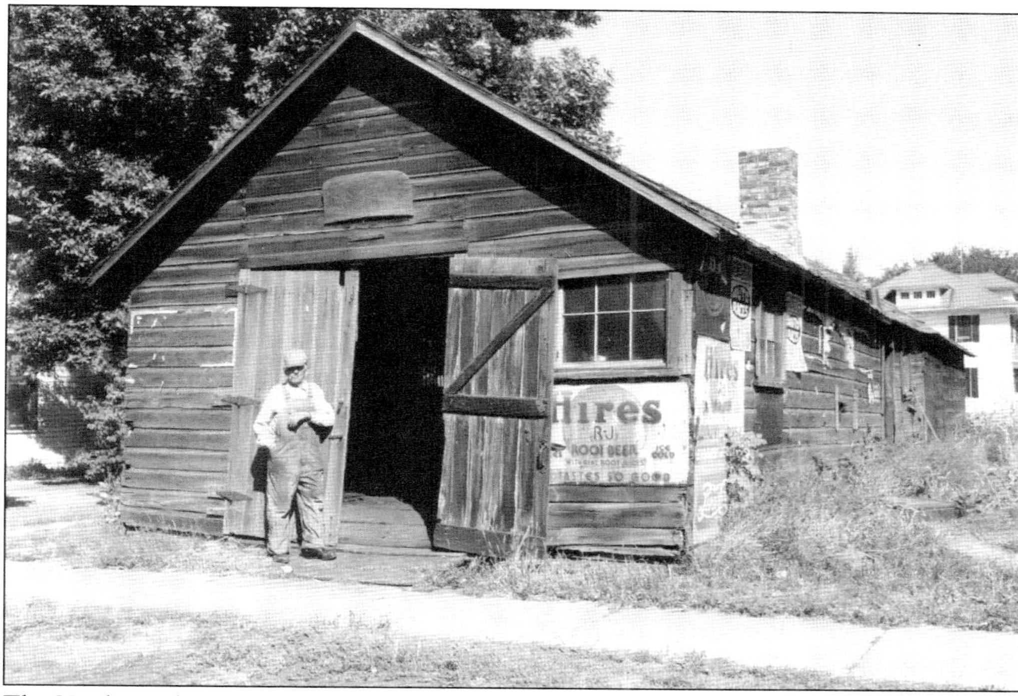

The Hawkins Blacksmith Shop began in Dakota City but, in the 1890s, moved down the hill to Humboldt and located on the northwest corner of Third Street and Sumner Avenue. Fred Hawkins is shown in front of his shop, which was removed in 1957 when Dr. Larry Dunscombe and Dr. Ken Pride built their offices at that location.

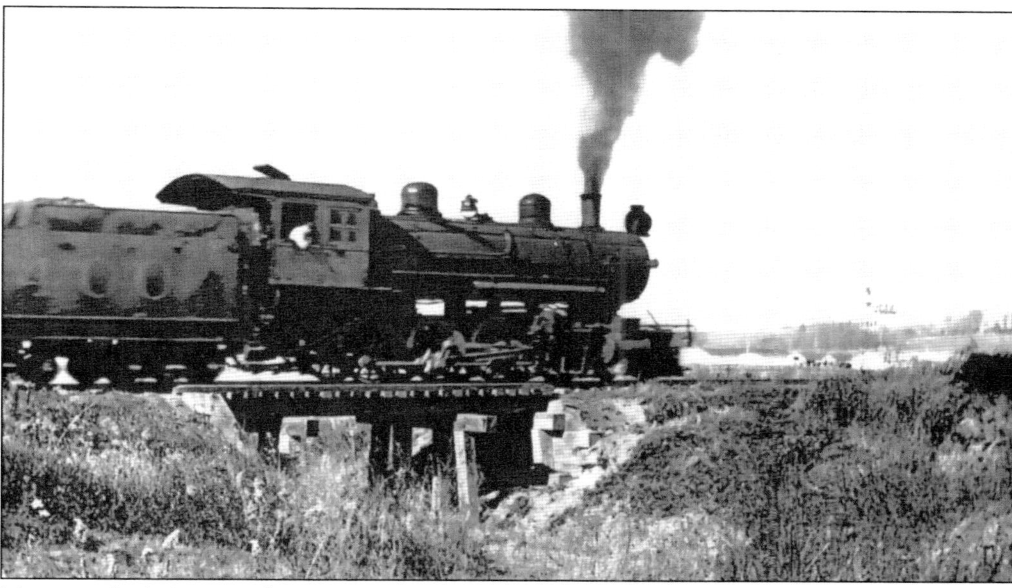

Minneapolis & St. Louis locomotive No. 400 climbs the grade out of Humboldt with the morning freight. The engine is passing over a small trestle spanning a gravel road that was and still is known as "the Rat Hole." In the distance behind the fairground barns are the main building and two dormitories of Humboldt College on College Hill.

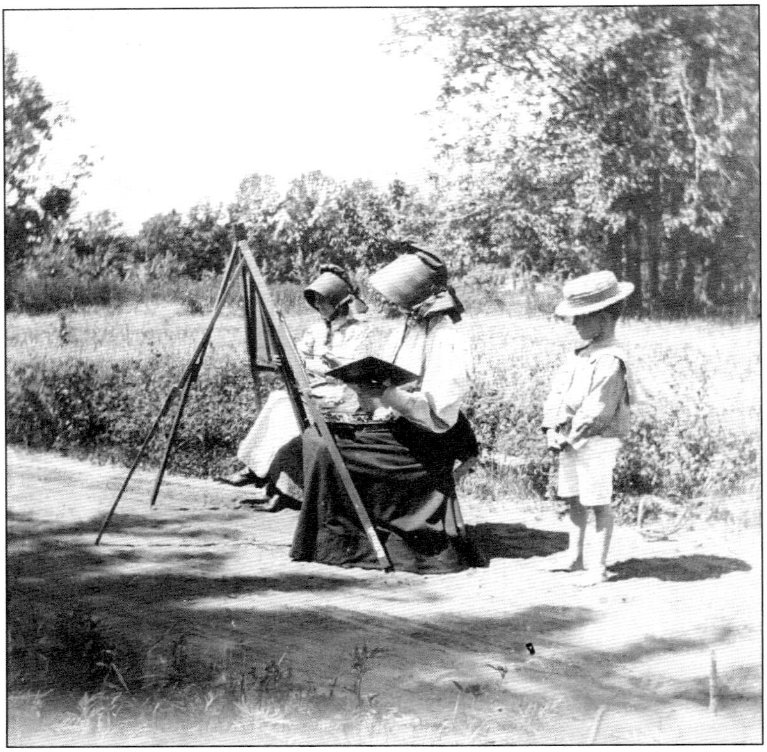

Clara Redmond Ray and a friend are shown sketching along the West Des Moines River in Humboldt. The boy is possibly Don Sterns. Ray was one of several talented artists, including Florence Prouty and Julia Nelson, whose paintings and drawings are on display at the Humboldt County Historical Museum.

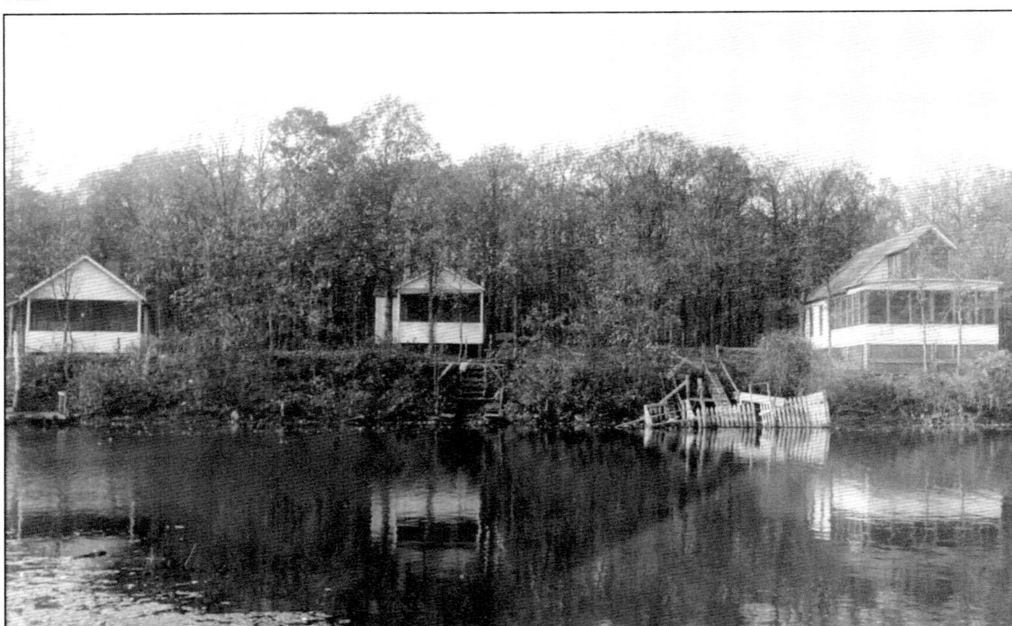

By the turn of the century, Lake Nokomis, located above the dam on the West Fork of the Des Moines River, was a popular recreational site. Cottages on the west side are pictured in 1903 by Frank Bicknell. The Pinney, Russell, and Sterns families owned them. Visitors took a boat from the ramp on the east side or hiked on the Indian Trail past Bicknell Woods.

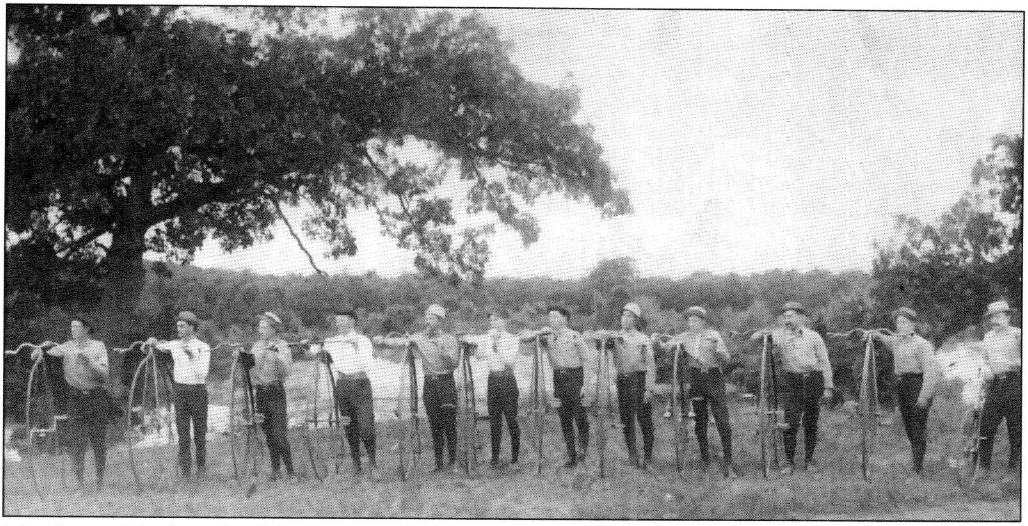

Members of the bicycle club, the "Humboldt's Scorchers," are shown in 1890 with their high-wheel bicycles by the old dam on the West Fork of the Des Moines River. From left to right are Elmer Peck, G.W. "Jud" Marsh, H.H. Perkins, L.D. Hack, Sid Taft, Fred Fairman, T.W. "Waylie" Rogers, John Rine, Ted White, N.H. Knowles, S.W. Smith, and Pete Saul.

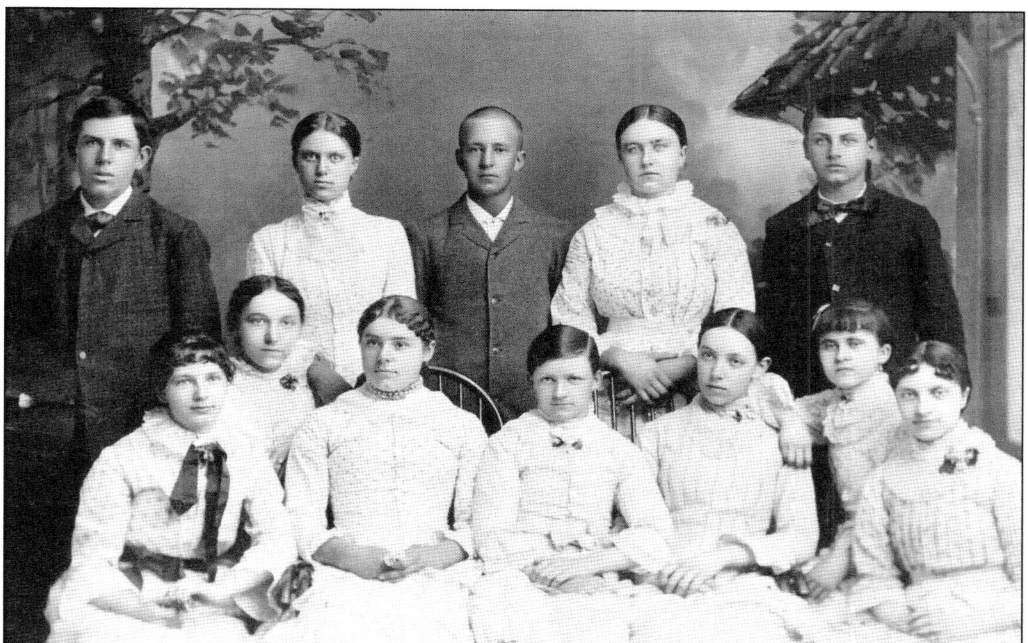

Humboldt eighth-grade graduates in 1883 are, from left to right, (sitting) Morda Stevens, Charlena Welch, Ophie Loomis, H.J. Cora VanVelsor, Mida French, Flora Young, and Carrie Lorbeer; (standing) John Rine, Fretta Winegarten, Ned Jones, Lottie Munson, and A.B. White. The first 10th-grade graduation came in 1888 with Clara Bicknell and Marian Thomas graduating; the first 12th-grade graduation was in 1892.

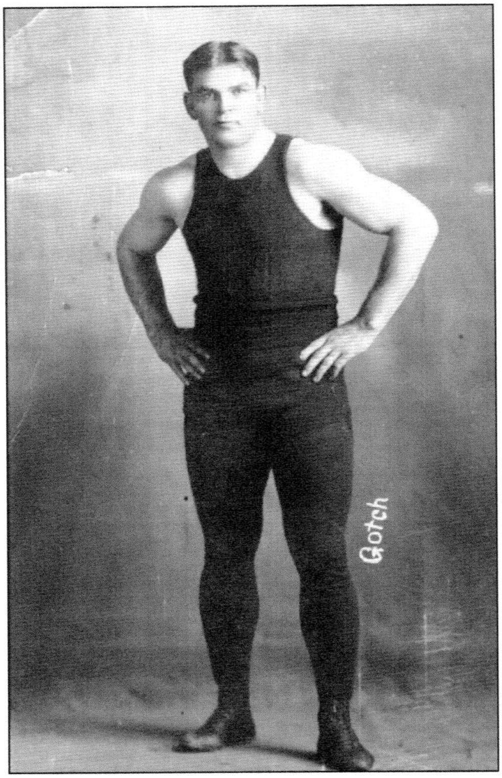

Frank A. Gotch attained national and international fame as a world champion wrestler. He was born in 1877 on a farm near the "forks" in Beaver Township and often wrestled with members of the neighborhood threshing crew. After a few public matches he took on "Farmer Burns" who defeated him but became Gotch's teacher and trainer. Gotch beat many state and national wrestlers and defeated European champion George Hackenschmidt in 1908.

In the summer of 1911, Frank Gotch established a training center in Bicknell Park. Many wrestlers and trainers were here, and great crowds gathered to watch. Shown are, from left to right, Emil Klank, Joe Rogers, Frank Gotch, Jeff Reimer, Jim Asbell, and Yussiff Hassan. After becoming world champion, Gotch retired in 1913 and formed an automobile agency with P.F. Saul and later Albert Wittman. Gotch died in 1917 at the age of 40.

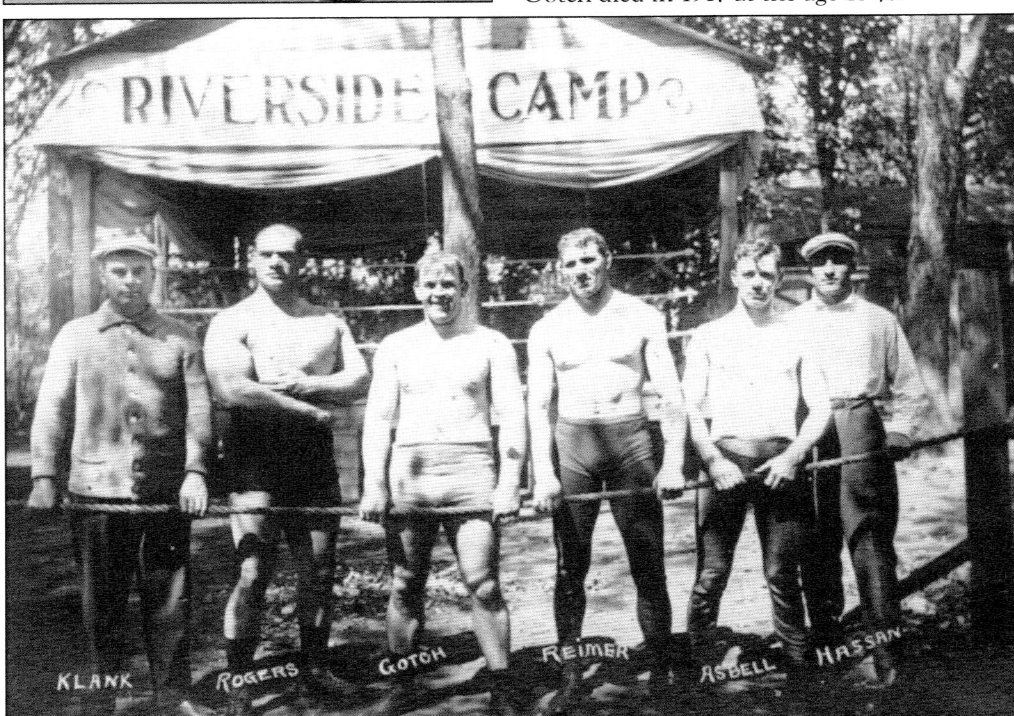

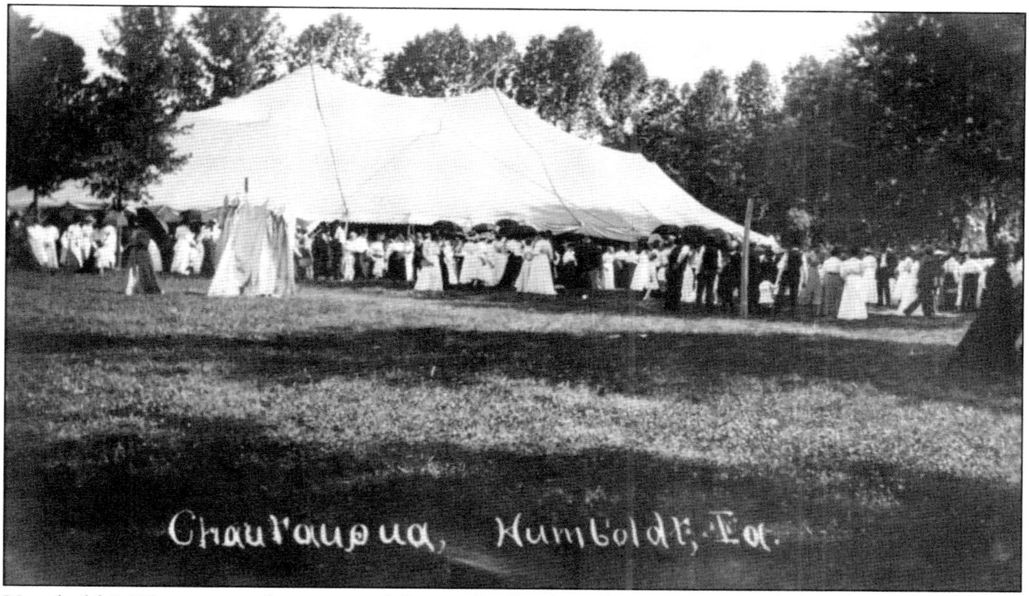

Humboldt's Chautauqua Literary and Scientific Circle is the oldest remaining circle in the nation. Led by Aurelia Wickes Lorbeer, who knew the organizers at Lake Chautauqua, New York, members began reading assigned books the year after the group was organized. Shown in August 1908 is the Chautauqua tent set up in Taft Park. It was there where many noted orators, musicians, magicians, and comedians performed for 10 days.

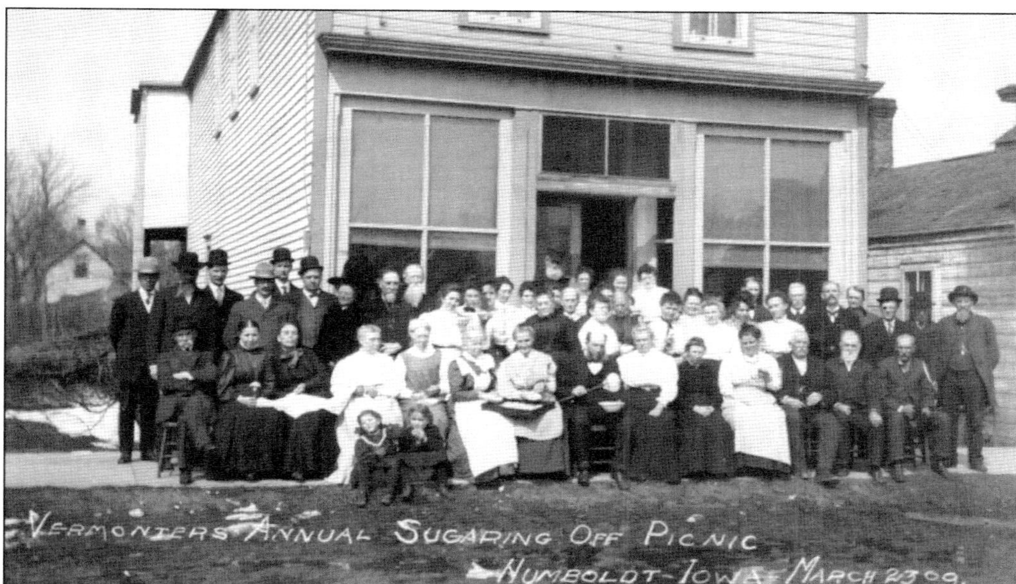

The 1909 Vermonter's Annual sugaring-off picnic is shown at 409 Sumner Avenue. The Vermont Society of Humboldt County organized the event in 1905, and the celebration continued until the beginning of World War I. The group purchased syrup collected from maple trees in Vermont and, on the designated day, met to boil it down and enjoy a New England boiled dinner. "Humboldt was like a New England Village," reported Frances Messer.

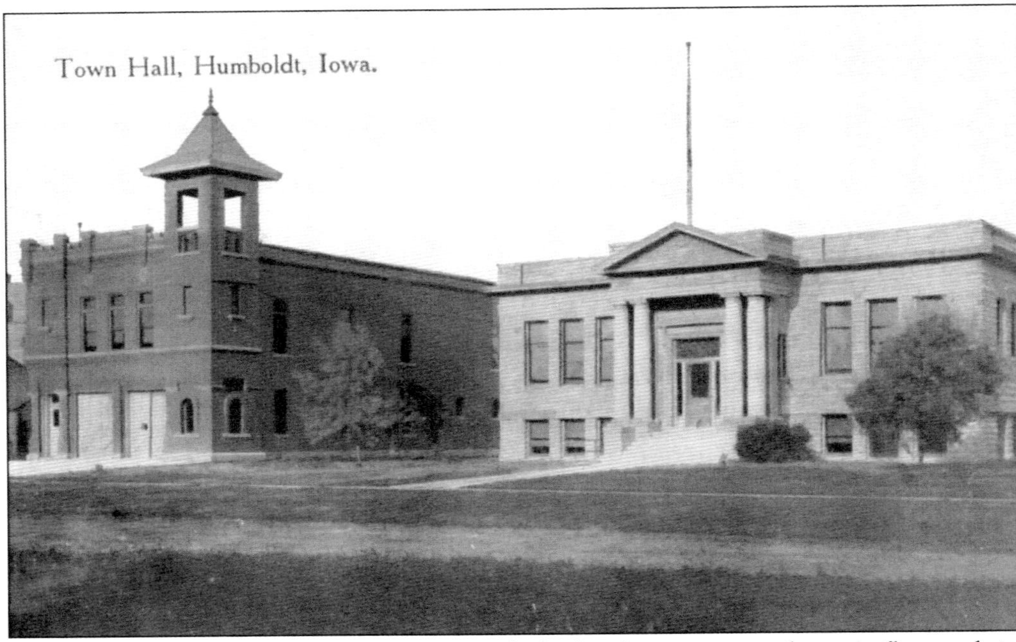

Humboldt City Hall (left) was built in 1912 with the fire department on the main floor and city offices upstairs. The Humboldt Carnegie Public Library (right) was dedicated in 1909 after a long campaign by civic groups. It was built of native stones dug from a quarry across the street to the north and was hand-hewn by the Mayer brothers. An addition was completed in 1992.

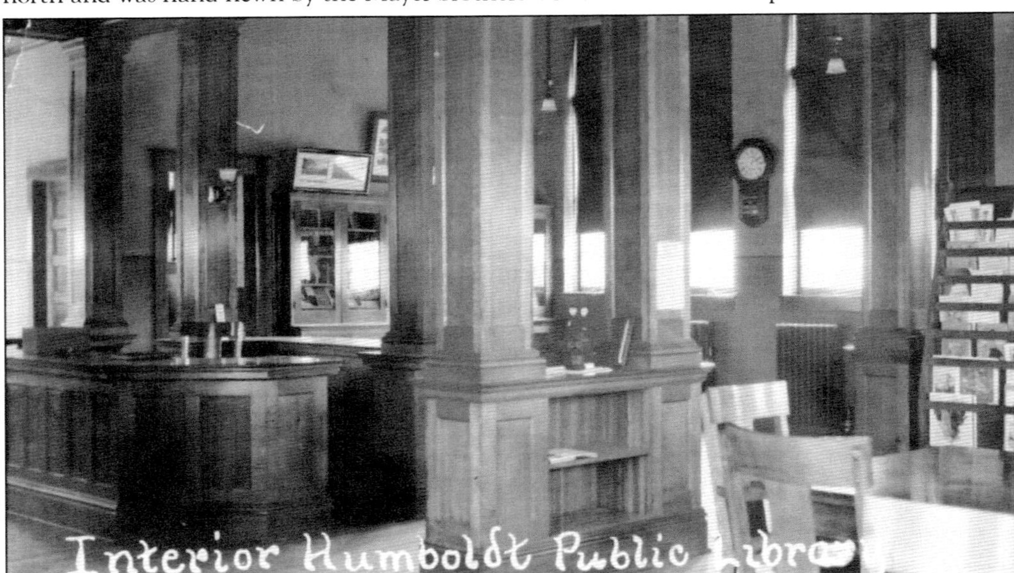

Behind this desk at the Humboldt Public Library, librarians including Grace Shellenberger, Nellie Pinney, Greta DeSmidt, Myrtle Parsons, Mary Lowder, Frances Messer, Grace Bennett, Margaret Oxborrow, Bill Verbrugge, Virginia Hart, Marilyn Fevold, Carol Larson, Vivian Hansen, Marilyn Lindemann, Stacey Lundsford, Demi Johnson, and Nikki Ehlers, checked out books. Laura Shellenberger, Louise Davis, Eunice Greuner, Lib Hadar, Irene Blair, Jean Holste, Martha Schmidt, and Sarah Evans were children's librarians.

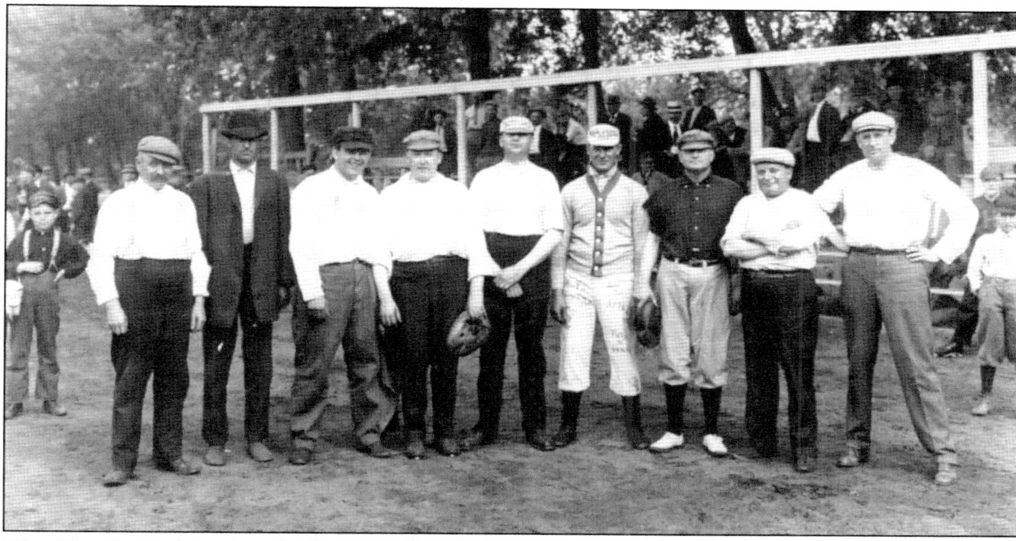

The Humboldt Fats baseball team played the Humboldt Leans team on the old fairground diamond. Bert White and Pete Saul of the Fats and Clarence McFarland and Ted White of the Leans could throw the ball hard and bat them far. The Fats are, from left to right, Will Strong, Robert Johnston, Frank Gotch, Ben McGee, Dr. VanVorhees, A. Lehman, A.B. White, Pete Saul, and Archie Wilder.

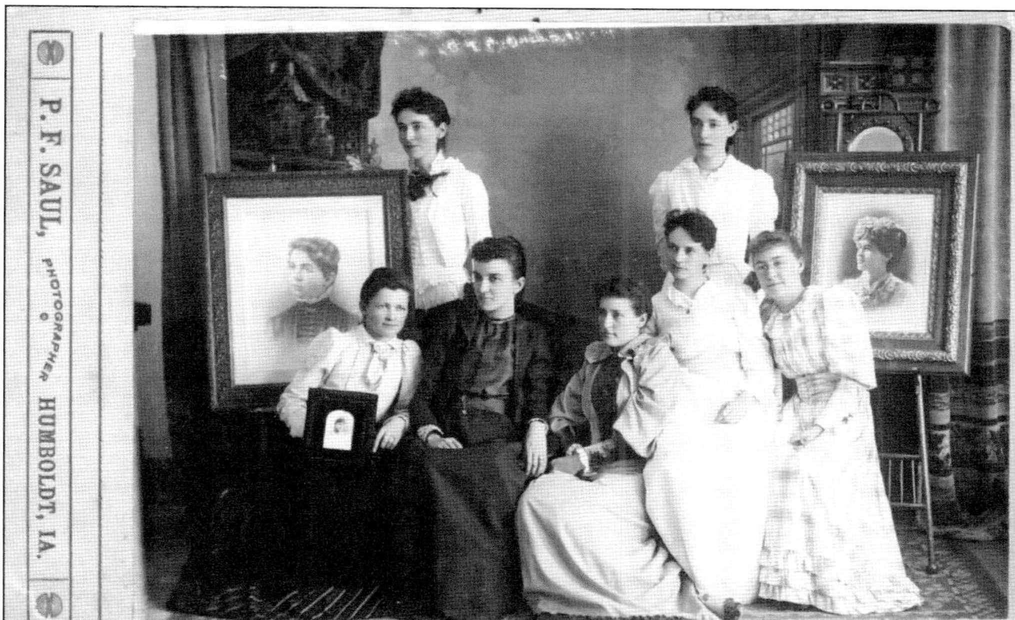

The Unity Club was afraid of no subject and tackled ancient and modern philosophers, higher biblical criticism, and Darwin. Some of the members included Charlena Welch, Mida French, Franklyn French, Mary Taft, Frankie Welch, Clara Berkhimer, Edith Prouty, Cora VanVelsor, Mary Collson, Morda Stevens, Marian Thomas, and Clara Bicknell, some of whom are shown above. LeRoy Berrier joined and went to prison for mailing his views on birth control to those who requested them.

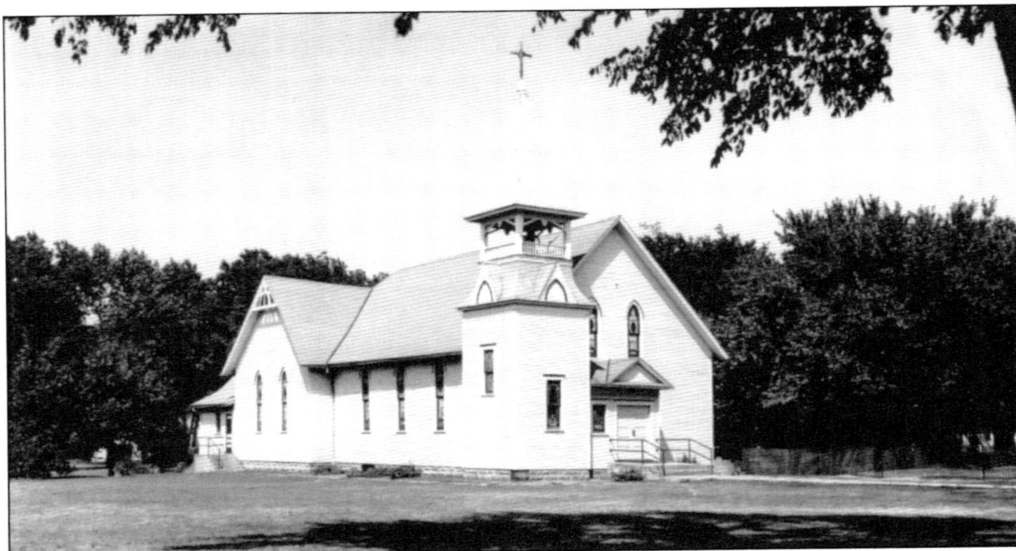

St. Mary's Catholic Church met first in Dakota City Town Hall. The congregation moved to Humboldt in 1904 and built a church on the northwest corner of Third Street and First Avenue South. St. Mary's School was built in 1920 at 305 Fourth Avenue North. In 1926, they moved the church next to the school (shown). A new edifice was built in 1961, and the new school was added in 1983.

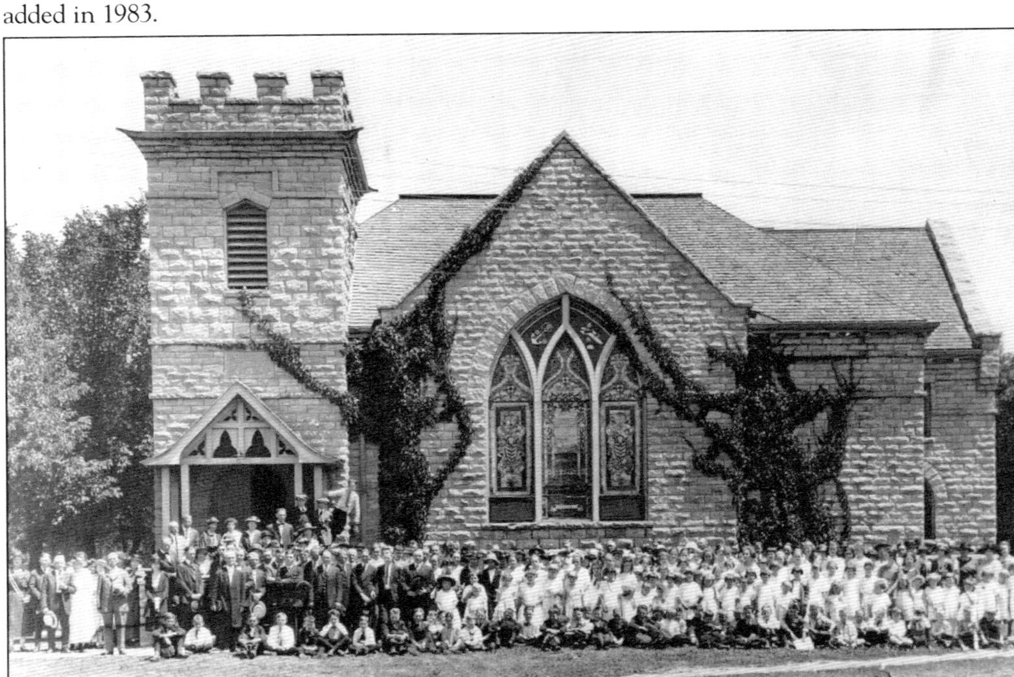

The new Humboldt Congregational Church is shown on Children's Day 1922. This church was built in 1904 from limestone quarried on the site. The stained-glass windows were made in Germany. Financed by the Ladies Circle, an addition to the south (church kitchen and "blue room") was made in 1921 when the church celebrated its 50th anniversary. (Courtesy of the Congregational United Church of Christ.)

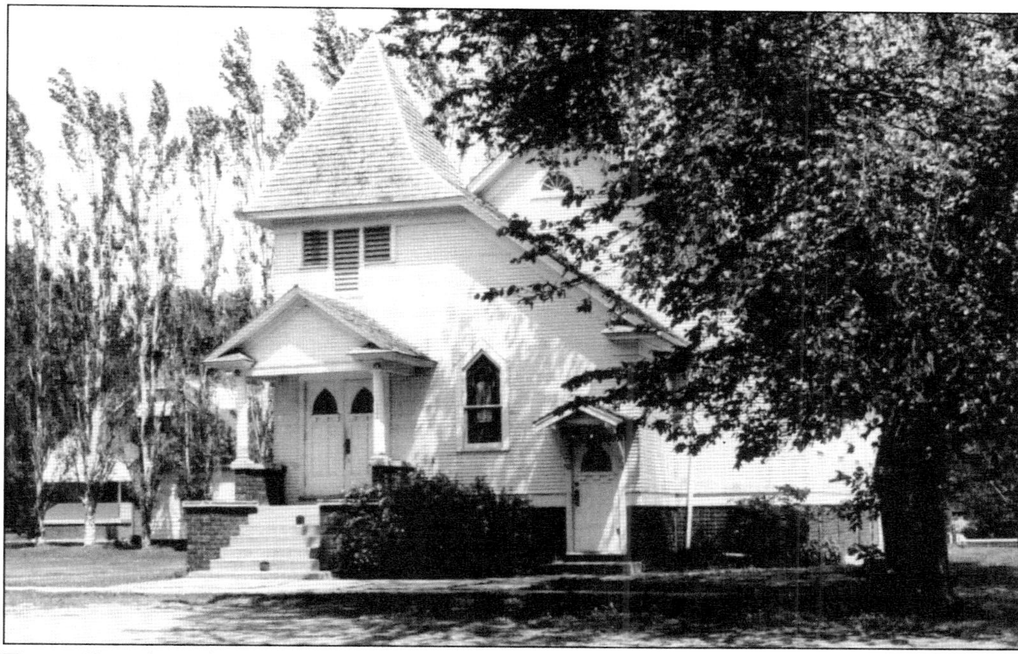

Trinity Danish Lutheran Church was built in 1923 at 407 Eighth Street North. The congregation often shared a pastor with the Trinity Danish Lutheran Church in Rutland. A Danish service was preached Sunday morning, and a sermon in English was given in the evening. The Trinity Danish Lutheran Church of Humboldt merged with the First Lutheran Church to form Our Saviour's Lutheran in 1959. Seventh Day Adventists and later the Abundant Life Christian Fellowship worshipped there.

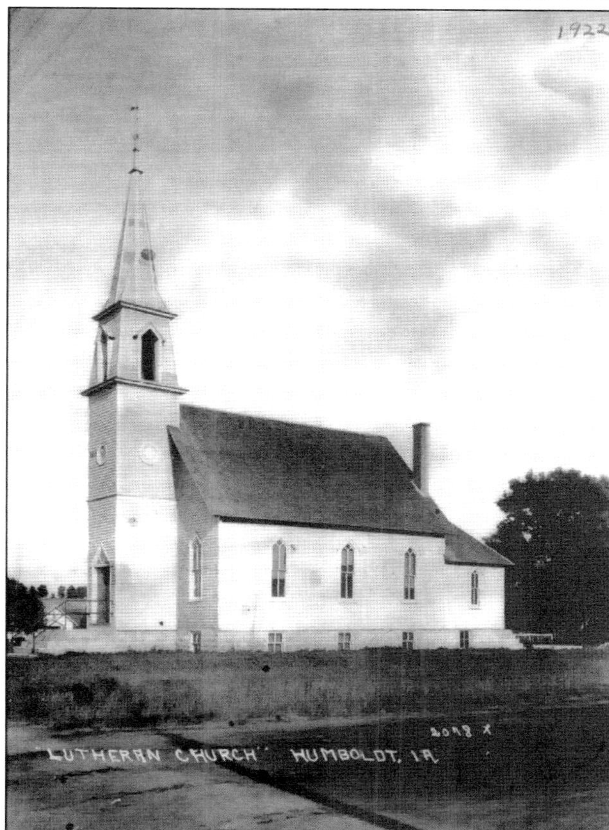

The First Lutheran Church was built in 1897 at 227 Sumner Avenue. Norwegian Lutherans first settled in northern (Delana) and southern (Corinth and Norway) Humboldt County townships. As time progressed, some settled in Humboldt and needed a town church. They were joined by Danish Lutherans in 1959 to form Our Saviour's Lutheran Church, which built a new edifice at 1212 Sumner Avenue Southwest.

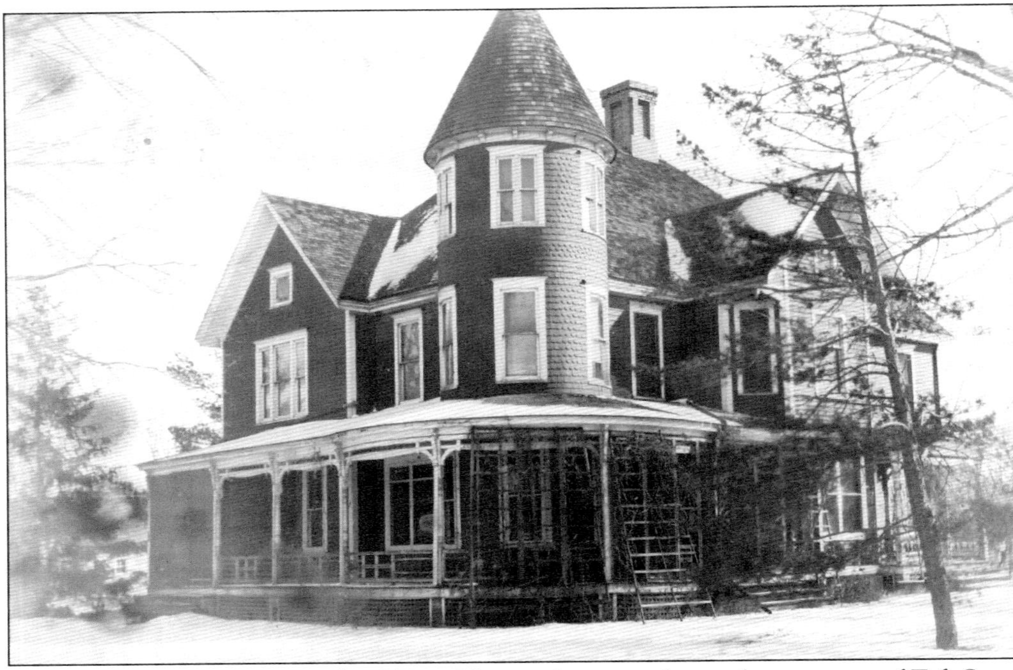

Avery house was built in 1891 by O.F. and Jennie Avery on the southeast corner of Taft Street and Second Avenue South. The three-story Victorian home, beautifully appointed with fine woodcarving, stained-glass windows, and an open stairway, became the home of their daughter Minnie, who delighted in entertaining. After her death, the house became a funeral home for the Duncan, Skaugstad, Bogaard, Lindhart, and Mason mortuaries.

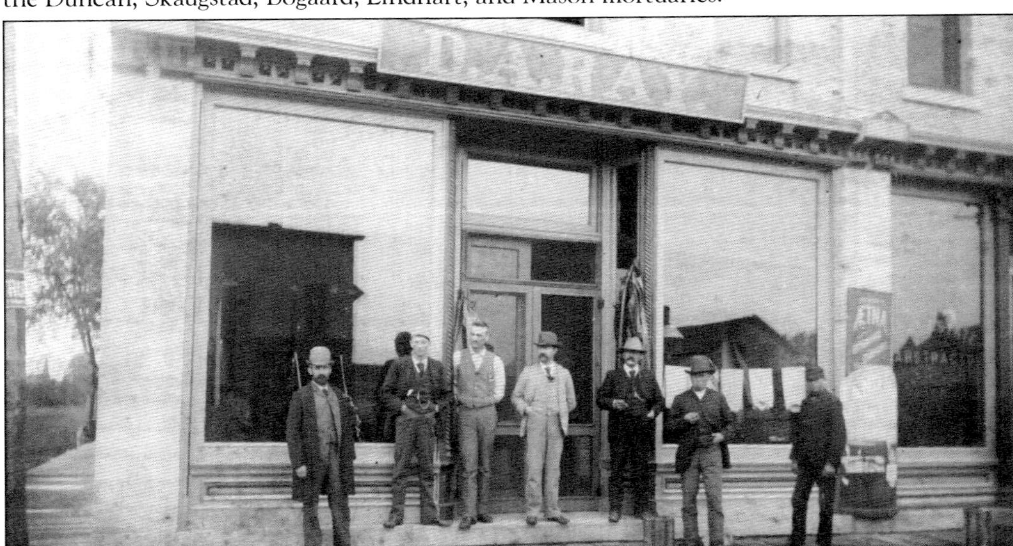

D.A. Ray's General Mercantile Store was in the Harkness Building, 627 Sumner Avenue, in 1890. Ray came to Humboldt with Frank E. Adams in 1882, and they established themselves with this business, which they successfully operated until 1898, when they sold out to E.A Wilder. Then, Ray was the postmaster, the mayor of Humboldt for three terms, and the president of the First National Bank.

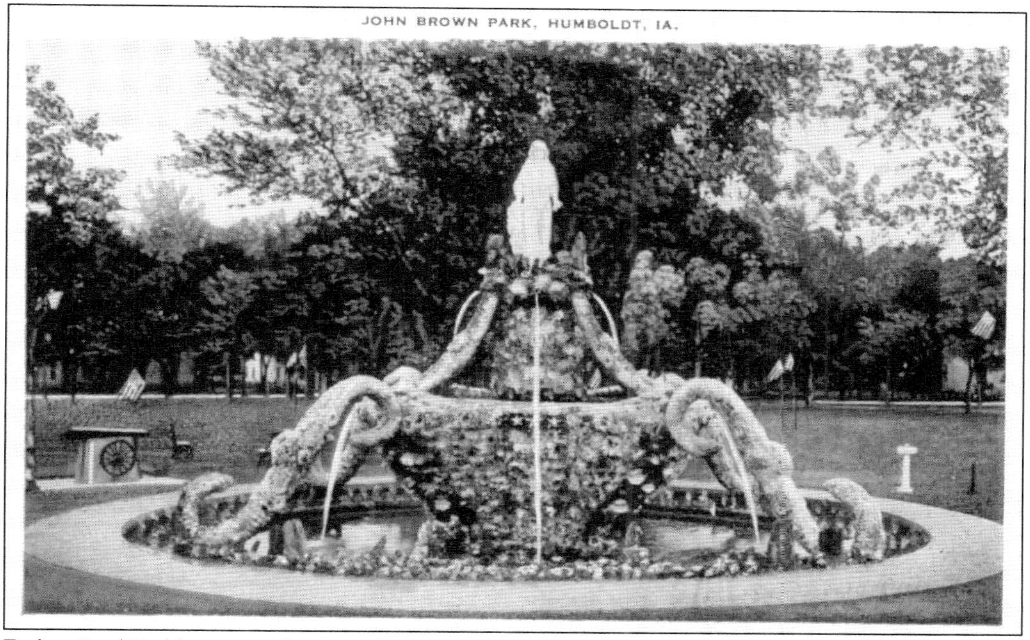

Father Paul Dobberstein, the famed builder of the Grotto at West Bend, constructed the Liberty Fountain at John Brown Park in 1918. The multiple aggregate fountain contains a wide variety of stones, minerals, seashells, and curiosities collected by Father Dobberstein. It is in the process of being restored in 2011.

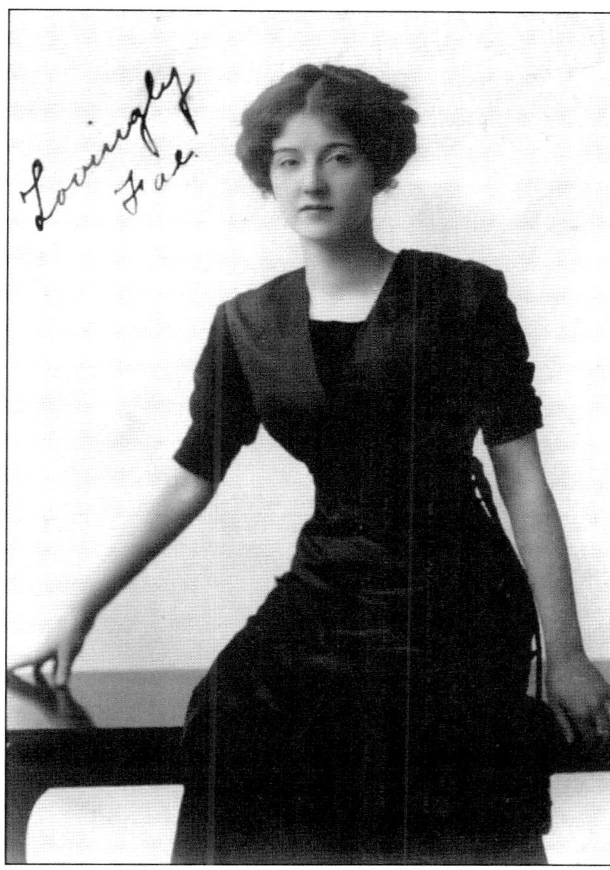

The statue on top of the fountain was sculpted in Italy and shipped to the United States. It is a memorial for Fae Hessian, a young girl from Humboldt who died in her early 20s after contracting tuberculosis in 1912. Her father, Dennis Hessian, commissioned Father Dobberstein to build the fountain. It is through the efforts of Ed Ruse, a local druggist, that the fountain was maintained through the years.

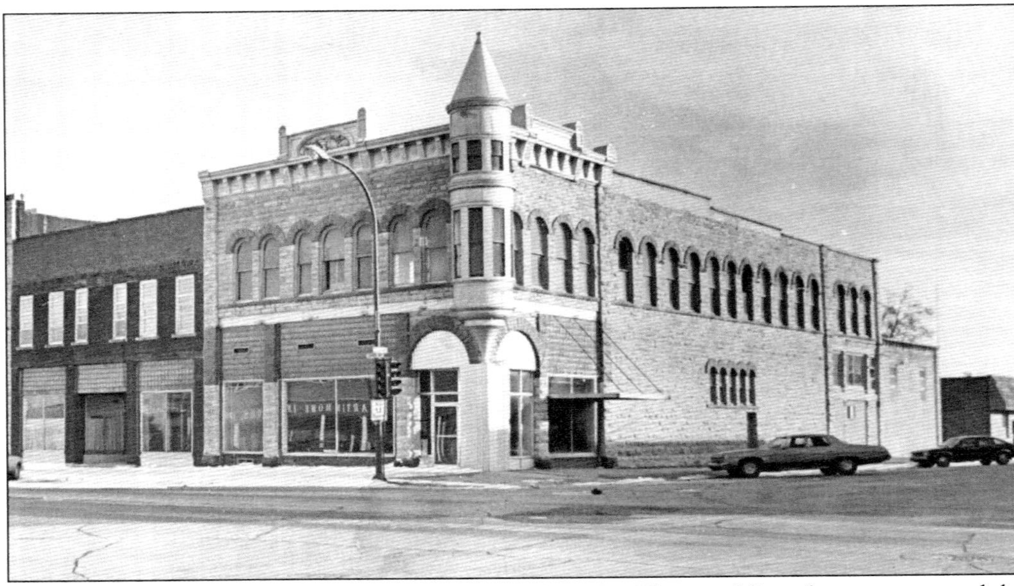

A.B. "Bert" White, who was long connected with the G.B. White and Sons firm, constructed the White Department Store in 1899. The mammoth building was two stories high with a cupola on the corner. A pressed steel ceiling was high above the first floor, and a balcony provided additional display space. An elevator went to the second floor, which was devoted to coats and carpets, and to the basement for heavy goods.

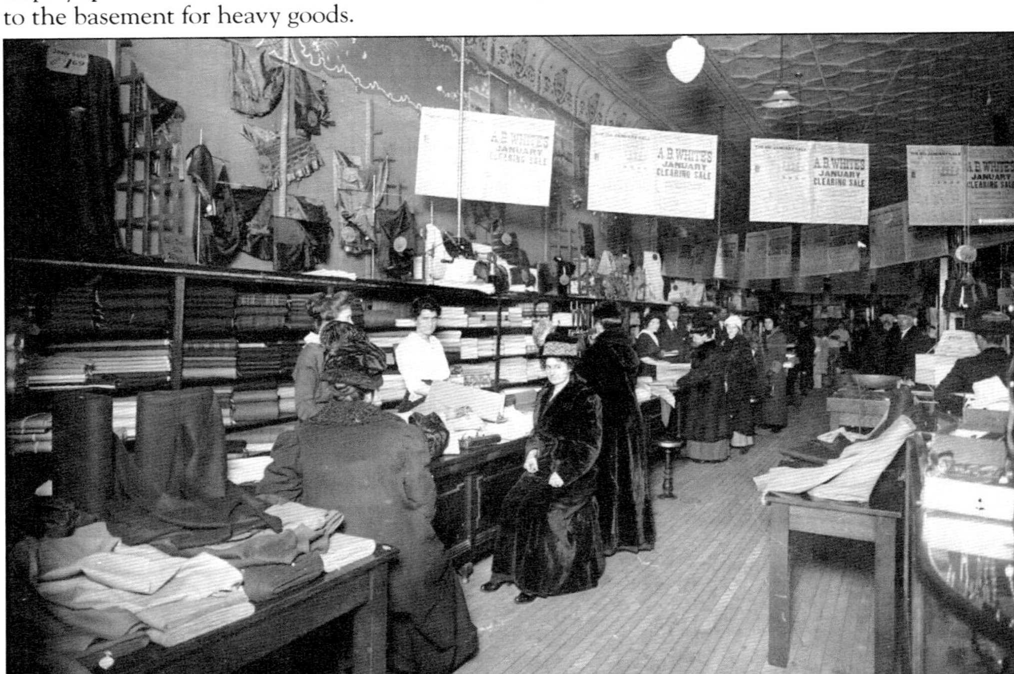

Women are seated at the fabric counter in the White Department Store during a January clearance sale in the 1920s. A system of vacuum tubes conveyed sale slips and money to the store office. An addition on the south end of the building provided space for a grocery department. The store became Johnson's in the 1950s, Gibson's in the 1970s, and finally Pamida. It was taken down in 1988.

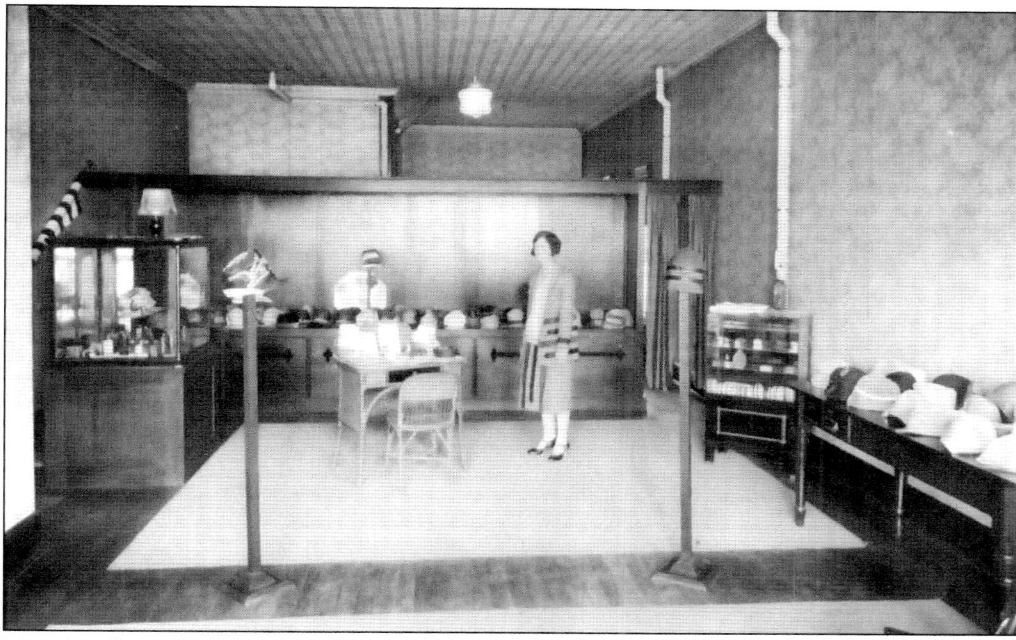

Most locally owned stores were small. Julia Nelson's Millinery shop was located at 508 Sumner Avenue in 1931. She was one of several women who created and sold hats of the latest fashion in the community. Clara Pierce Harkness, Miss L.J. Simmons, and Mrs. J.M. Spayde were some who realized that women could run their own businesses on Main Street.

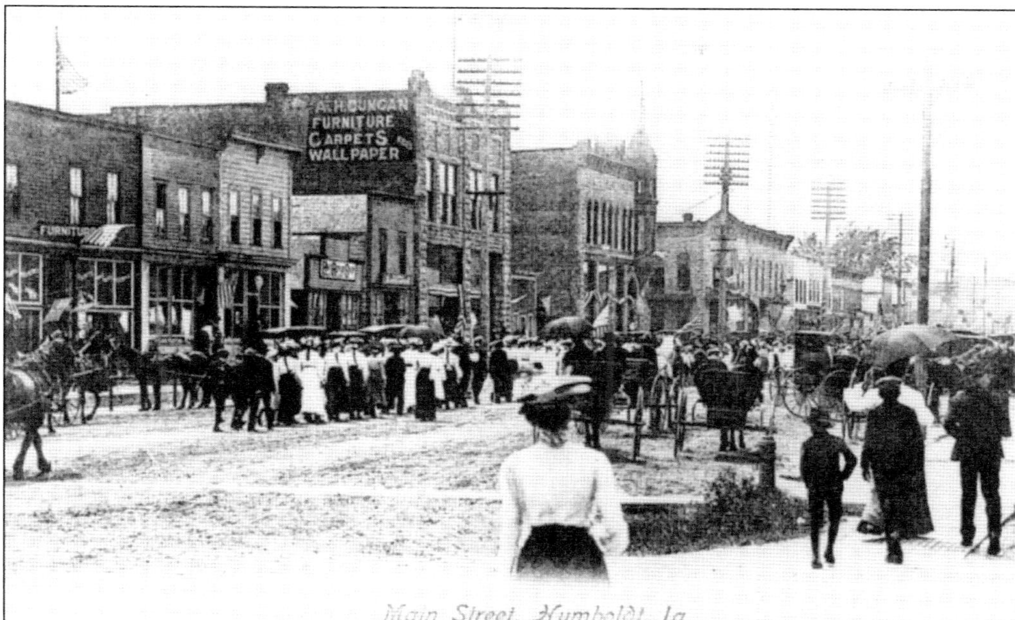

Flags are waving as a parade passes on Sumner Avenue in about 1908. The stores include, from left to right, a furniture store, printing office, dressmaker, furniture repair, millinery, Duncan Furniture, implement dealer, and White Department Store. The town had to wait until 1920 to have the street paved, forcing skirts to be hemmed several inches above the dirt.

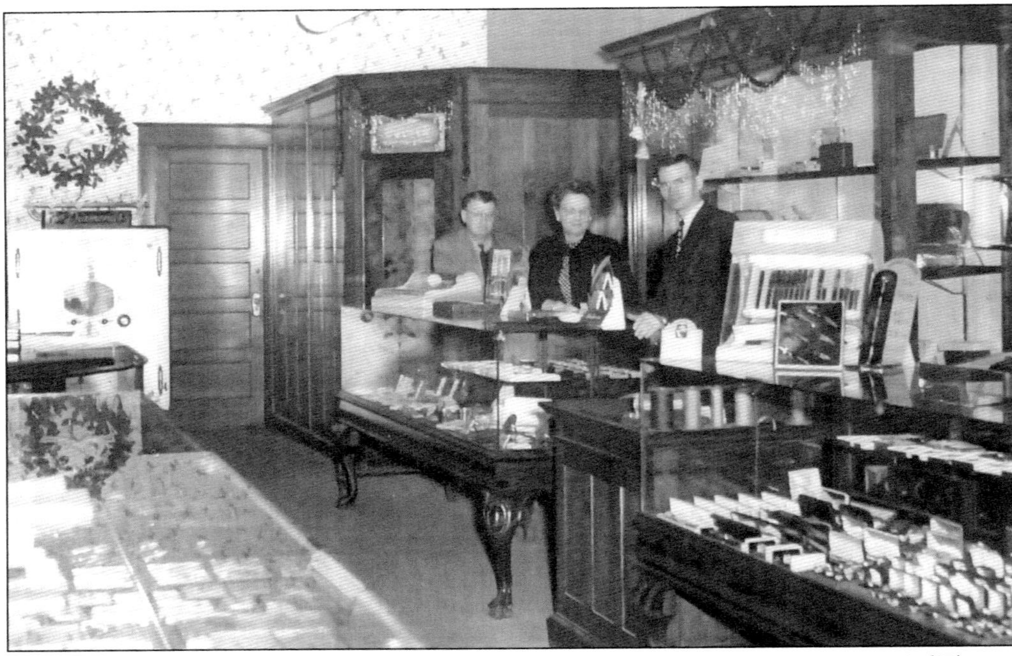

Art and Lucille Hof are shown in 1954 with Bob Thomas, their new partner in Hof-Thomas Jewelry. Thomas became full owner in 1964. After his death, daughter Susan Eggerich took over. N.H. Knowles began his jewelry store in 1880. Around 1900, John A. Reed began his jewelry store at 626 Sumner Avenue. He bought out Knowles, built a new store at 608 Sumner in 1914, and sold it to Art Hof.

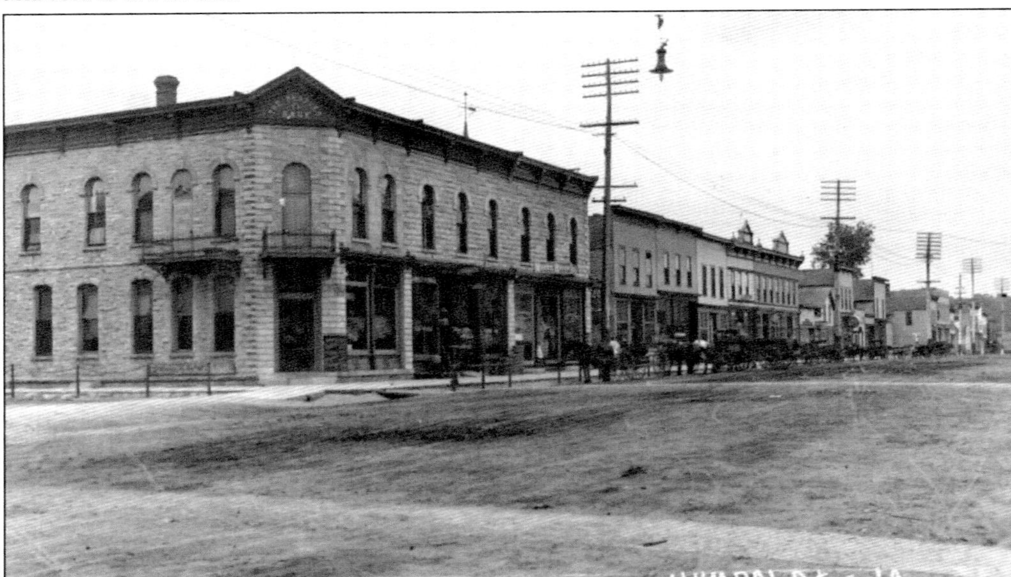

The south side of Sumner Avenue is shown about 1908. From left to right are the People's Bank, C.E. Ward Hardware, C.J. White Clothing, O.K. Restaurant, Smith and Rogers Meats, B.E. Stong Grocery, Otto Matthies Jewelry, Otto Windrath's, Hackley Cleaners, John Reed Jewelry, Pinney Lumber, and Ray Morgan's Café.

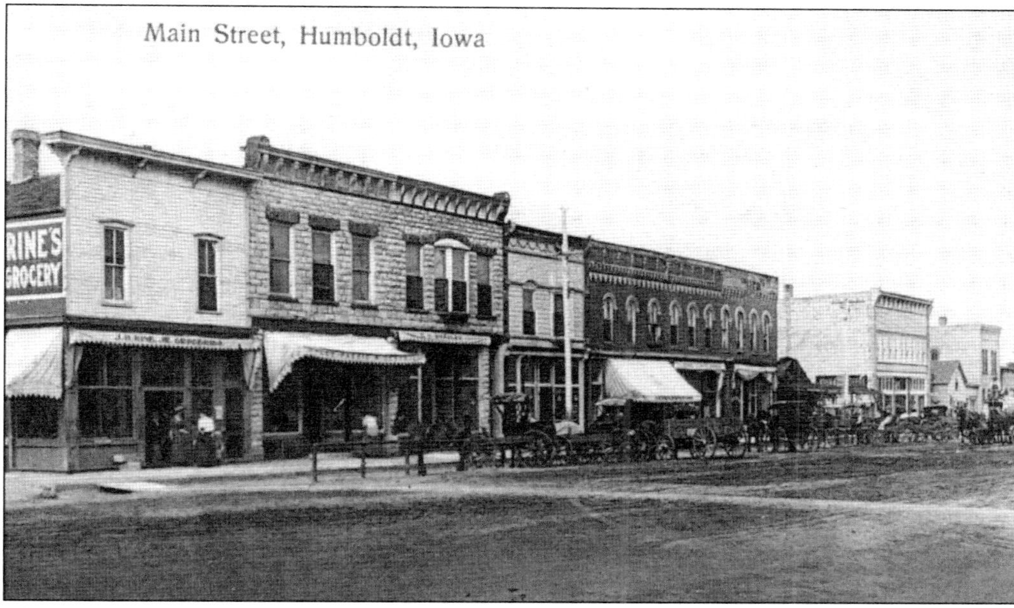

The block of Sumner Avenue between Fifth and Sixth Streets North is shown before 1912. From left to right are John Rine Grocery, Miles and Passig Clothing, E.O. Bradley Grocery, John Tour Tailor Shop, Harness Store, a paint store, N.V. Glenn Variety, a dwelling, Bellows Implement, the Cream Station, Humboldt County Abstract Office, and the office for the *Humboldt Republican* newspaper.

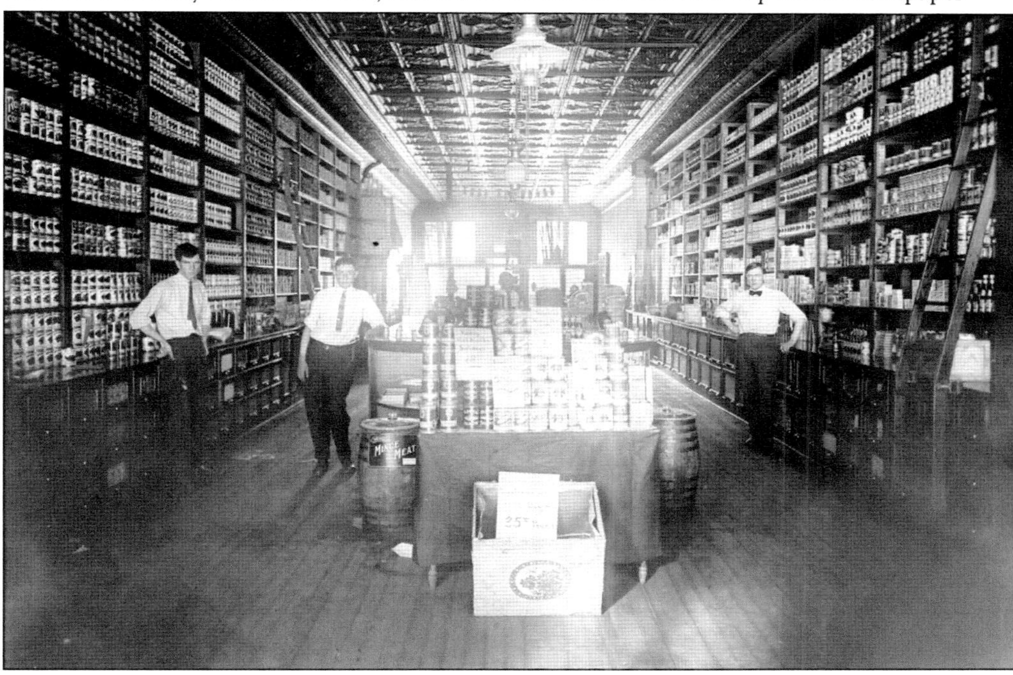

The E.O. Bradley Grocery was located at 525 Sumner in 1912. Bradley began as a clerk for clothier D.A. Ray where, because he spoke Norwegian, he could translate the needs of the immigrants. Later, he partnered with William Wallace and Louis Kinseth. Most grocery stores were not self-service. The customer told the clerk what he or she wanted, and the clerk found it on the shelves.

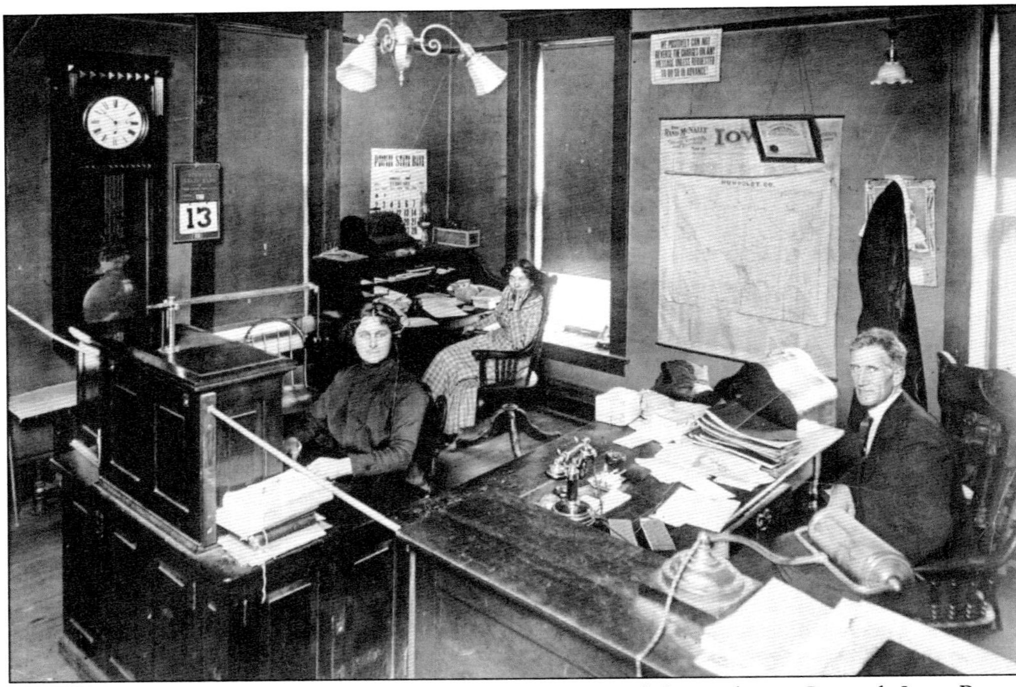

The office for the telephone company is shown in 1913. From left to right are Gertrude Lane Boore, Blanche Simpson, and Hugh McCauley. A single-wire long-distance line from Fort Dodge provided the only service from 1888 to 1899. Then, newspaperman Albert M. Adams built a telephone exchange. In 1902, the exchange was sold to the Royal Union Telephone Company, which consolidated into the Iowa Telephone Company in 1917 and became Northwestern Bell in 1921.

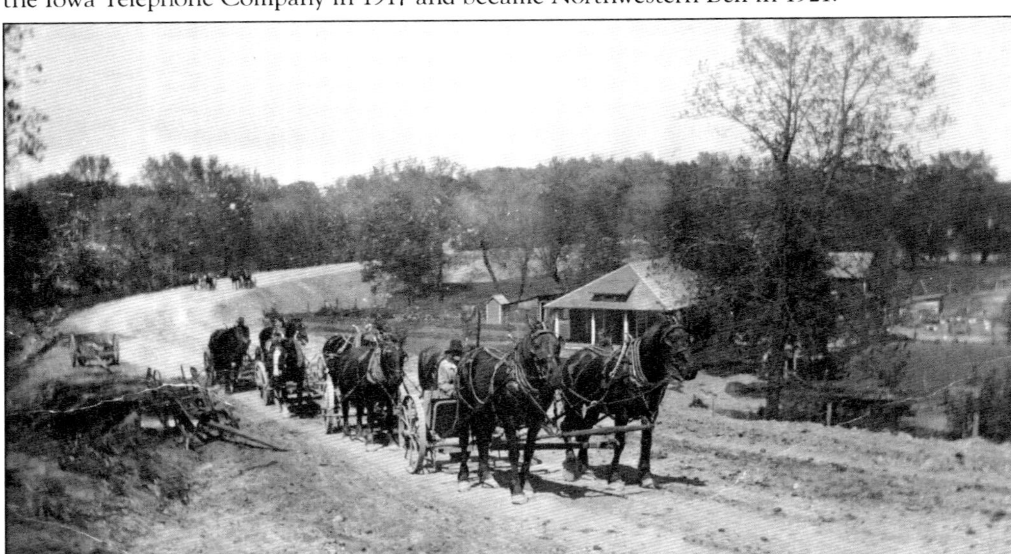

Sumner Avenue was paved in 1919, and the bridge was finished in 1920. Sumner Avenue is shown being extended up Johnston Hill. A big cut into the bluff was made by steam shovel in 1920, and in 1921, sand and gravel were added. The fill at the bottom of the hill had to settle before teams of horses and scrapers (shown) could finish the job in June 1922.

Five

A New Generation of Leaders Takes Charge

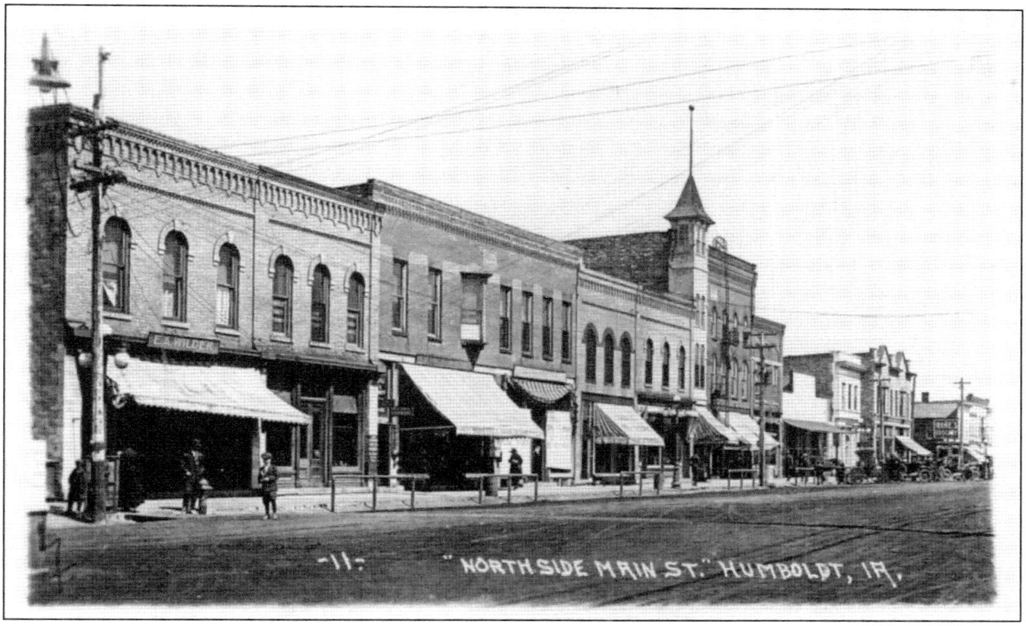

The 600 block on the north side of Sumner Avenue is shown sometime after 1911. From left to right are the E.A. Wilder General Store, Safety Savings Bank, Hubbard Drugs, Krouskup Clothing, Hilsenoff Cigar Factory, Humboldt State Bank, Stanhope Grocery, the post office, Sherman Meats, a pool hall, Sampson Hardware, Clark Restaurant, First National Bank, and McNamara Drugstore.

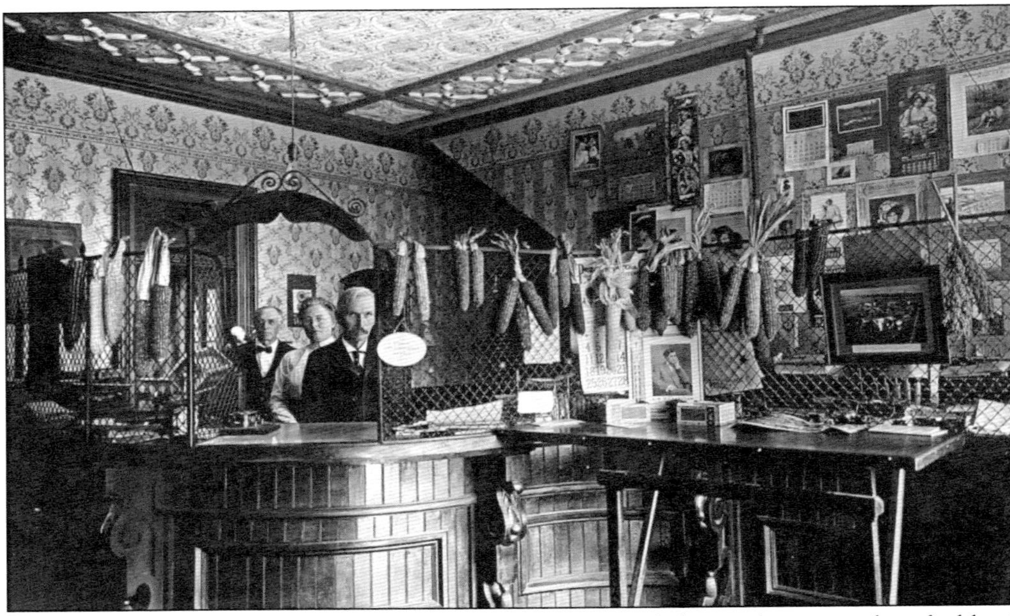

An interior view of the Humboldt State Bank shows, from left to right, an unidentified bank employee, cashier Mary H.S. Johnston, and bank president Robert Johnston in 1910. In 1872, John Dickey and others organized the bank at 617 Sumner Avenue across from the courthouse, and in 1876, the bank was moved to this location. John's nephew P.M. Dickey took over in 1884 and sold it to the Johnstons in 1898.

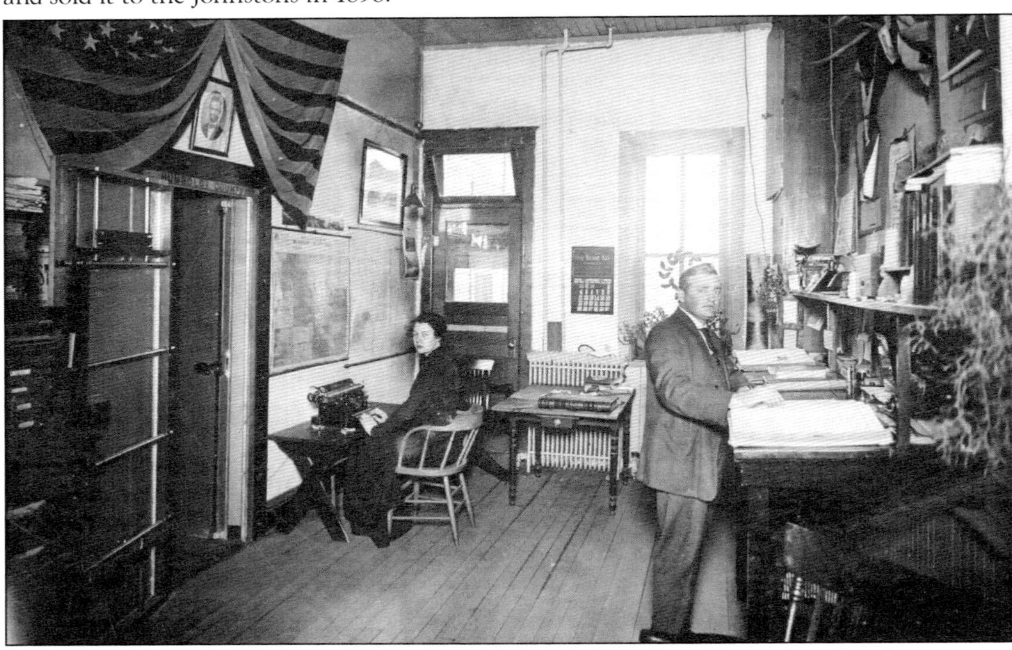

The Humboldt County Abstract Office is shown in 1915. Myrtle Parsons is seated at the typewriter and J.A Parker is at his standing desk. The abstract office is still located at 503 Sumner Avenue on the main floor of the stone building that was constructed by Fred Taft in 1879 for his newspaper the *Humboldt Kosmos*.

In 1897, state senator Parley Finch erected the first of two stone business buildings on the north side of Sumner Avenue (right). This structure was two stories high with rooms for the Humboldt Businessmen's Club on the second floor. The second building (left) was erected in 1899 and boasted a third story and a pointed cupola. This was prompted by competition with the White family to erect the grandest building in town.

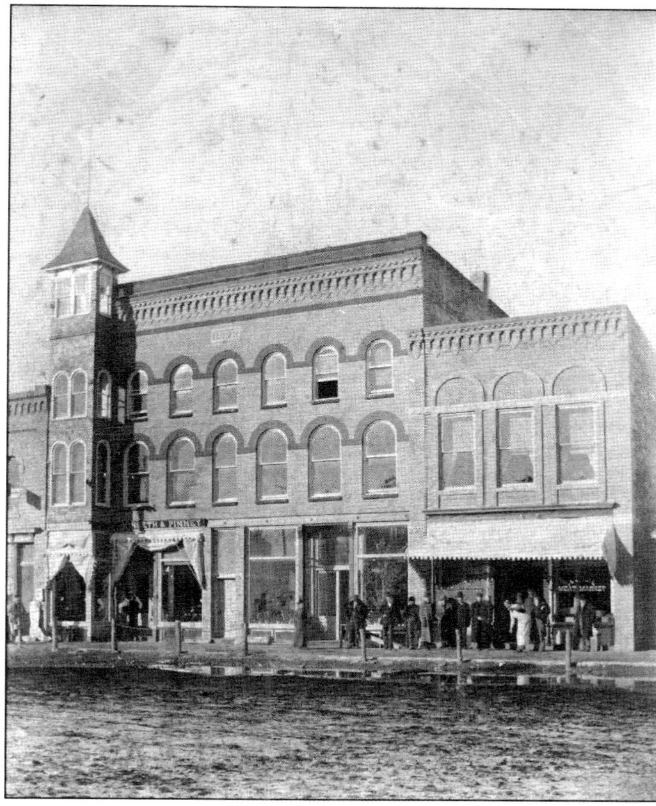

Roy Chapel and Jim Morrison are shown in their barbershop in 1937. It was located below the Clayton Variety Store in the 1899 Finch Building. Several business and professional offices were located in the basements and second floors of the two Finch Buildings, taking advantage of the Sumner Avenue location during the busy years.

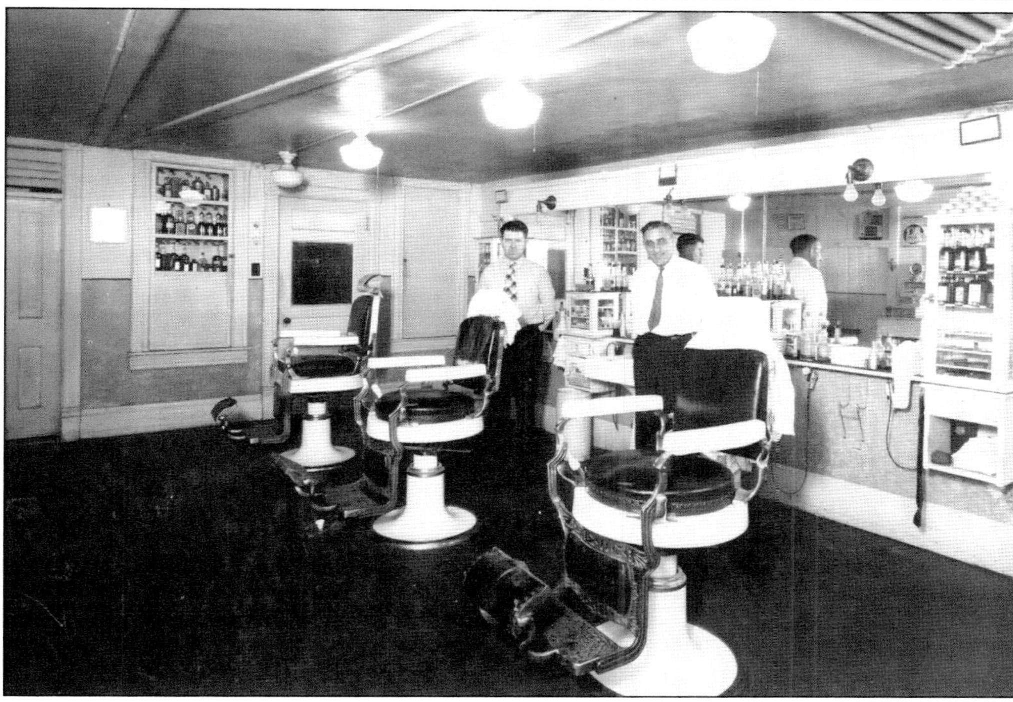

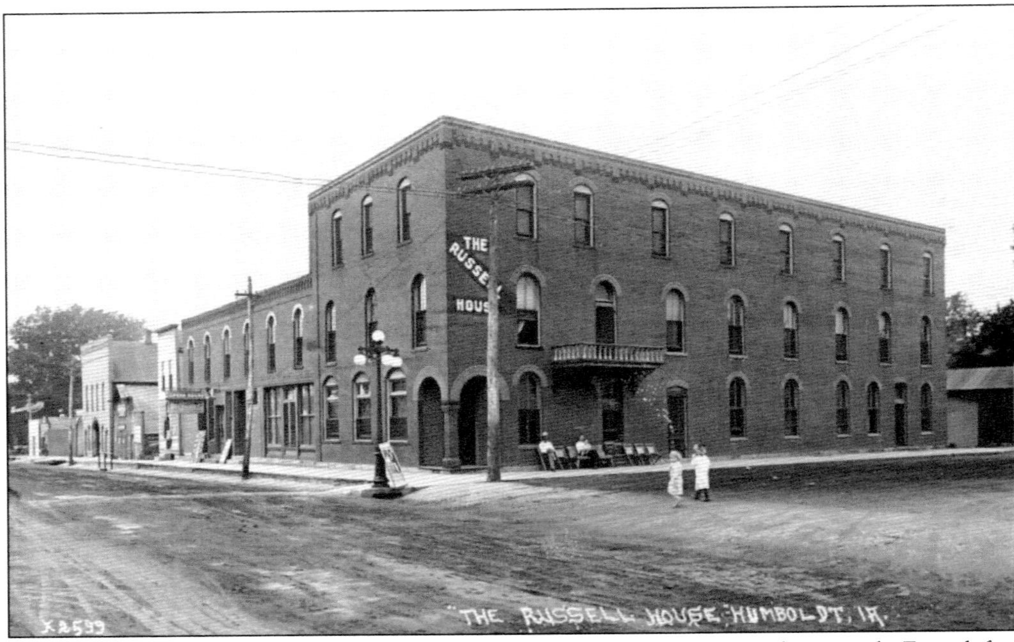

The block between Eighth and Taft Streets North is shown in this 1915 photograph. From left to right are Caille Blacksmith and Wagon Shop, a feeding shed, livery, Hardy Cleaners, a harness shop, an opera house, and Russell Hotel. The hotel, built in 1887 by Herman Russell, son of "Doc" D.P. Russell, was originally two stories high. A third floor was added after 1900. The hotel and the opera house burned in 1928.

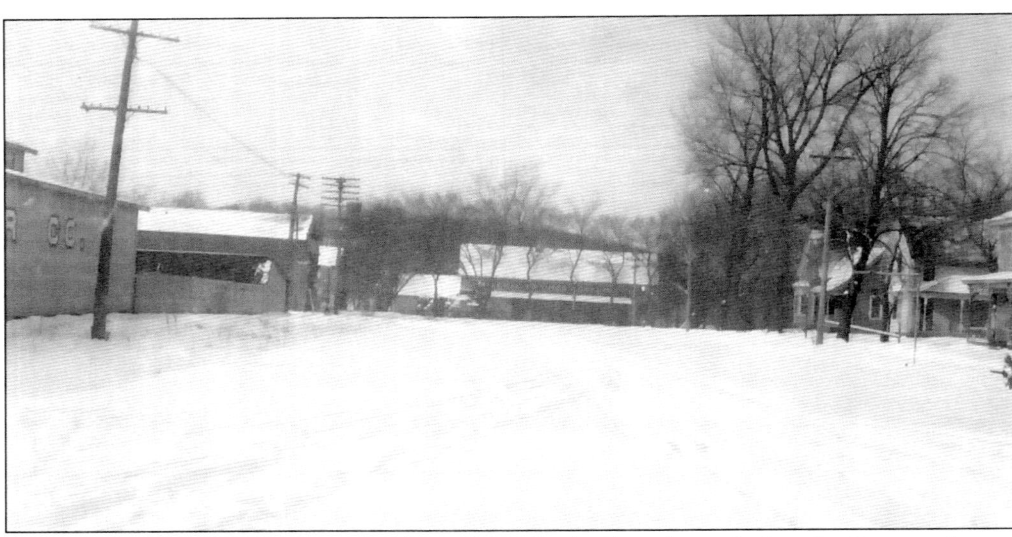

The west end of Sumner Avenue in downtown Humboldt is shown before the Sumner Avenue Bridge was built in 1920. Landmarks recognizable today are the lumberyard (left) and three houses (right.) The center building is the Mineral Springs Bottling Company, which moved west of the lumberyard so that the bridge could be built. Later, it became the Coca-Cola Plant.

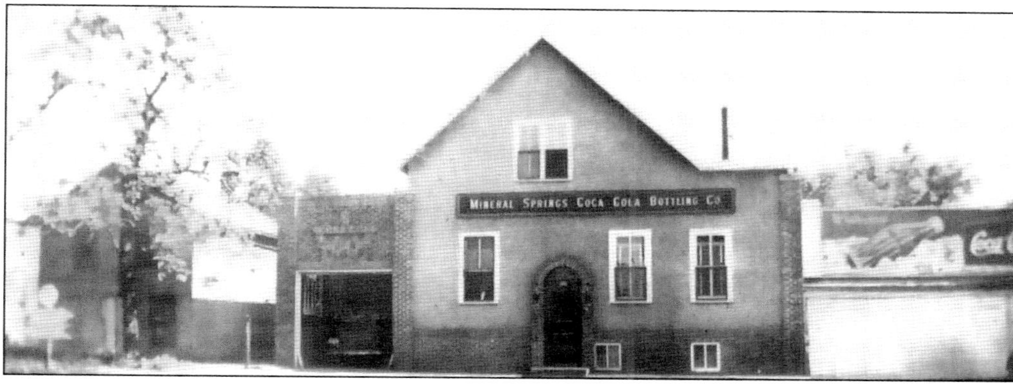

The Mineral Springs Bottling Company was established in 1887 by "Waylie" Rogers and was later led by Bime and Ralph Bellows. The plant drew water from a huge, natural spring. The business was located at the west end of Sumner Avenue, but when the bridge was built in 1921, the bottling company relocated south of it (above). Coca-Cola was first bottled there in 1924. A new building was completed in 1939 with Art Deco decor (below). The plant filled 10,500 bottles per hour, which were inspected by a person with a huge magnifying glass seated near the front window. The glory days of Coca-Cola took a hit during World War II because of sugar rationing, and by the 1950s, the plant was sold. In 1963, the building was used for school administration offices. It is currently an art museum.

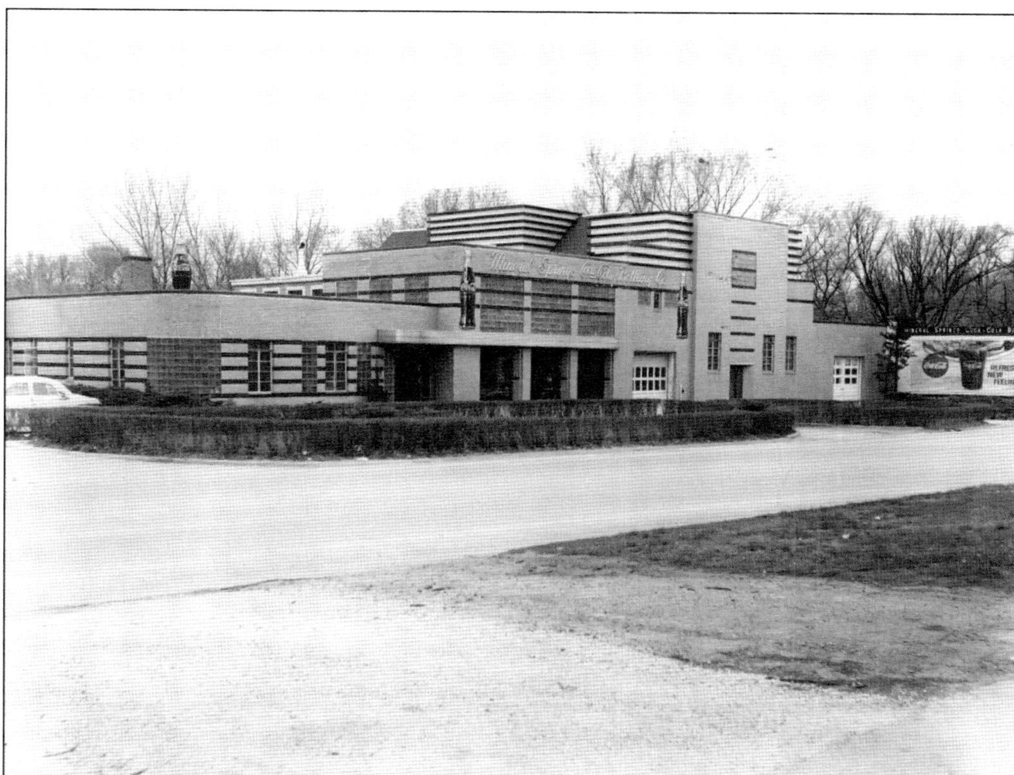

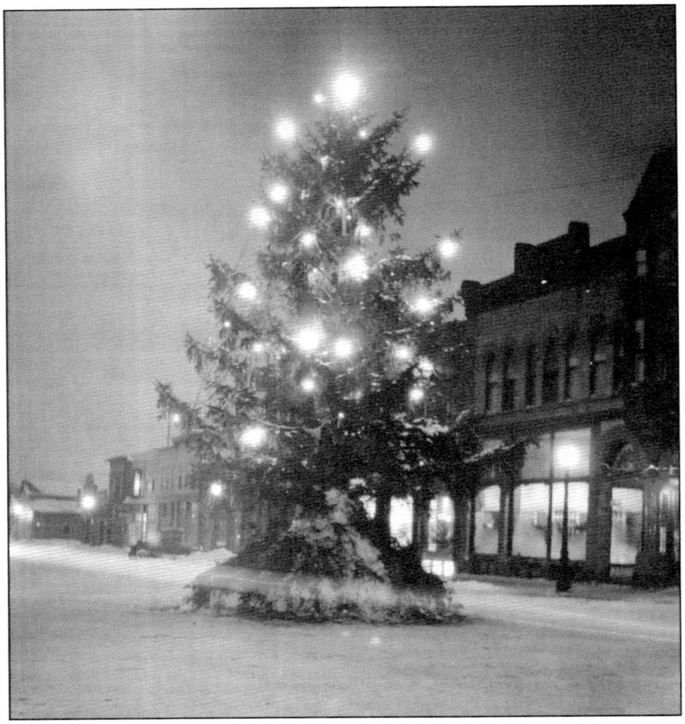

In 1925, the Humboldt Community Christmas tree was placed in the middle of the 500 block of Sumner Avenue. Stores in the background are, from left to right, Mason Hat Shop, Bruhn and Wrisberg Meat Market, Ernest Wykes Plumbing, Gabrielson Shoes, Brighton Millinery, Duncan Furniture and Undertaking (behind tree), Miles and Sexe Clothing, Central Iowa Power and Light, and the White Department Store.

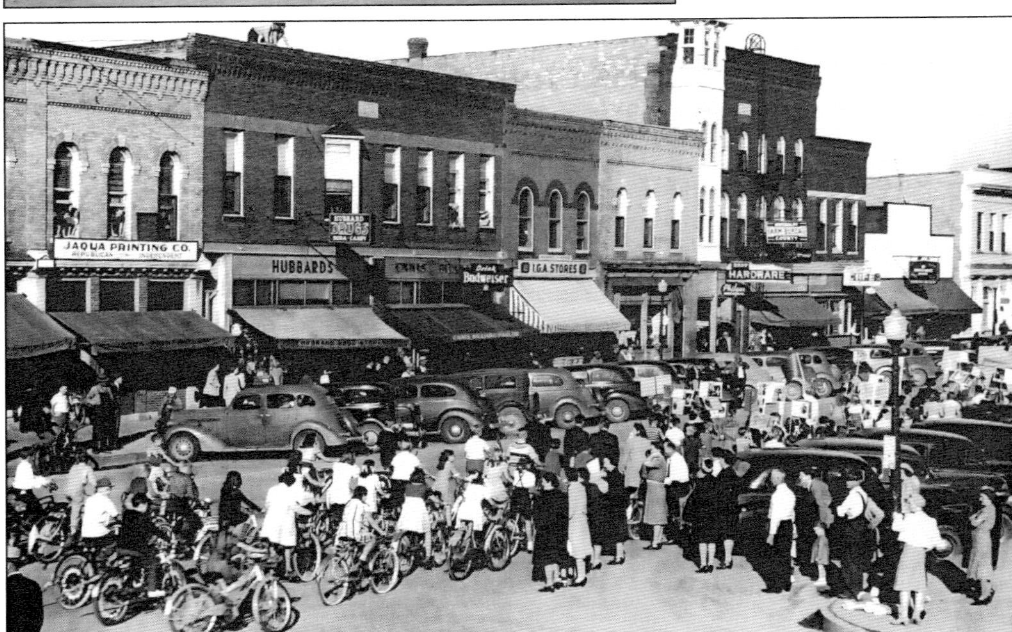

Humboldt High School's homecoming parade down Sumner Avenue featured a band and students on bicycles in 1940. The Nokomis yearbook first mentioned a homecoming celebration, which was usually associated with a football game in October, in 1933. The event grew to honor a homecoming queen and (later) a king, a dance, and weeklong celebration of events. (Courtesy of Tim Smith.)

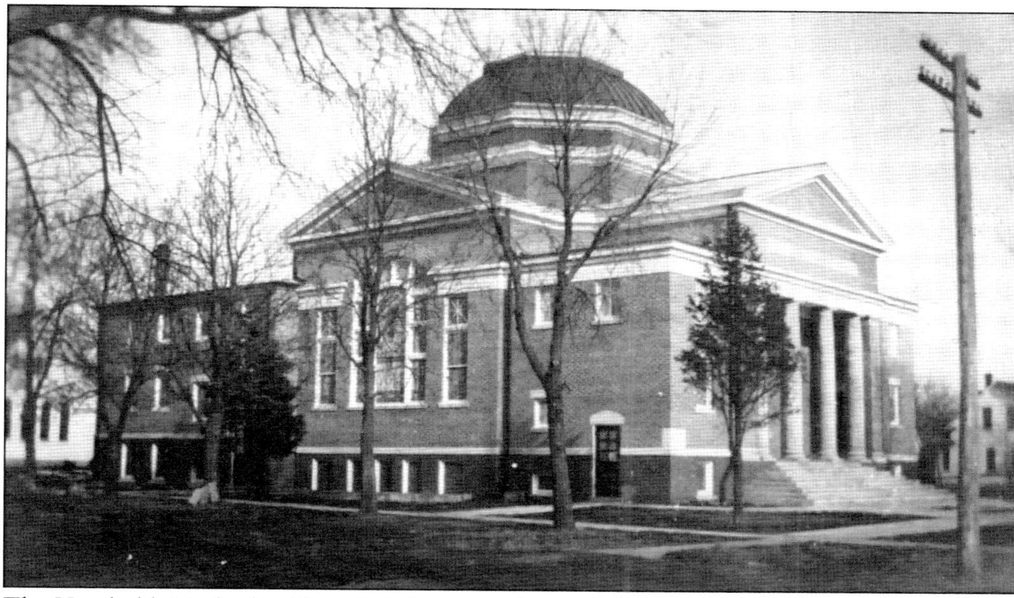

The Humboldt Methodist Church is shown while it still had its dome on top. The first church, built in 1883, was sold to the Baptists in 1919. Also that year, this church was built. In 1967, the Morehouse Hall addition provided more space. In 1982, the current structure was built. The church became Faith United Methodist Church, combining the Methodist congregations in Bradgate, Gilmore City, Rutland, Humboldt, and Livermore.

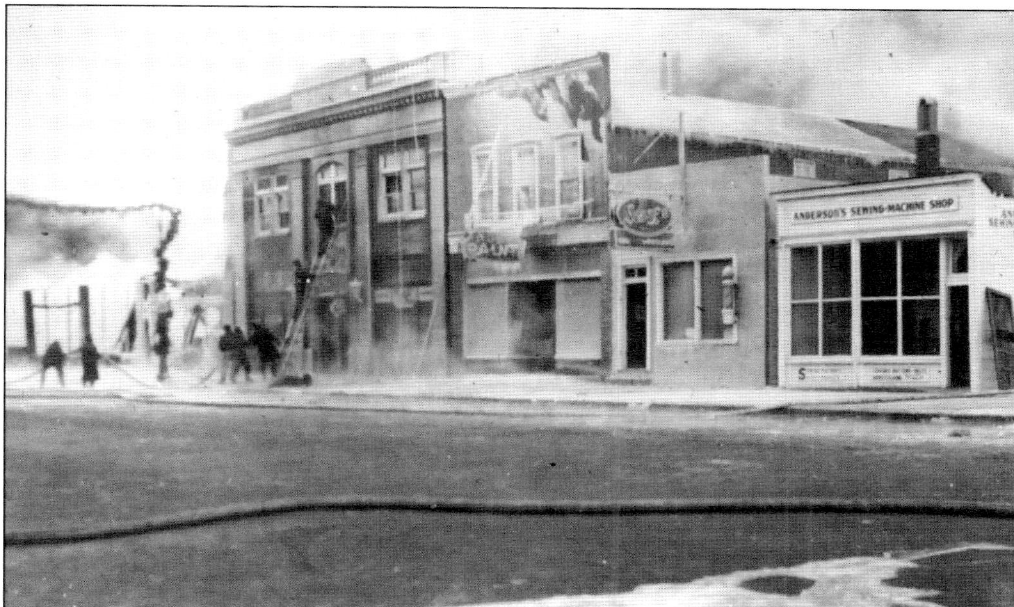

Humboldt's big fire took place on Christmas Day 1948. Discovered about 3:30 a.m., it raged through the Ben Franklin Store, McEntaffer Jewelry, Jensen Paint, Coast-to-Coast Stores, and the Legion Building, which was almost completely destroyed. Clark A. Lane Jr., age 11, passed out warm gloves to firemen who worked in sub-zero temperatures to halt the blaze. Those living in upstairs apartments lost possessions but were lucky to get out.

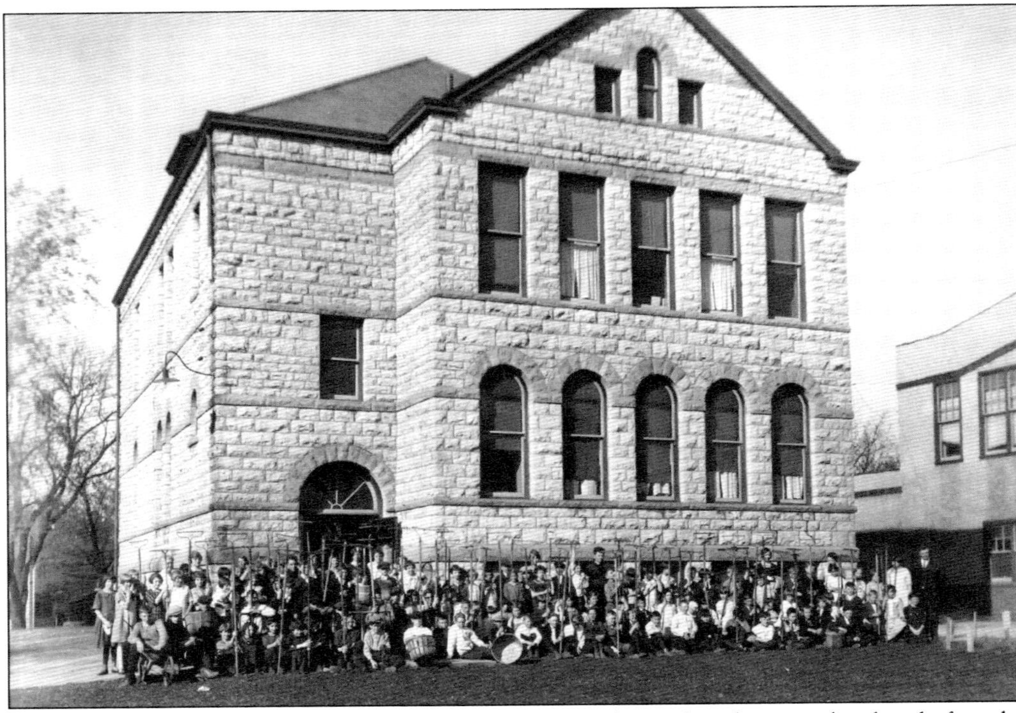

"Old Stoney" students are ready to rake and clean up parks in this photograph taken before the 1938 gymnasium was built. Constructed in 1909, it had four good-sized classrooms, two on each floor; an attic; and a janitor's room and nurses' station in the basement. It housed home economics and art departments and served intermediate students until 1979. It was torn down because the walls were pulling away from the structure.

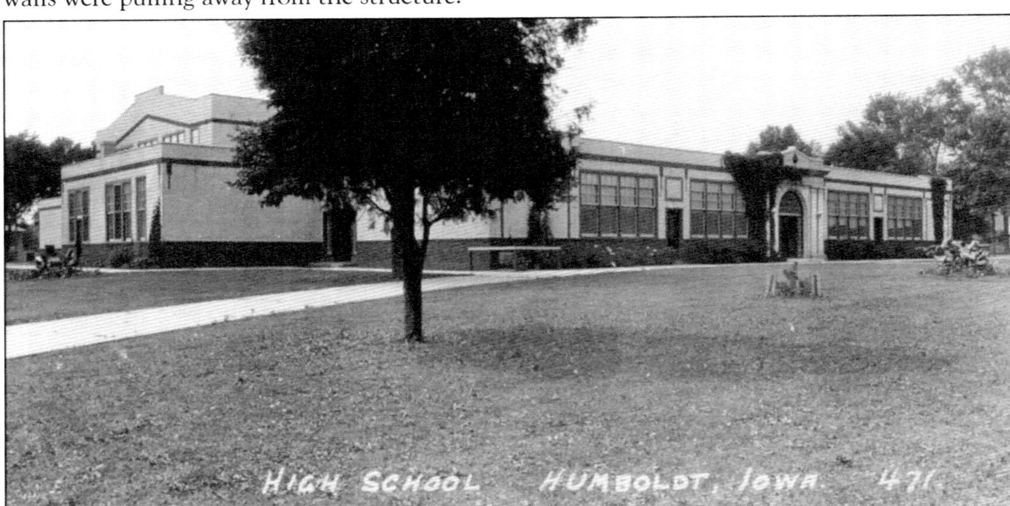

In 1919, Humboldt built a new school that contained the primary department, two study halls, rooms for home economics and manual training, a science laboratory, 11 other classrooms for junior and senior high students, a gymnasium, and an auditorium. Remodeling projects adapted the structure to the needs of the students. In 1938, a gymnasium was built next to the school, and the former gym and auditorium were altered to provide additional rooms.

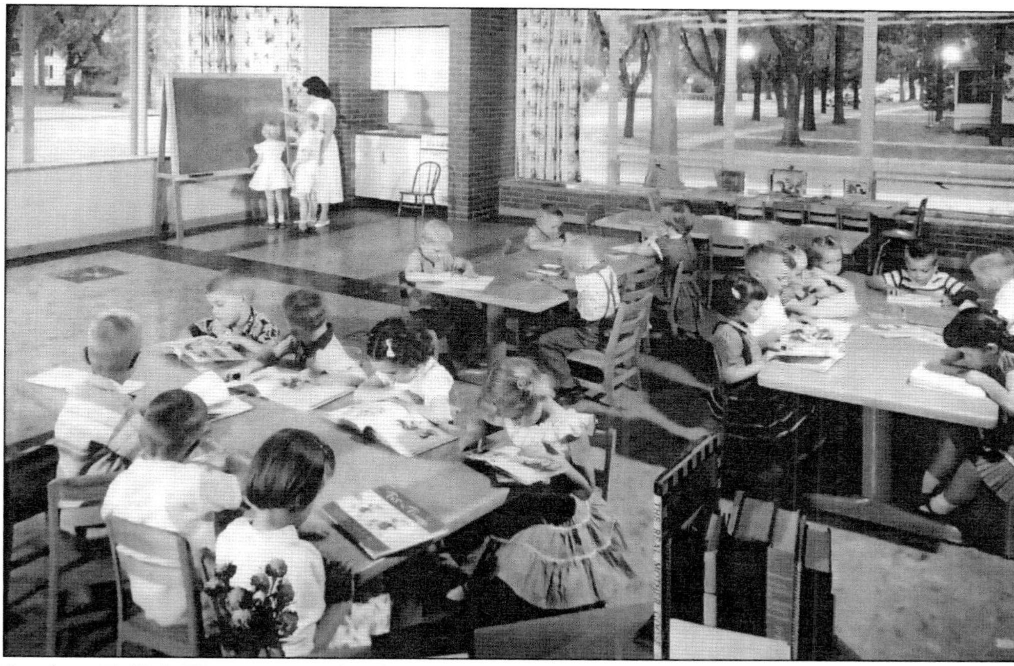

Stephen H. Taft Elementary School was built in 1953 for pupils from kindergarten through the fourth grade. Students used the multipurpose room for lunch and physical education and also an activity room with a stage. Special education and remedial teaching were offered. In 1958, a new wing was added for the fifth and sixth grades, with a total pupil load of 650 students.

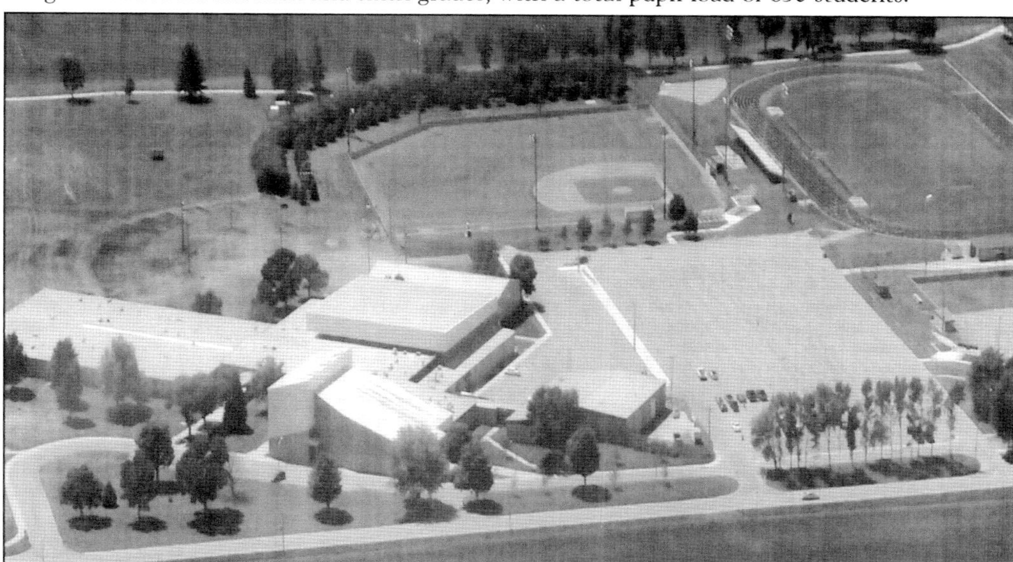

The Humboldt Community High School was dedicated in 1964. The new location away from the center of town provided space for three basic structures, which housed classrooms, a shop, gym, and cafeteria. A music room was located north of the cafeteria. An open court in the building was later used for classroom space. An auditorium was added in 1981. In 2012, the junior high school will be completed next to the high school.

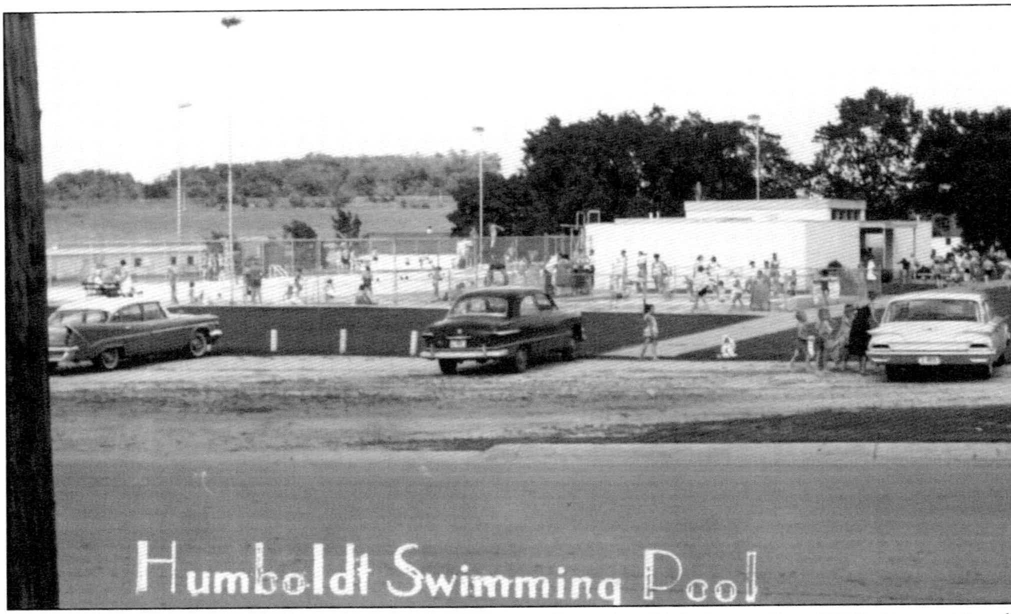

The Humboldt Municipal Swimming Pool, located south of Highway 3 at Fifth Street North, opened in 1954 after a campaign lasting 10 years. Nancy Robinson Jensen was crowned pool queen over a court of 20 attendants. The pool was enlarged and updated several times, enabling it to serve for over 50 years before being replaced in 2006 by the Humboldt Aquatic Center on Sumner Avenue.

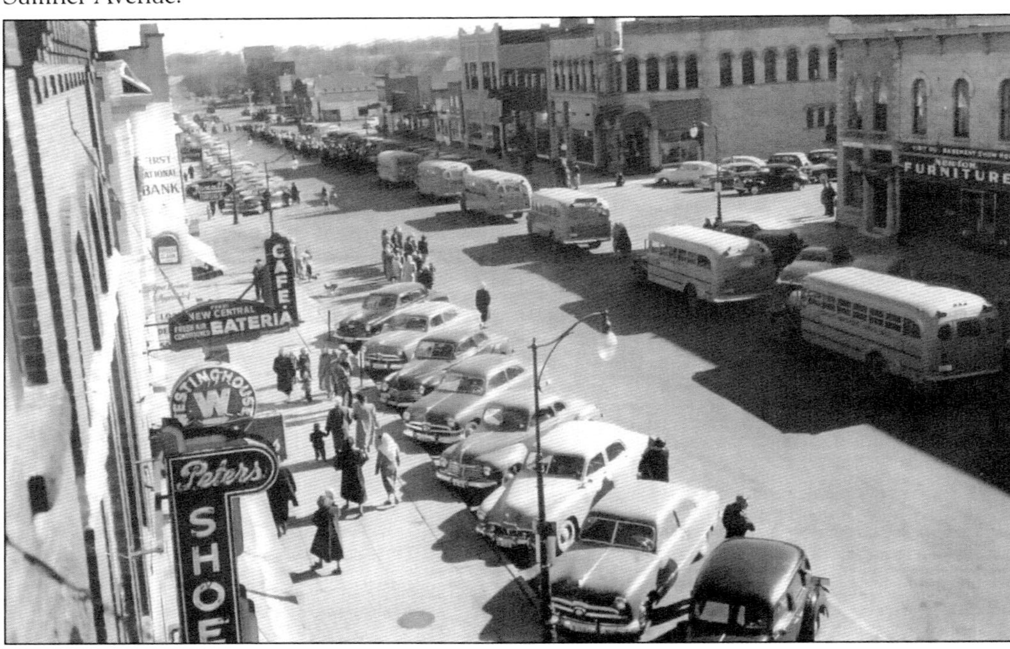

A line of school buses, probably part of the homecoming parade, is shown progressing east along Sumner Avenue in the early 1950s. Humboldt began busing students from the surrounding rural school districts several years before the districts merged, thus making the transition to merged districts easier. This photograph was taken from a third-floor window of the Finch Building cupola.

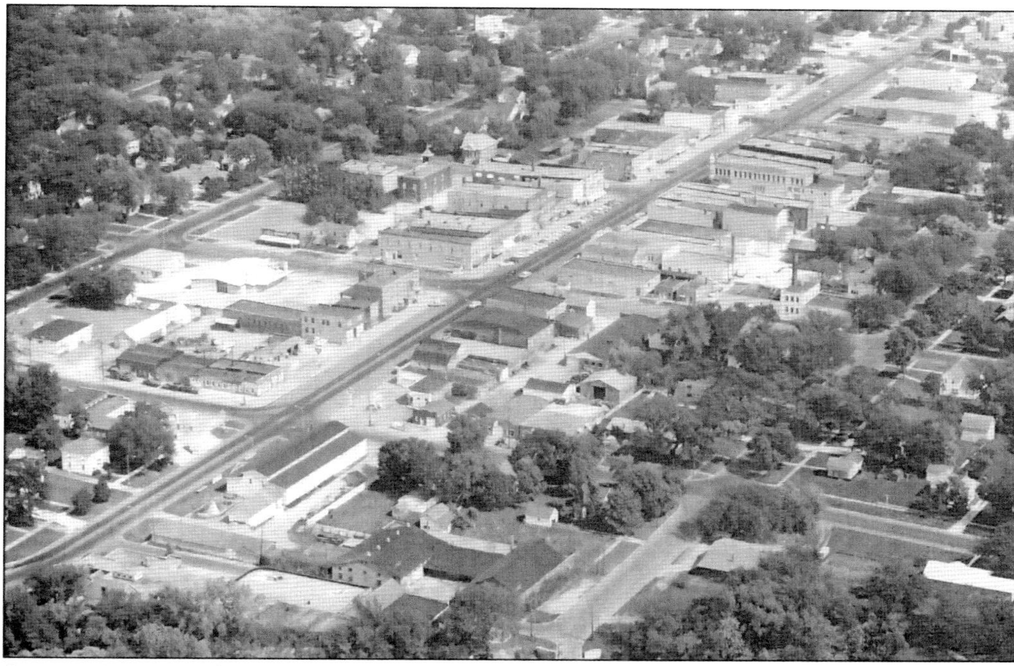

Sumner Avenue is shown in 1963, which was 100 years after the city of Humboldt was founded. From left to right are the intersections of Ninth Street, Eighth Street, Taft Street, Sixth Street, Fifth Street, and Fourth Street, with Third Street at the top. (Courtesy of Jaqua photographers.)

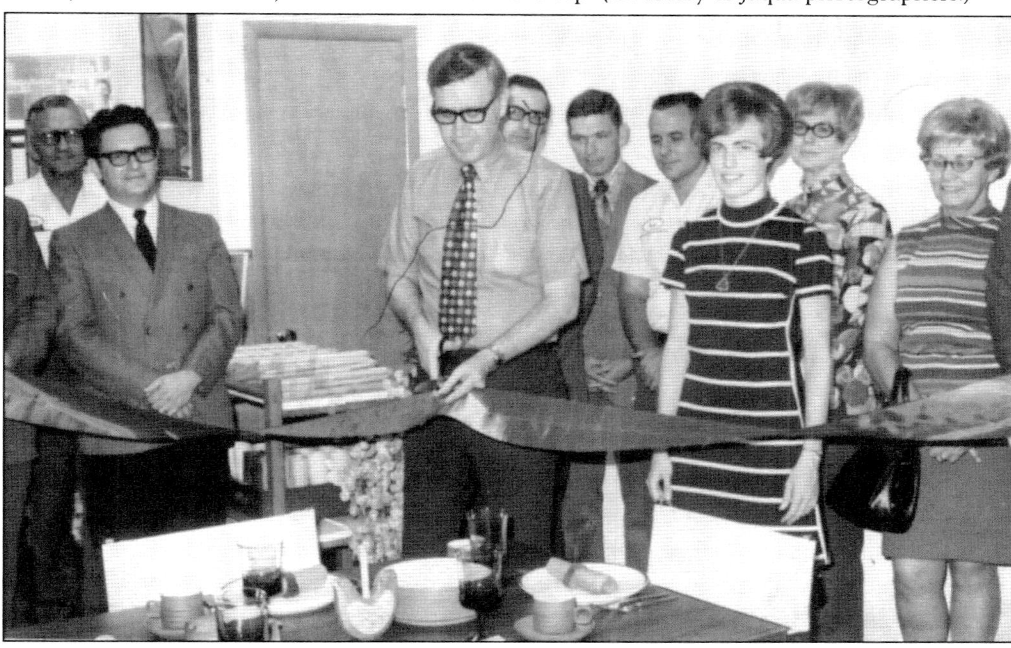

The grand opening of the Design Center in downtown Humboldt took place about 1971. Located in the west side of the Legion Building, it was owned by Pat and Jay Hospers and featured Scandinavian designs. From left to right are Henry Christensen, Dick Barnes, Al Thompson, Roger Day, Clark Lane Jr., Russ Christensen, Pat Hospers, Edna Fowler, and Dorothy Tellier.

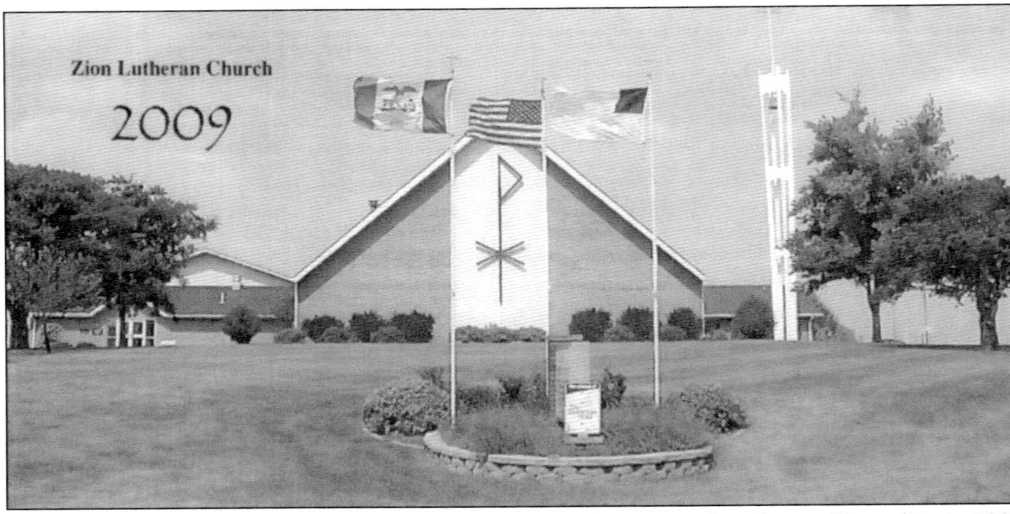

The Humboldt Zion Lutheran Church, Missouri Synod, organized in Beaver Township in 1884 and built its first church. A cemetery and church school were soon placed nearby. In 1926, a new brick church was constructed, and in 1969, the congregation purchased the former Unitarian church on Taft Street in Humboldt to serve town members. In 1971, they built the present edifice at 1005 Eleventh Avenue North, which was enlarged in 2009.

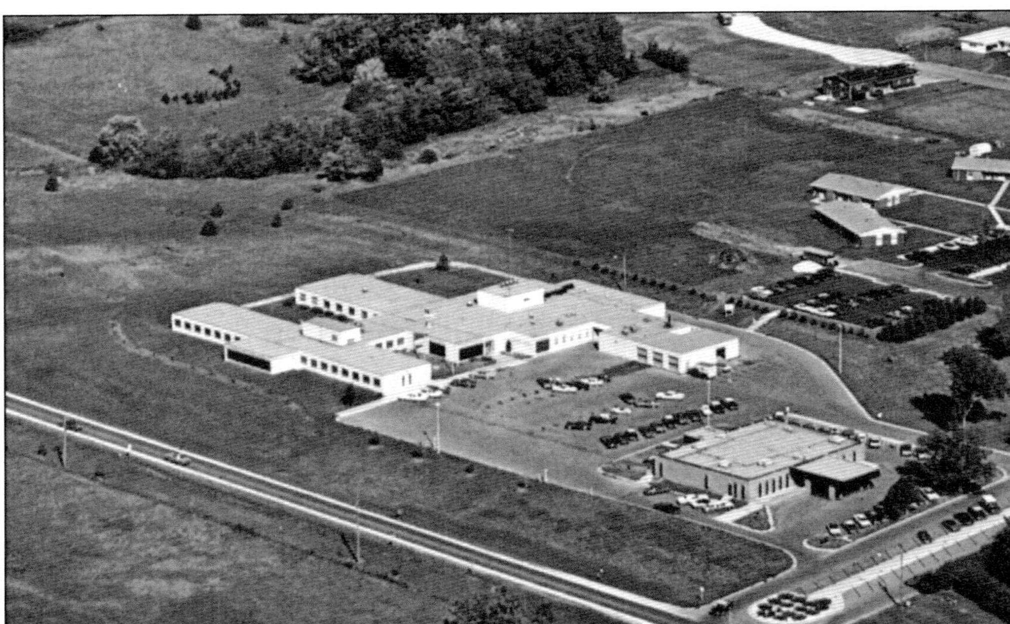

The Humboldt County Memorial Hospital is shown after it was built in 1970 following a campaign that began in 1946 and succeeded with the help of funds from Minnie Hanna's estate. Doctor's Park Medical Clinic is seen at right. In 2010, the building was completely remodeled. With Springvale Senior Living Center and Assisted Living facilities nearby, the medical needs of Humboldt County citizens are served.

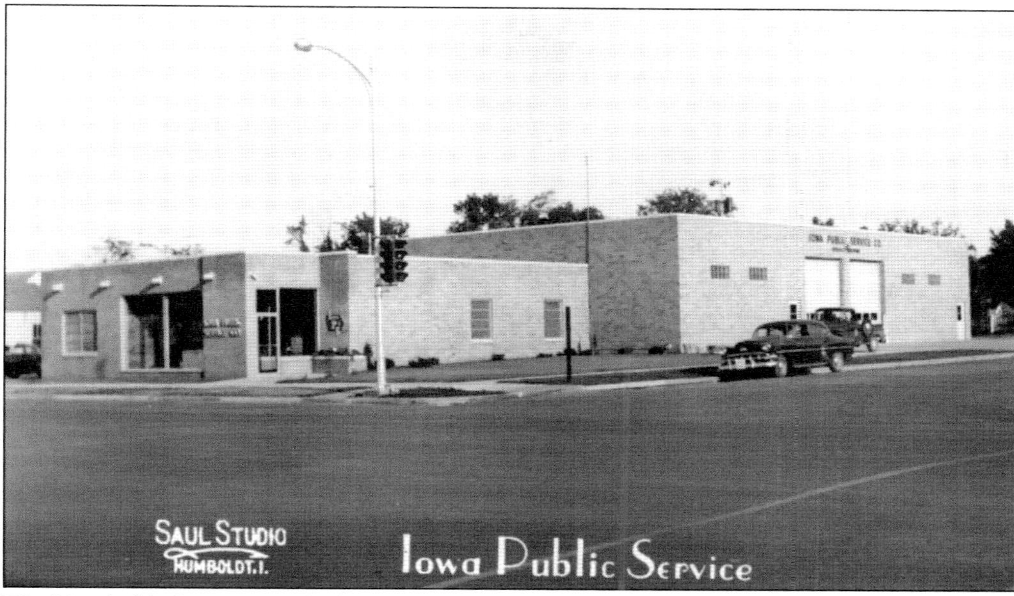

The Humboldt County Law Enforcement Center, 430 Sumner Avenue, is shown after it was built in 1957 as the office for the Iowa Public Service (now MidAmerican Energy). Demonstrating cooperation of city and county services, it now houses the Humboldt County Sheriff's Department, the City of Humboldt Police Department, and the Humboldt County Jail.

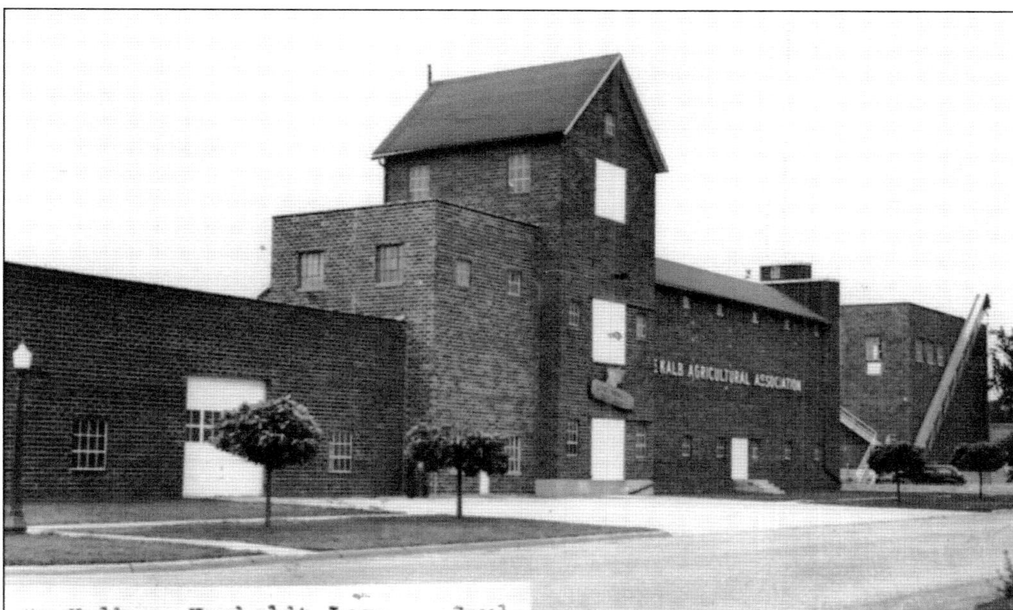

The DeKalb Plant added dignity to Humboldt's main street. DeKalb served the community beginning in 1922. The plant was built at 302 Sumner Avenue in 1938 and processed grain for Humboldt County's farmers and provided employment for many. In 1984, it became DeKalb-Pfizer Genetics and was dismantled in the late 1990s. The aquatic center is located there now.

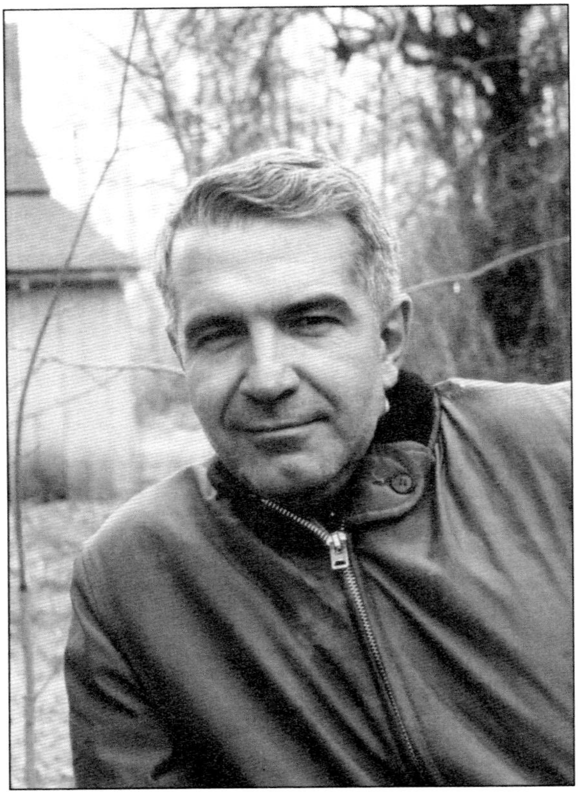

Newscaster Harry Reasoner, born in Dakota City, enjoyed visiting his grandparents in Humboldt. Harry started in television in 1954, working with ABC and CBS. Don Hewitt, his producer, recalled, "Harry Reasoner was not the only broadcaster from the Midwest, but he was the only broadcaster who brought the Midwest with him to television. He not only had craggy good looks but also that Iowa sense of what's important."

The Northwest Industrial Park in Humboldt is shown in 2007, one of several created by Humboldt County Development Association for over 30 industries that manufacture agricultural-related equipment and precision machines, and make use of local minerals and farm products. Industries are attracted to Humboldt County by its skilled labor force, work ethic, and quality of life.

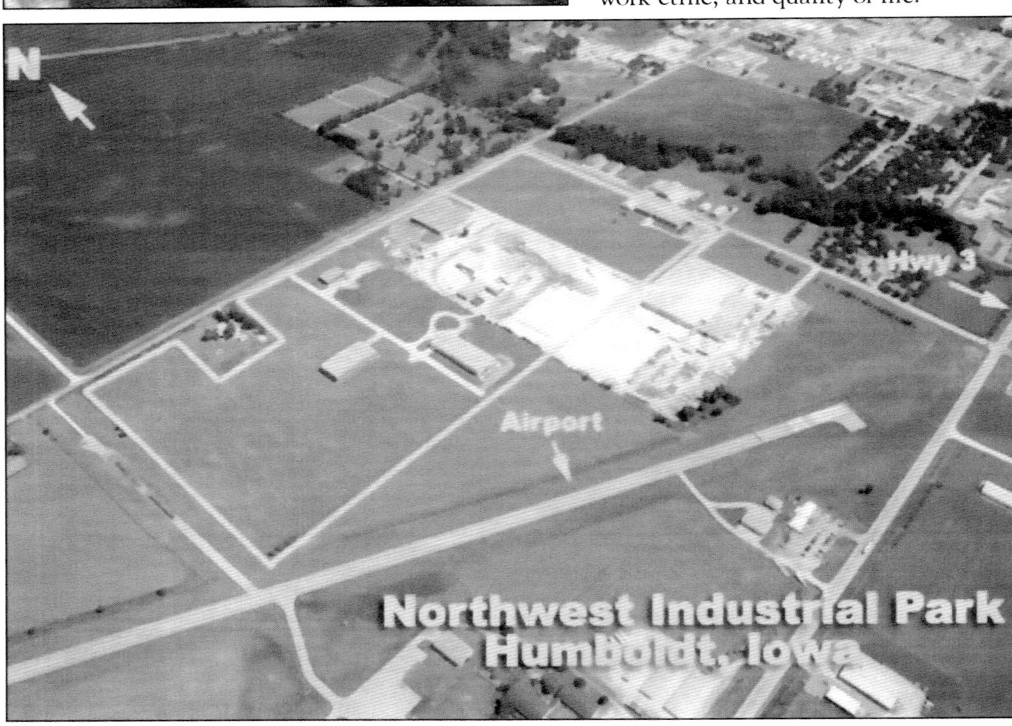

Six

Small Towns and Rural Areas Prosper

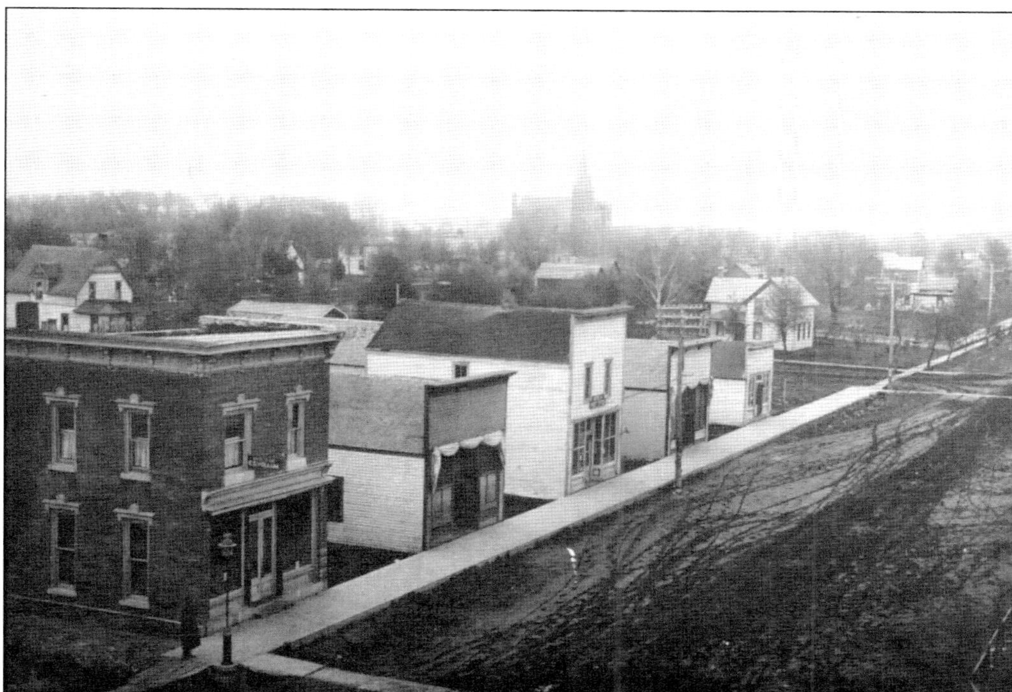

The city of Bode was platted in November 1881 by the Burlington, Cedar Rapids & Northern Railroad. Torkel Rossing established several early businesses, which included a general merchandise store, lumberyard, and creamery. Other businessmen were Kinseth Brothers, M.O. Monson, and Nels Johnson. The scene above is of the east side of Humboldt Avenue. Dr. Vollum's office is on the left.

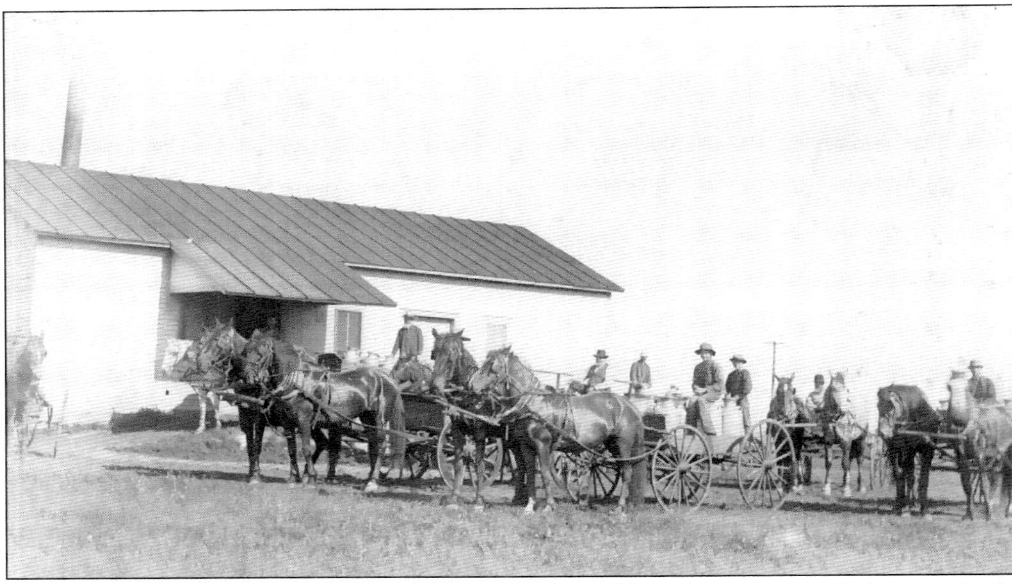

Arnold Creamery, located in the northern part of Grove Township, was an early business in the small town. Other businesses included two general stores, two elevators, a blacksmith shop, and a Methodist church. The town, originally called Grove, was renamed in 1900 for early settler Hiram Arnold. It was located on the Minneapolis & St. Louis Railroad.

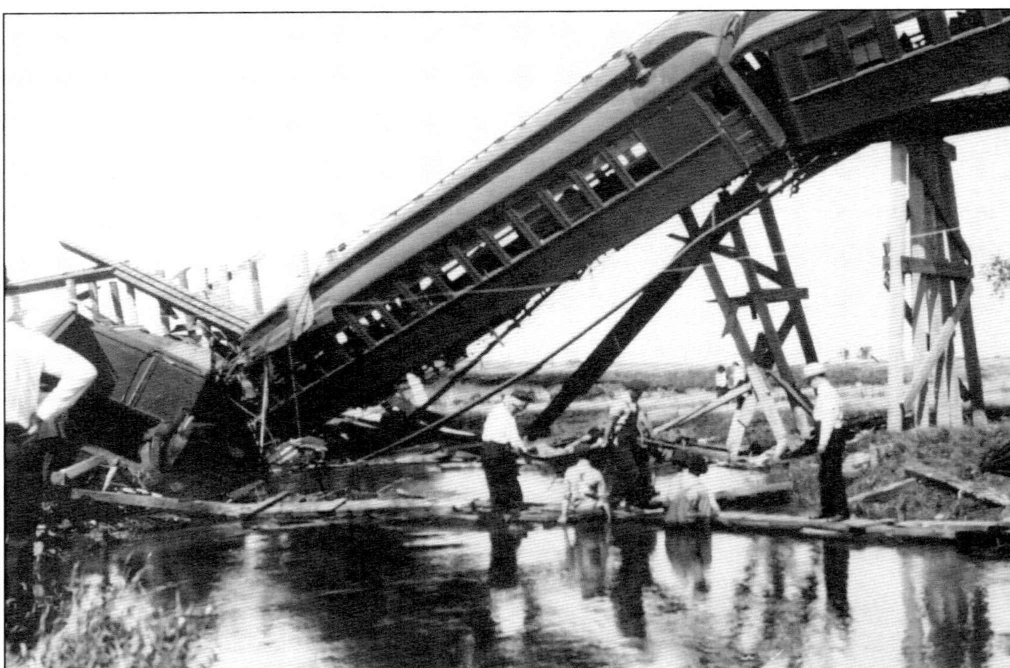

On July 3, 1920, a horrible train wreck occurred a half mile north of Arnold. As a train crossed the bridge over Bloody Run Creek, the engineer felt it shake. He sped up, hoping to get the train safely across. The bridge gave way, and several coaches fell to the creek bed below. Eight passengers died, with many more injured. Numerous people in the area gave assistance.

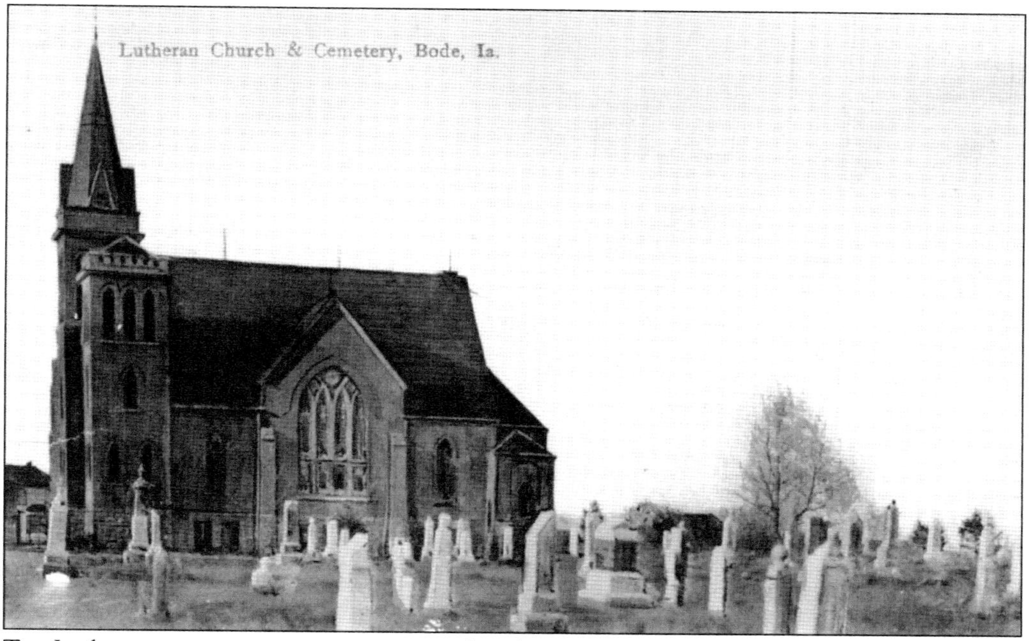

Two Lutheran congregations were organized in the Lotts Creek area about 1870. Five years later, they merged to form St. Olaf's Norwegian Evangelical Lutheran Church in Bode. The congregation dedicated its first building in 1877. They established a cemetery near the building with the burial of John Olson in 1877. The present building was dedicated in 1901. Both buildings were debt free at the time of dedication.

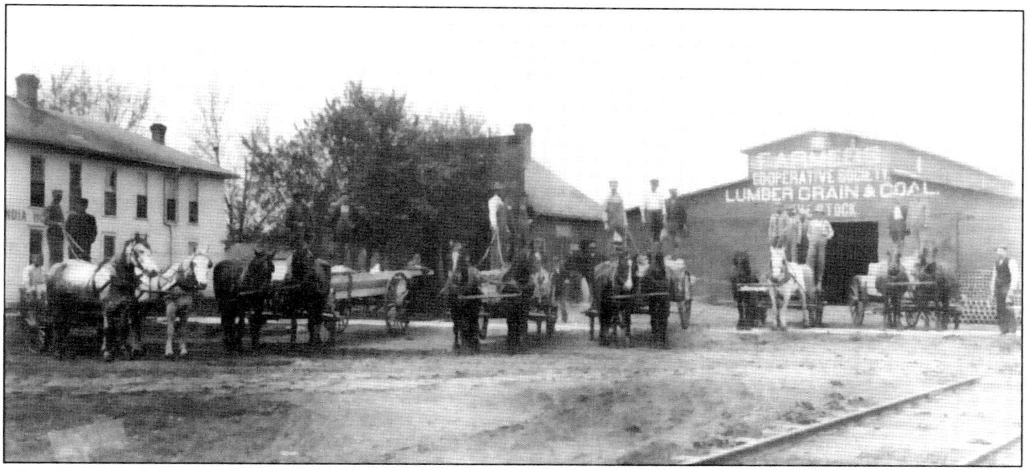

The Farmers' Cooperative Society played an important role in the life of the Bode community and surrounding countryside. They sold needed agricultural items and helped farmers ship grain to market. To the left is the Scandia Hotel, which was built in 1881. It was the overnight home for many travelers, including railroad personnel, entertainers, and salesmen. The building was torn down sometime in the 1980s.

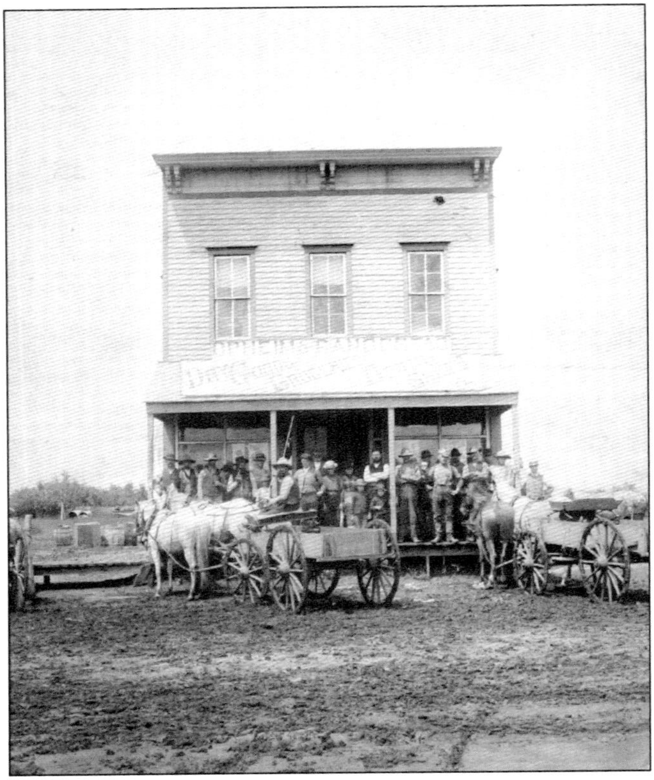

Lars Opheim and James Gangstad constructed the second store building in Bode in June 1883. They operated a general mercantile business for 11 years. Lars purchased his partner's share of the business when James moved away. He ran the store until 1909, when he sold out to John Pederson and Company. His sale offered men's suits for $14.88, felt shoes for $1.37, and caps for $1.19.

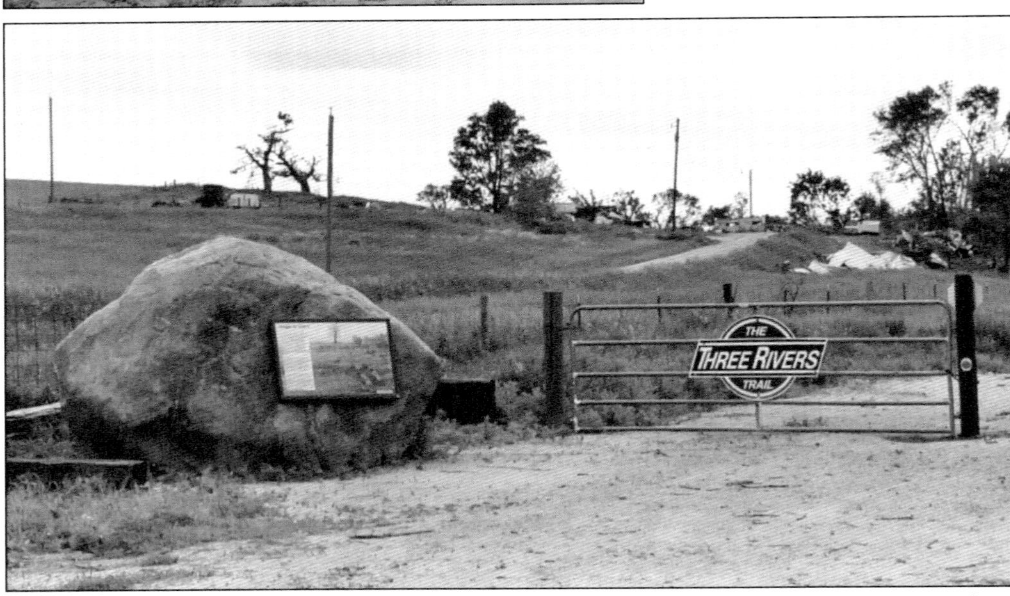

The last battle in Iowa between two Indian tribes occurred near Bradgate. In 1853–1854, a band of Winnebago were camped west of town. Nearby Sioux heard about the camp and attacked their enemies during the night. Luckily for the Winnebago, a warrior awoke and sounded the alarm. A desperate hand-to-hand fight then took place. Ten Winnebago were killed while the number of Sioux killed is unknown.

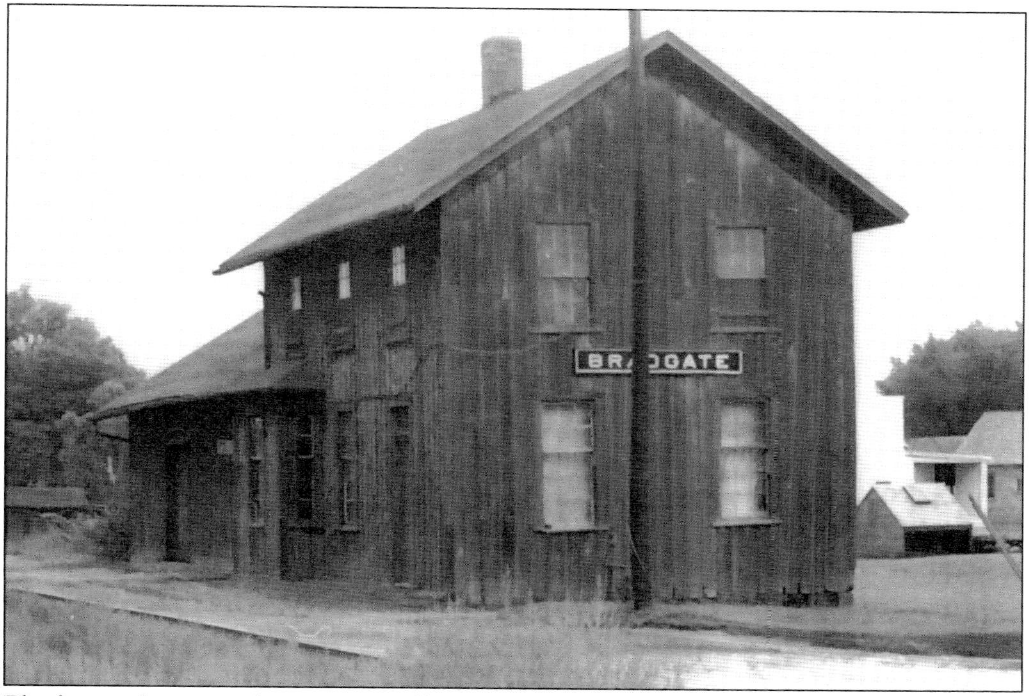

The first settlement in the area was Willow Glen, which had a post office and a one-room school. Bradgate was laid out in 1882 by the Chicago & Northwestern Railroad. There were four passenger trains each day plus several freight trains. It was said that people from towns near Bradgate came here to shop, making the round trip by train.

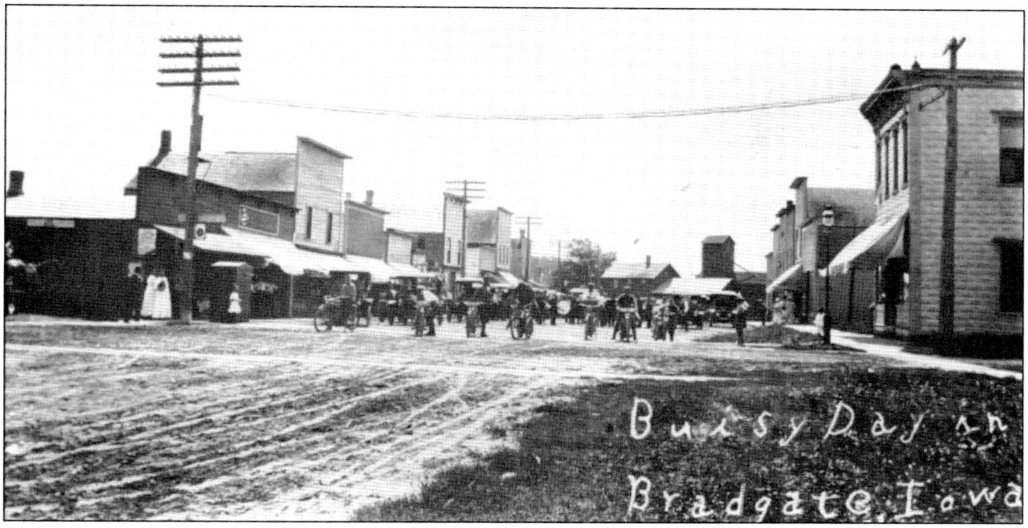

Bradgate around 1900 was a busy place with three general stores, two millinery stores, two elevators, two churches, two restaurants, two barbershops, a telephone office, lumberyard, drugstore, harness shop, livery stable, hardware store, bank, and post office. In addition, the town had a doctor, photographer, blacksmith, and drayman. For entertainment, the town had a band, which played Saturday nights in the summer. Early citizens included Cord King, John King, Charles Jarvis, and Charles and Jerome Tilton.

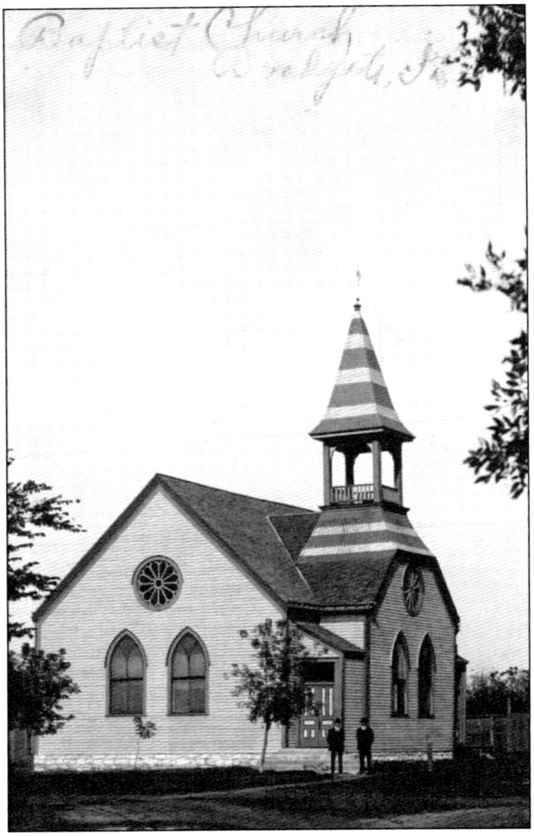

At first, Baptists in the Bradgate area attended church services held in the schoolhouse. Some traveled to Rutland for church. In 1883, they organized a church of their own in Bradgate. Early members included the Sharp, Coffin, King, Mowe, Godden, Van Horne, and Billings families. Their church was built by 1890 and served the congregation until 1937, when they decided to close due to declining membership.

The first school in Bradgate, which also doubled as a church, was a building moved from the country. A two-story wooden school built in 1892 served the community until 1917, when a new brick school was completed. On moving day, students carried books from one building to the other. A gym-auditorium was added in 1953, which gave more room for athletic events and school plays.

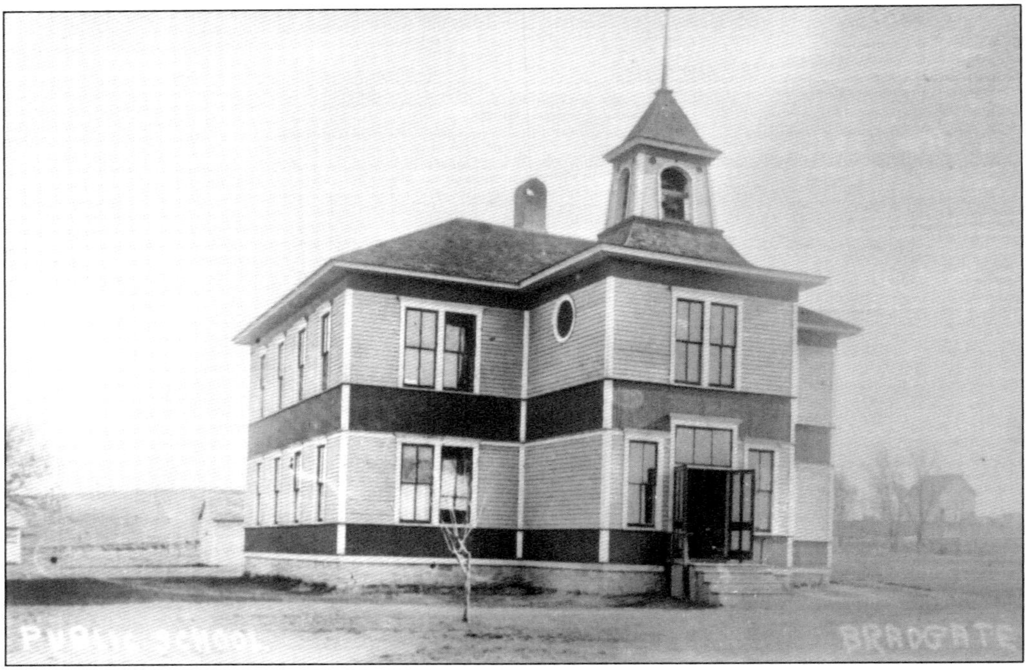

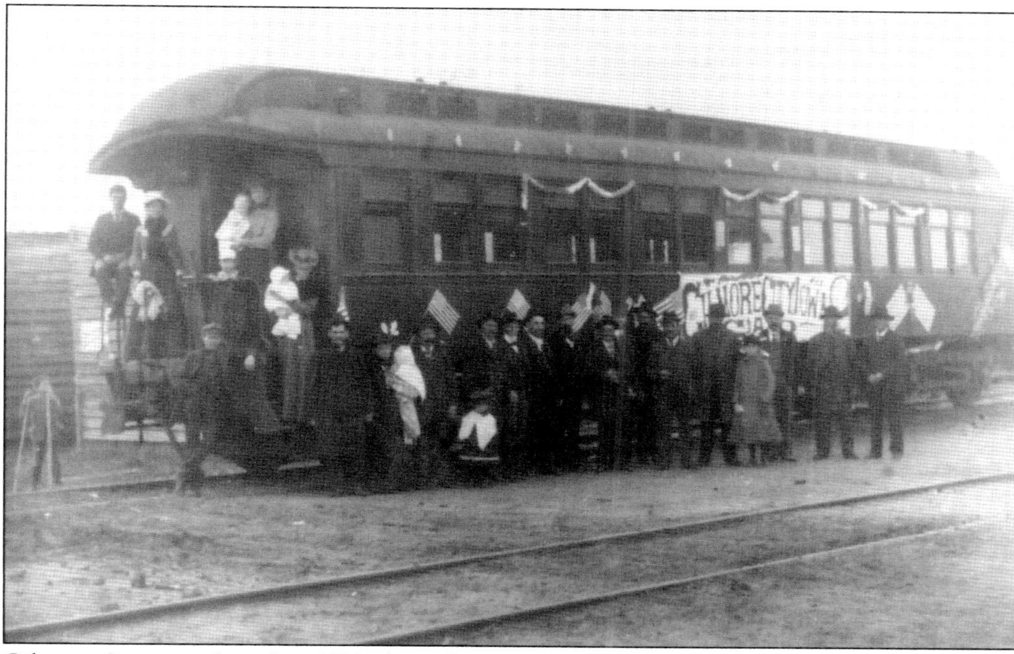

Gilmore City was platted in 1882 along the Des Moines & Fort Dodge Railroad. The original name, Blooming Prairie, was changed to honor railroad official C.N. Gilmore. The town has the distinction of being located in both Humboldt and Pocahontas Counties as Gilmore Street is on the county line. Pictured are people who traveled by train to attend the 1904 World's Fair in St. Louis, Missouri.

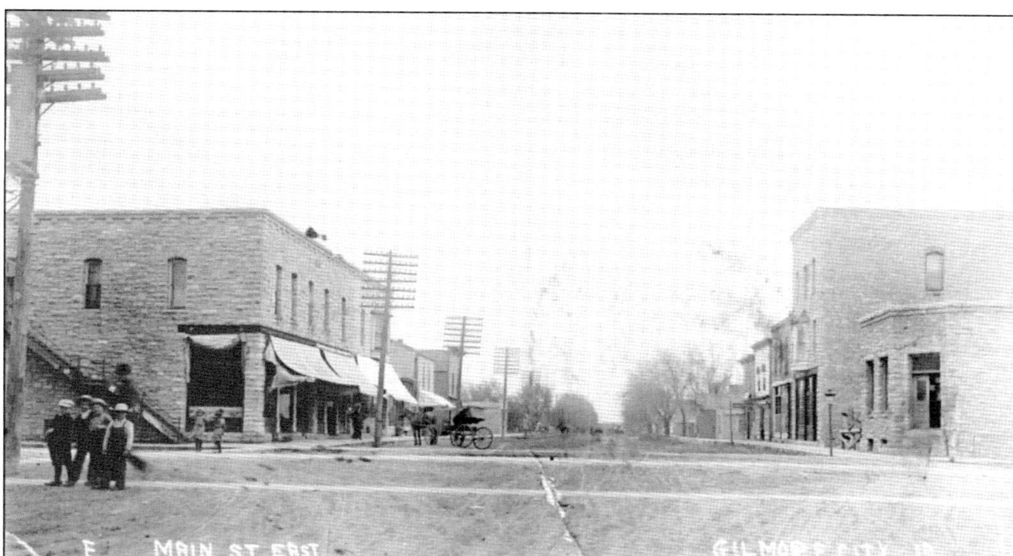

C Avenue in Gilmore City was busy around 1900. The limestone building in the right foreground held Security Bank, established in 1894 with officers Rollin Van Alstine and Francis and Lyman Beers. Next door was a three-story building erected by Andrew Bull, which housed Gilmore Hotel. The International Order of Odd Fellows met on the second floor. The building in the left foreground was Seavers Furniture and Undertaking.

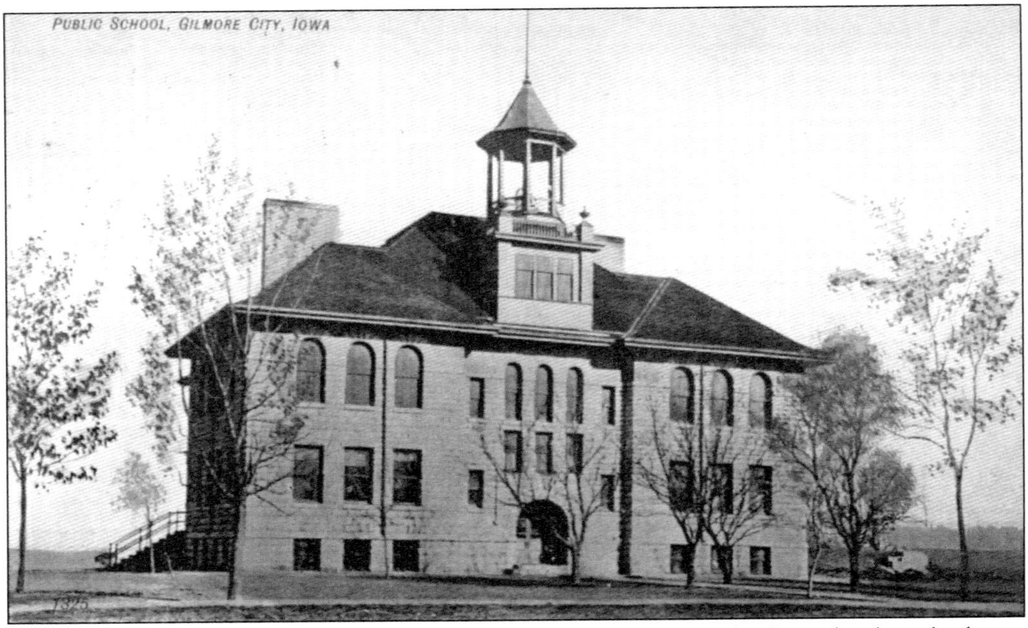

Gilmore City Independent School District was established in 1885. The first school was built two years later. In 1905, a new school building was dedicated. Limestone from a nearby quarry was used in its construction. Sadly, principal Elma Edgington lost her life when the building burned in 1943. Classes were held in various places around town until the present school was built in 1949.

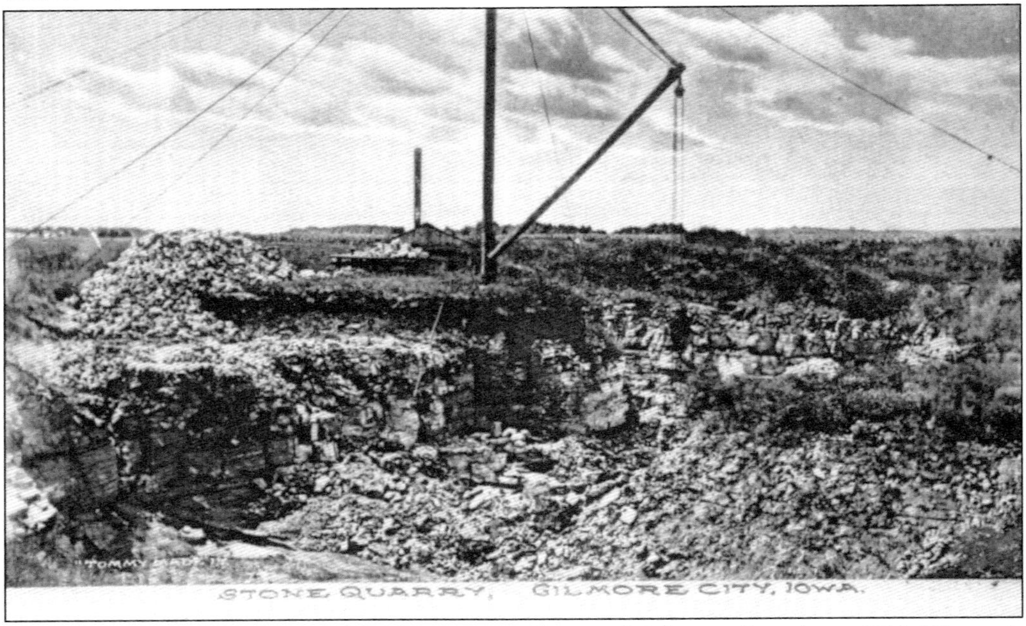

A limestone quarry was opened for business northwest of Gilmore City about 1880. The rock was used for railroad and building purposes. A cement plant was the next business to use the quarry. Midwest Limestone opened its doors in the 1940s and produced road stone, concrete stone, and agricultural material. Gilmore City limestone has been determined to be among the best in the state.

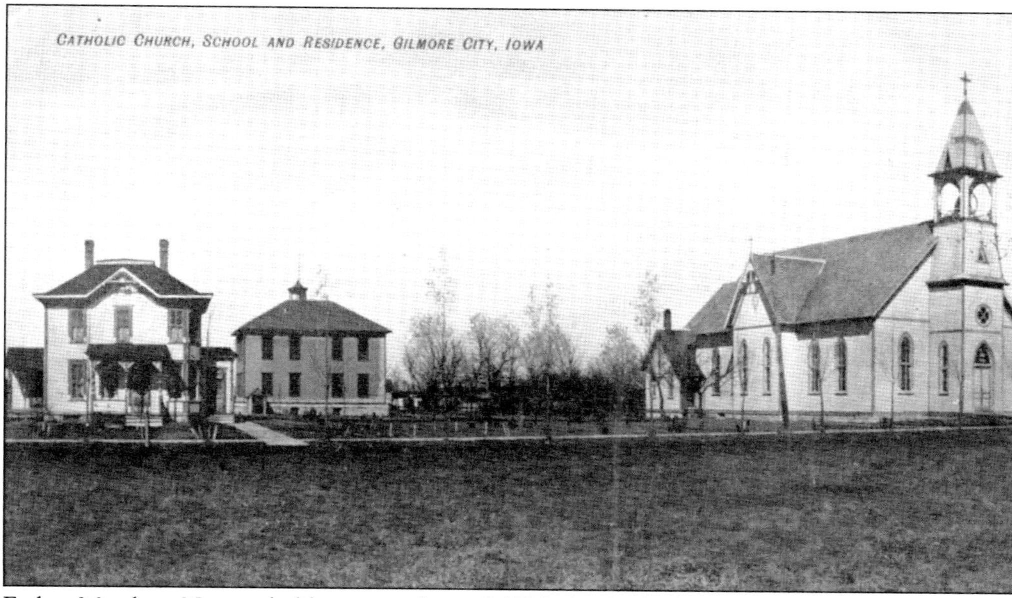

Father Matthew Norton held mass in the mid-1880s for Catholics in the Gilmore City area. St. John's Parish was a part of his circuit. The congregation built a church in 1889. They purchased the original public school building, moved it to the church grounds, and opened an eight-grade school in 1911. Five years later, the first senior class graduated from high school.

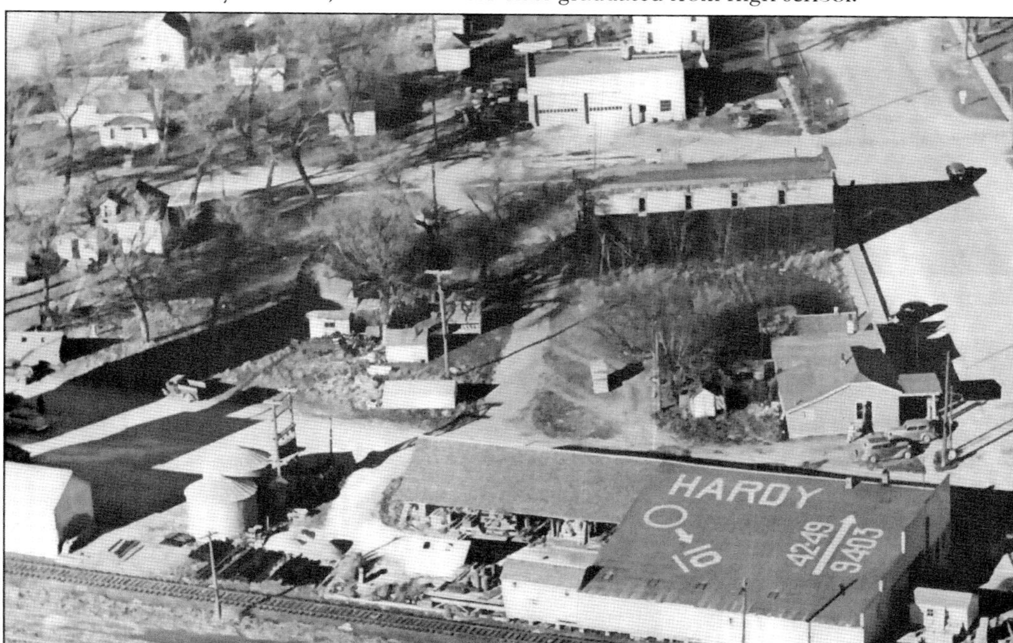

Hardy was laid out in 1881 on Section 4 of Lake Township by the Burlington, Cedar Rapids & Northern Railroad. The depot was the first building in town. W.H. Foley and Company opened a general merchandise store in 1882. A post office, originally located at Viona, was moved to town in 1882 with J.H. Foley as postmaster. In 1881–1882, the Viona Methodist congregation built a church in town.

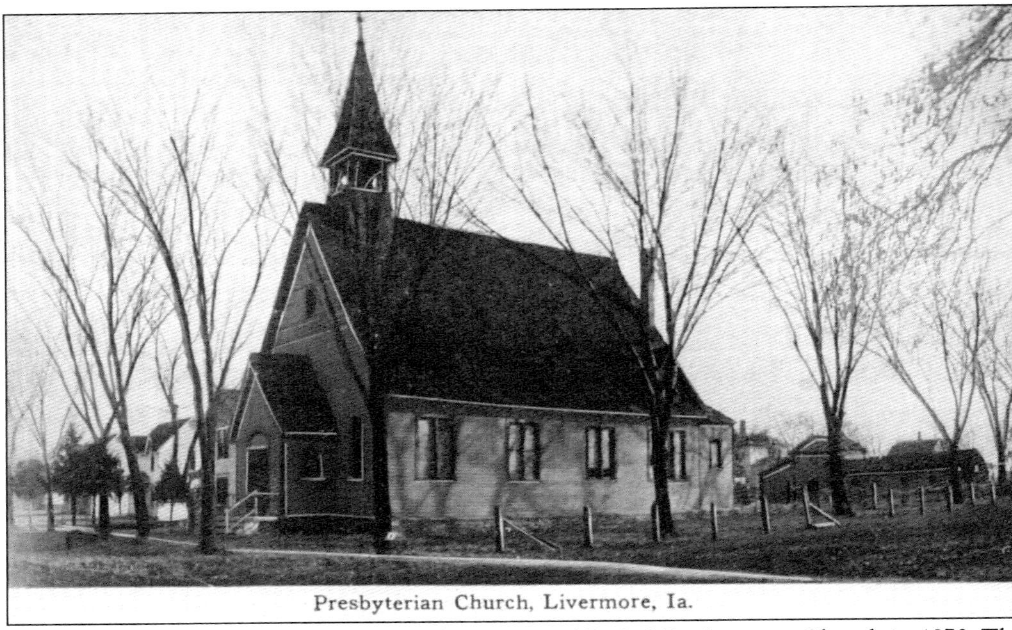

Rev. Walter Lyon, an early-day circuit rider, organized Bethel Presbyterian Church in 1870. The congregation met in schools and homes until they moved into Livermore shortly after the town was platted. They built a church, which was completed in 1885. Charter members included the Sinclair, Rutherford, Batten, Taylor, Miller, and Davidson families. Due to dwindling membership, the church was dissolved in 1978.

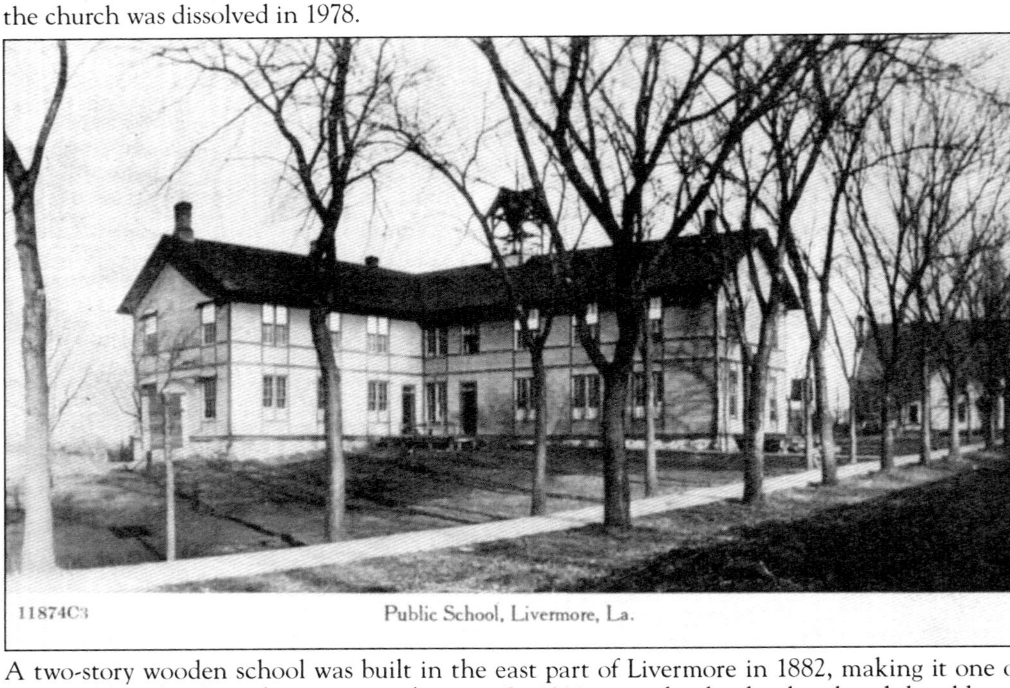

A two-story wooden school was built in the east part of Livermore in 1882, making it one of three public schools in the county at the time. In 1914, a new brick school replaced the old one. Dallas Clark, who played for the National Football League's Indianapolis Colts, attended the brick school. By becoming an excellent role model, he brought honor to his hometown.

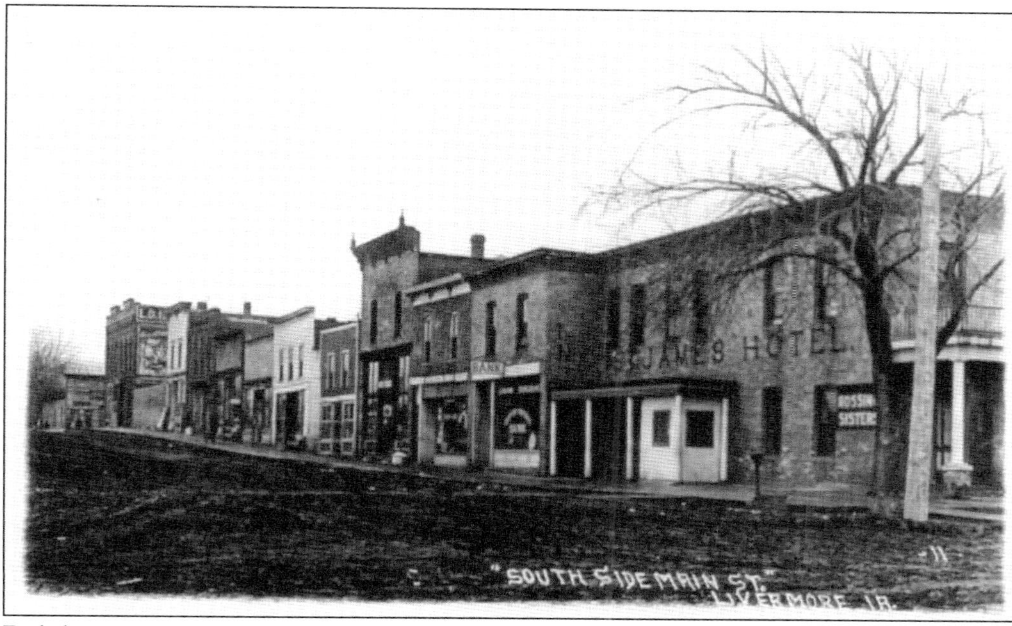

Early businesses were established north of the Minneapolis & St. Louis Railroad in Livermore. In October 1882, fire destroyed several of them, including the saloon, Meagher General Merchandise, Goddard Lumberyard, and McCauley Dry Goods. Stores were rebuilt one block south between the railroads. Dr. Daniel Russell erected the St. James Hotel. He soon sold it to John Zentz. Next door was Farmers Savings Bank, which was operated by Frank Miles and Ed Capesius.

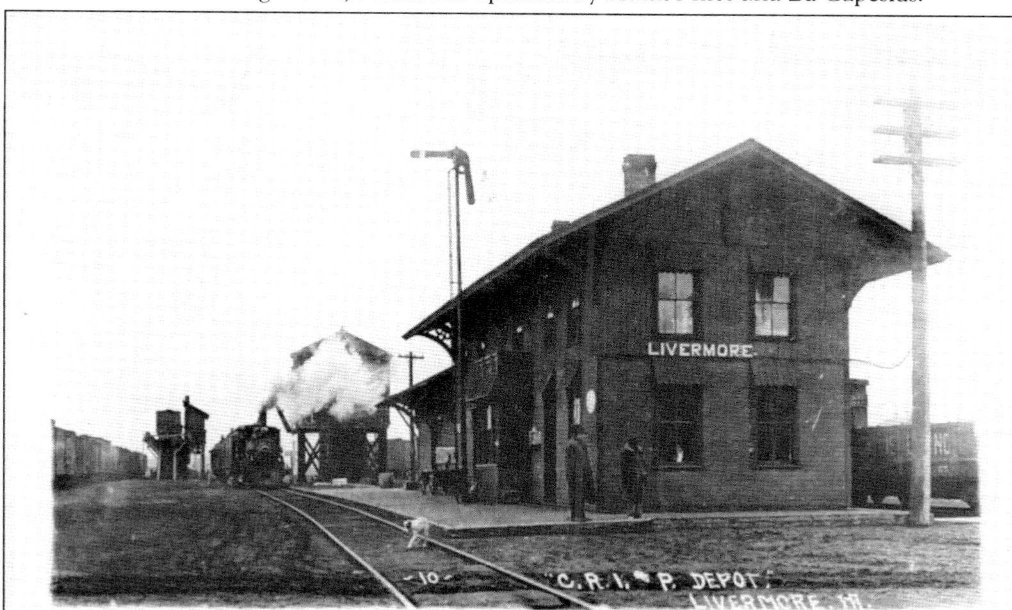

Livermore is located at the junction of two railroads. In 1879, the Minneapolis & St. Louis Railway reached the small town named for C.C. Washburne, who influenced the right of way. The Burlington, Cedar Rapids & Northern Railroad arrived in 1882. By then, the name had been changed to Livermore. Two railroads and two depots made for a bustling town.

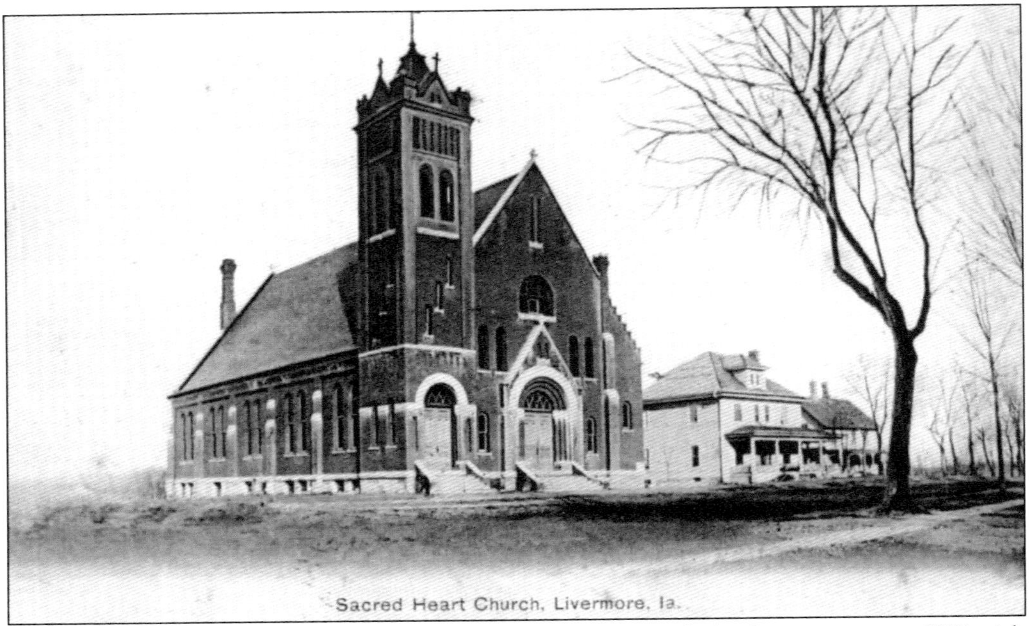

Father Zigrang of St. Joe organized Livermore's Sacred Heart Catholic Congregation in 1881 with the help of Ed Hines, John Murphy, John Berry, William Cox, Ed Sherman, and John Dunphy. They built a church the following year. A new brick church was dedicated in 1896 and served its congregation well until fire destroyed the building in 1919. The present church was dedicated in 1922 due to the generosity of many.

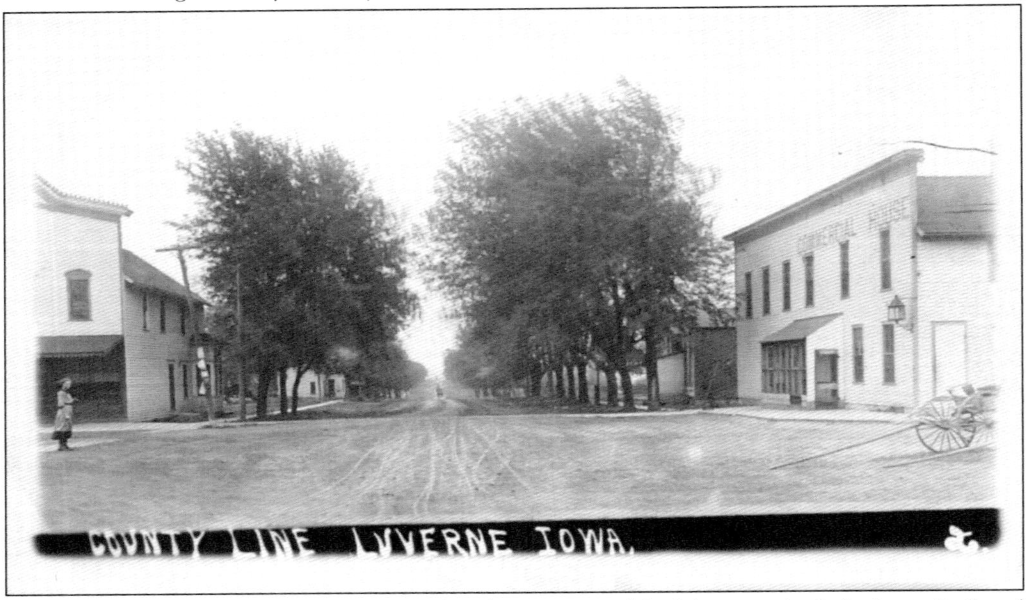

LuVerne, platted in 1880–1881, was located at the junction of the Minneapolis & St. Louis Railroad and the Chicago & Northwestern Railroad. It outgrew the close towns of Vernon and Whitman due to its enterprising businessmen. Early businesses were Hanna and Bliss General Store, Hanna Hardware, Burtis Lumberyard, Lovell Harness Shop, Eggerth Furniture, Dunlap Drugstore, and Preston Blacksmith Shop. The town is divided between Kossuth and Humboldt Counties.

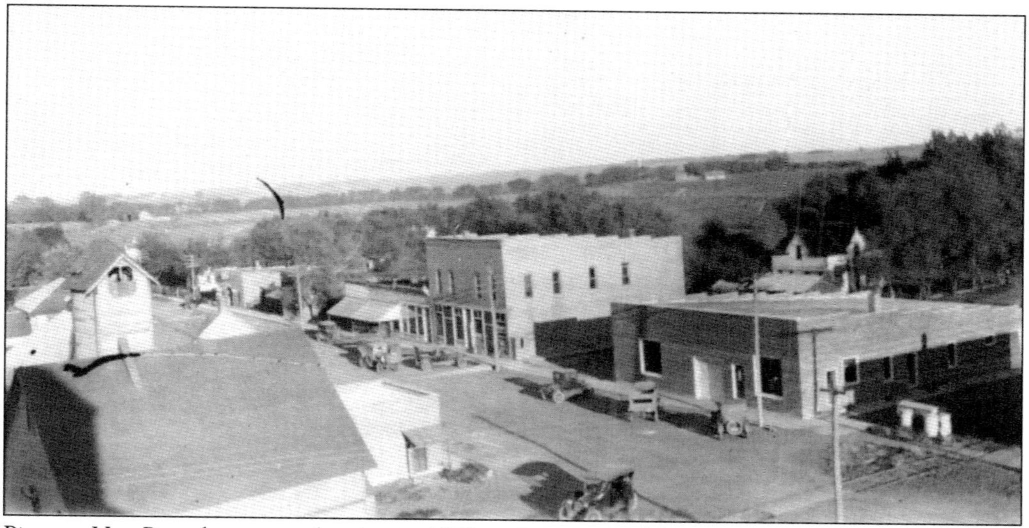

Pioneer Hay Press began production in 1882 and was one of the largest of its kind in northwest Iowa. The town, named for the hay press, was platted two years later in 1884. Some early businesses were Pioneer Hotel, Wittman General Store, Farmer Savings Bank, a telephone company, several restaurants, and an automotive garage. The Methodist Episcopal Church was built in 1894 and the Christian church in 1900.

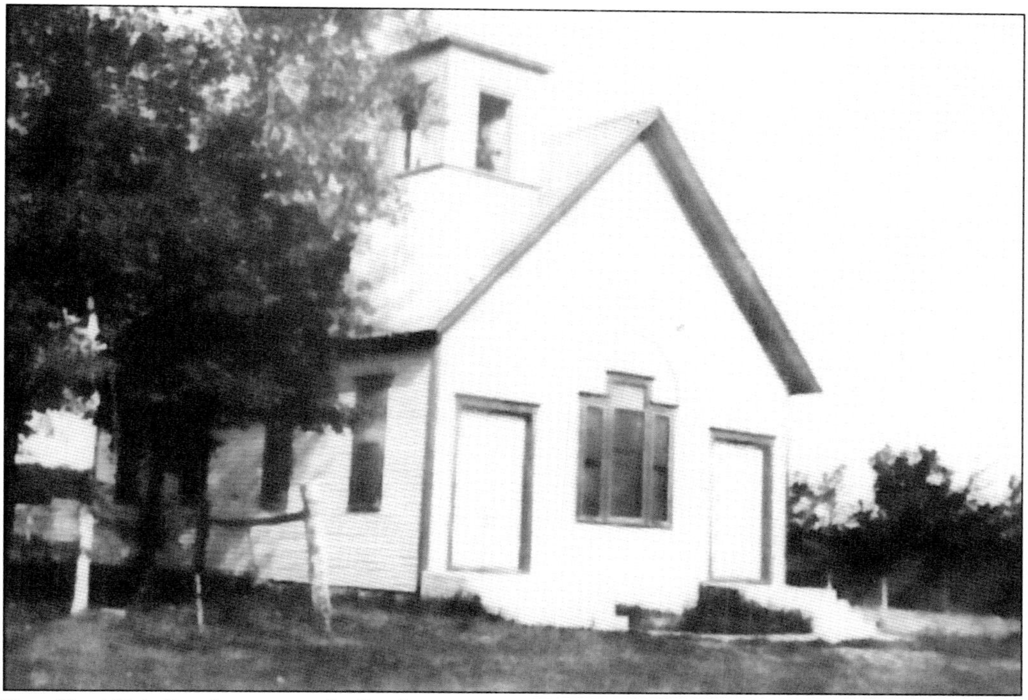

Rev. David McComb organized a Presbyterian congregation at McKnight's Point in 1856. He was noted as an exceptional speaker and active tobacco chewer who had a tendency to spit on the floor. The group met in homes until 1895, when they moved into McKnight's Chapel, which they owned jointly with the Methodists. The congregation eventually disbanded. Ottosen Presbyterians moved the building into town in 1924.

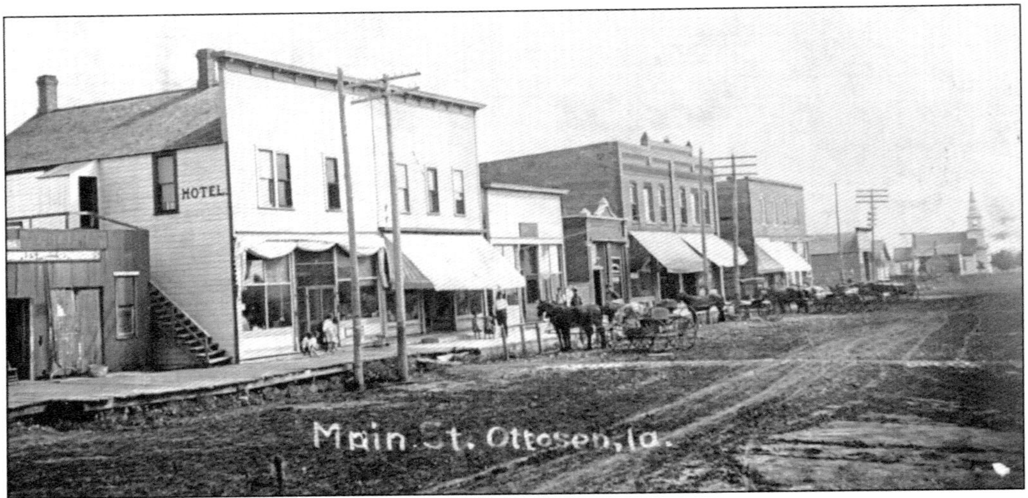

Main Street in Ottosen was the center of a bustling community. Property sold quickly, and building began in earnest in the fall of 1896. By 1901, the town was noted as having more brick buildings than any town in the county except Humboldt. Some of the better known businesses at that time were Quimby Hotel, Ottosen Savings Bank, Vohs Drugstore, Kenyon Brothers, and Cooper Stock Buying Company.

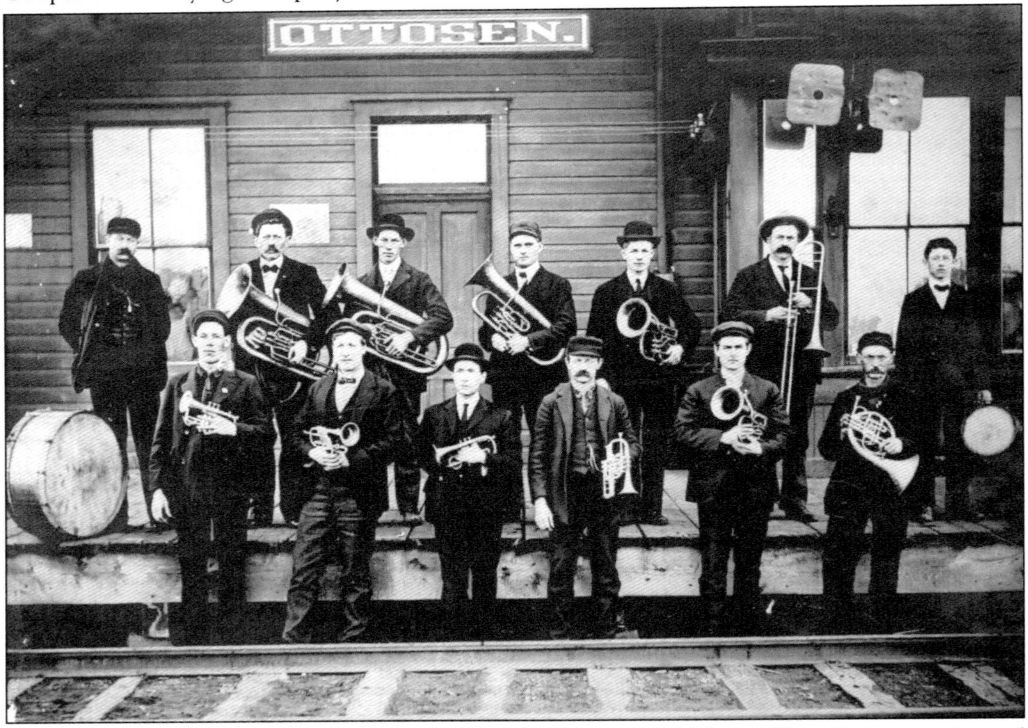

Ottosen Band was organized about 1902 under the direction of Murray Russell, an experienced band man and prominent area farmer. The group entertained at many events. From left to right are (first row) Charley Graves, Gus Vohs, Charles Miller, Joe Turner, Carl Morrison, and J.C. Bing; (second row) Joe Williams, George Goldner, Roy Graves, Joe Schumpp, Sylven Stone, Frank Howe, and Elmer Anderson.

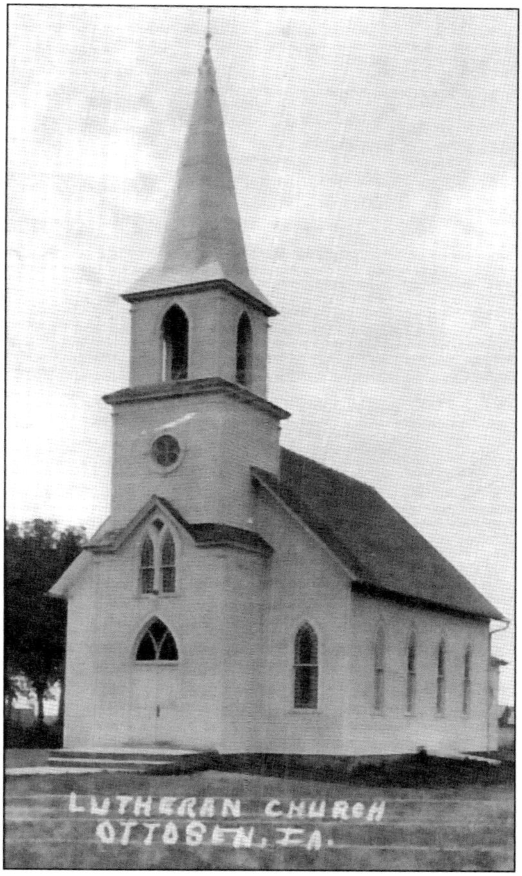

Reverend Wigdahl organized Ottosen's Trinity Lutheran Church in 1900. Two years later, the congregation was able to lay the cornerstone of its new church. Ladies Aide was organized soon after and contributed much to the spiritual and financial strength of the church. The church was struck by lightning and burned in 1927. This industrious congregation built a new church the next year, which is still in use.

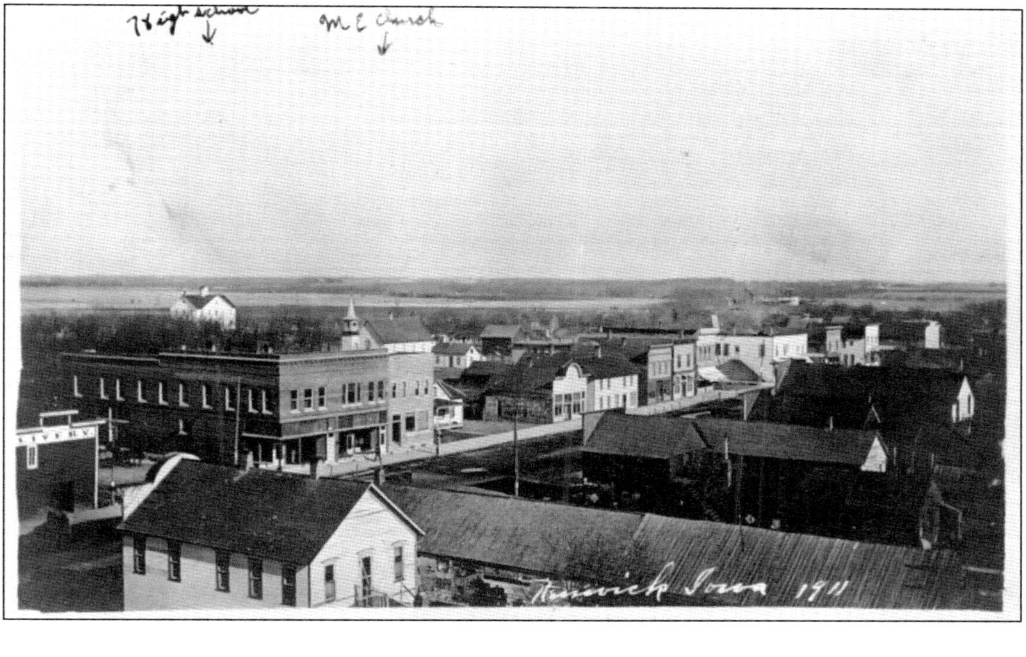

Renwick, platted in 1881 by the Chicago & Northwestern Railroad, was named for a crewman on the first train that steamed into town. By 1883, the town was booming. Early businesses were Martin Hotel, Stoddard Brothers Groceries, Drennan Hardware, Murphy Blacksmith Shop, Renwick Mill, Needham Creamery, Hoyt Lumber, Griebel Furniture, Richardson Dry Goods and Groceries, Brink Real Estate, and Mrs. Barbara Klassie Dry Goods Store.

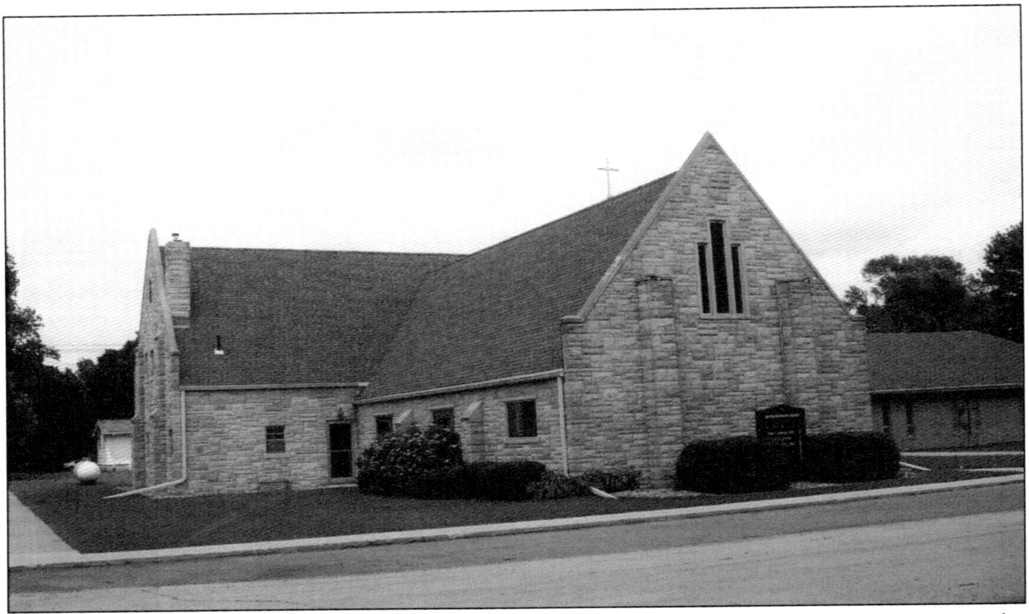

Swiss residents of Vernon Township constructed a building in 1890, which was known as the First Evangelical Church in Renwick. It became Evangelical United Brethren in 1945 when those two denominations merged. Methodists organized a congregation and built a church in 1891. When the Methodist and Evangelical United Brethren denominations merged in 1968, the local congregations chose to use the newer church (pictured), which was built in 1952.

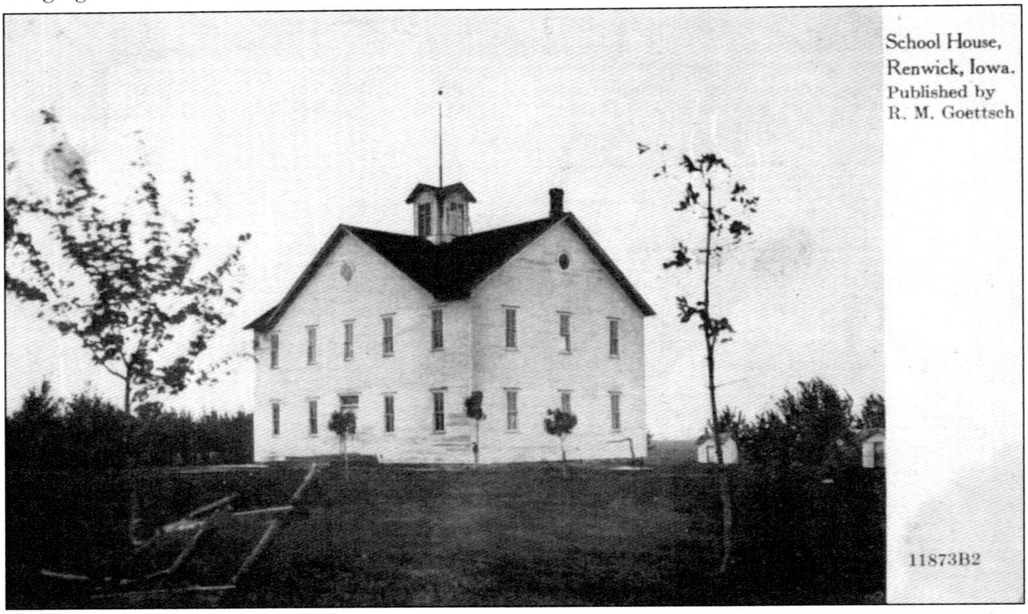

Renwick Independent School District was organized in 1892. The first school, constructed in 1893, was a two-story frame building. In 1916, a two-story brick building was built on the north side of town. The school board added a gym in 1935. In the mid-1950s, Renwick, Hardy, and Vernon Consolidated merged school systems under the name Boone Valley. Due to declining enrollment, this district dissolved in 1988.

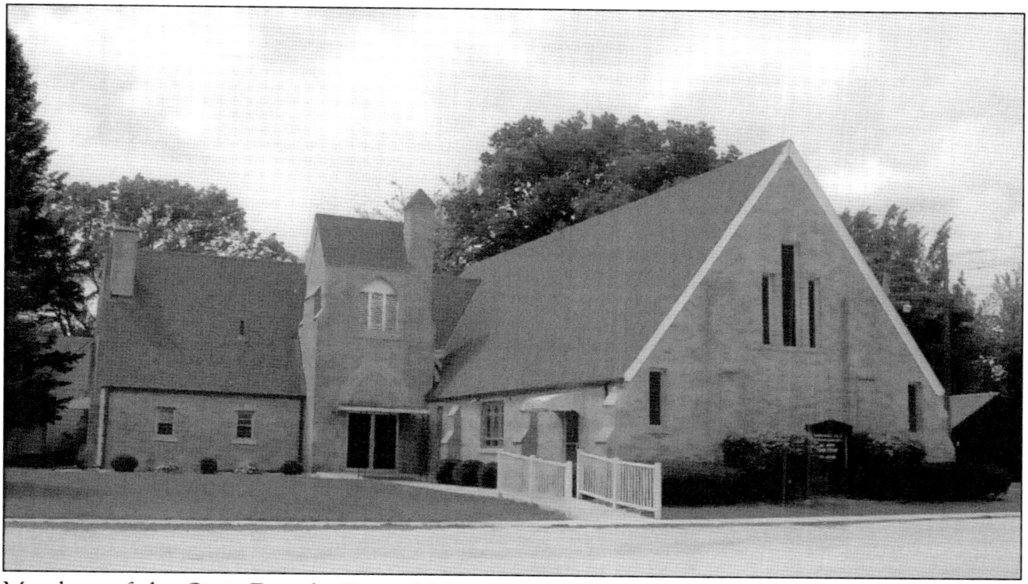

Members of the Orris French, Samuel Merithew, Lucy Stone, C. Ward, and Miner Schofield families established a Baptist congregation in the Prairie Creek area about 1872. This was the first Baptist church in Humboldt County. Soon after Renwick was platted, the members moved their worship services into town. The church they built in 1883 was destroyed by fire in 1948. They dedicated a new building (pictured) four years later.

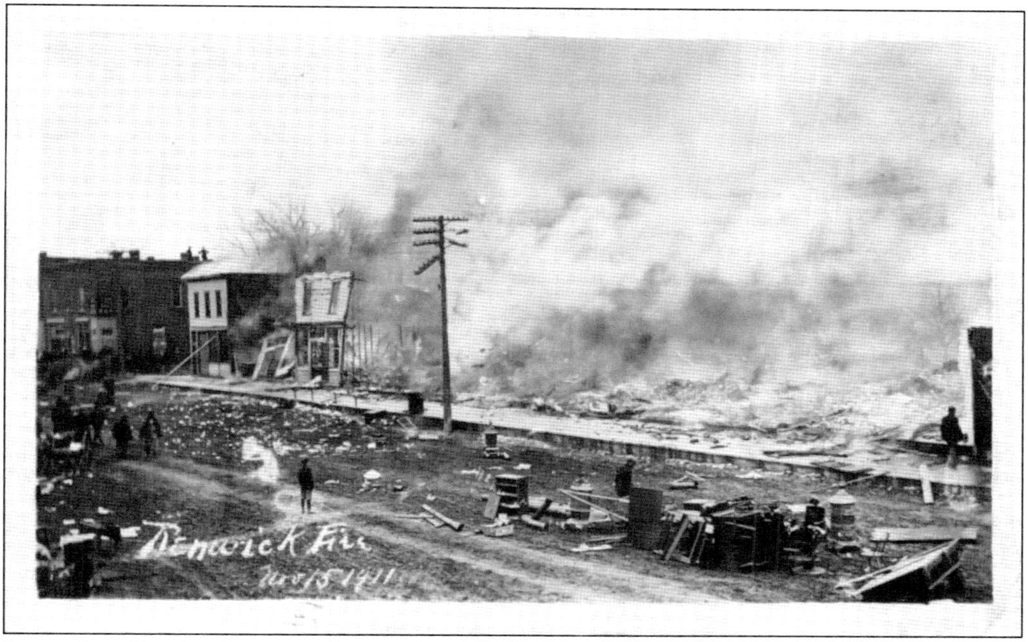

Renwick suffered a disastrous fire in November 1911, which burned almost an entire block on the north side of Main Street. The loss of businesses and household goods was estimated at $30,000. Among the buildings burned were Thompson Furniture Store, Walker's Restaurant, Renwick Times Printing Office, Rowther's Harness Shop, First National Bank, the post office, a barbershop, and a rooming house.

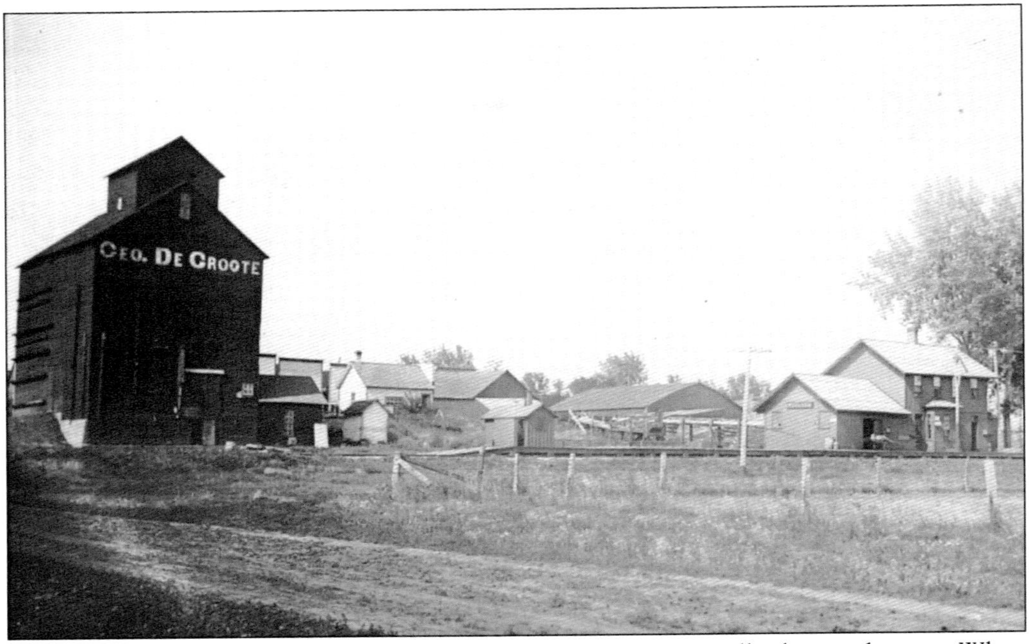

Rutland was laid out in 1869 by H.G. Bicknell. The town was originally close to the river. When the Chicago & Northwestern Railroad arrived in 1881, the business district was moved near the depot. Early citizens included Patrick Sheridan, William Locke, Daniel DeGroote, James Oxborrow, John Goodell, George Whipple, Wesley Davenport, and Charles Sherman.

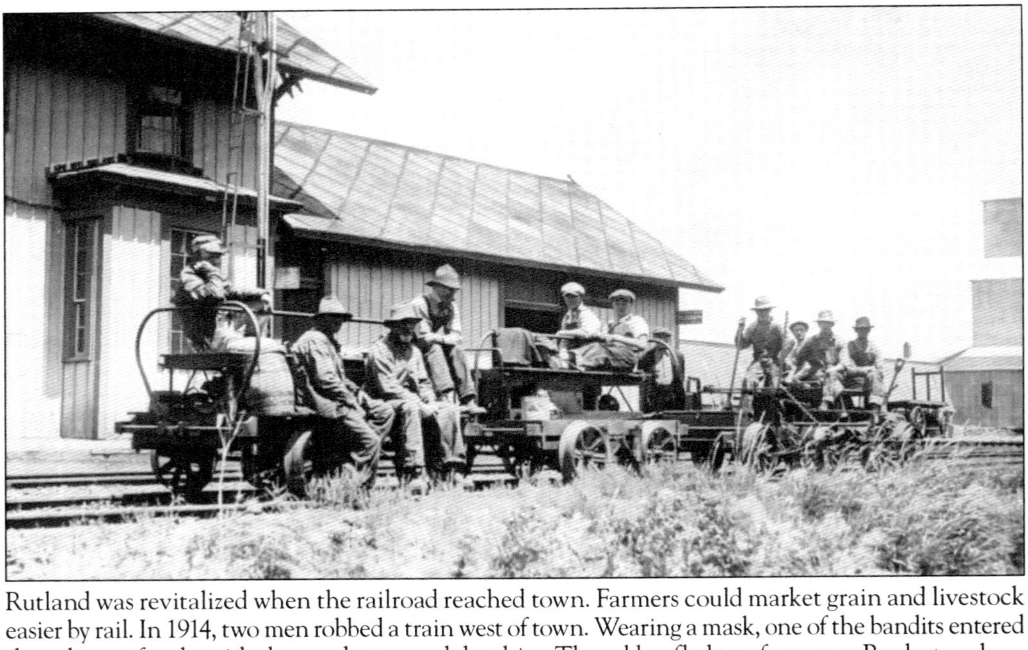

Rutland was revitalized when the railroad reached town. Farmers could market grain and livestock easier by rail. In 1914, two men robbed a train west of town. Wearing a mask, one of the bandits entered the caboose, fought with the conductor, and shot him. The robber fled to a farm near Bradgate, where he was apprehended with the use of bloodhounds. His accomplice later turned himself in.

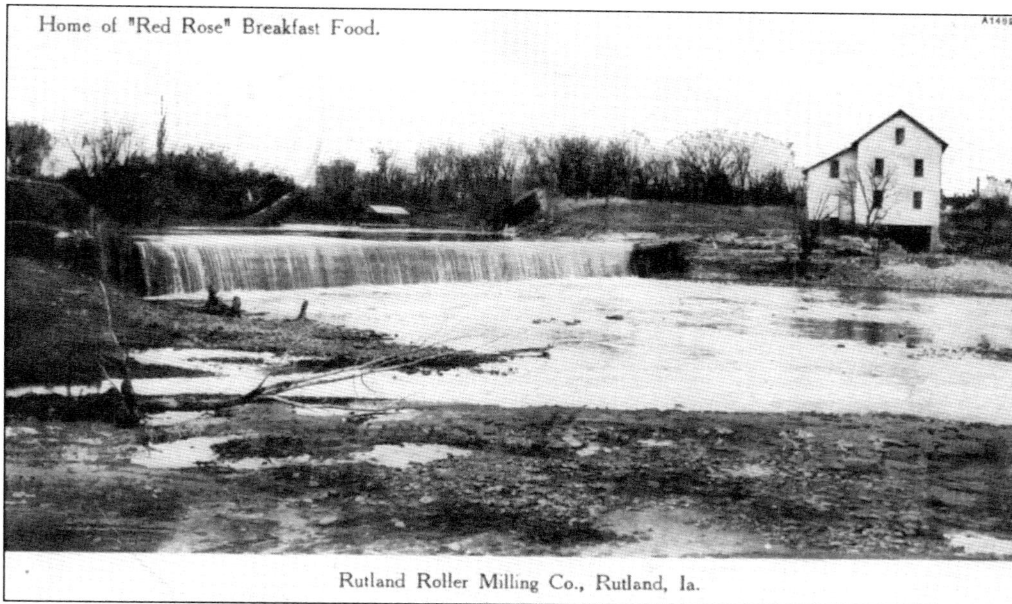

Rutland Mercantile and Manufacturing Company built a flour gristmill in 1871. It ran until 1881, when high water washed out the dam. Rutland Roller Mills was rebuilt in 1898. Red Rose and White Rose flours were produced. It was said that both of the flours came from the same bin, but one was priced higher. Ice broke the dam in 1916, which ended the business.

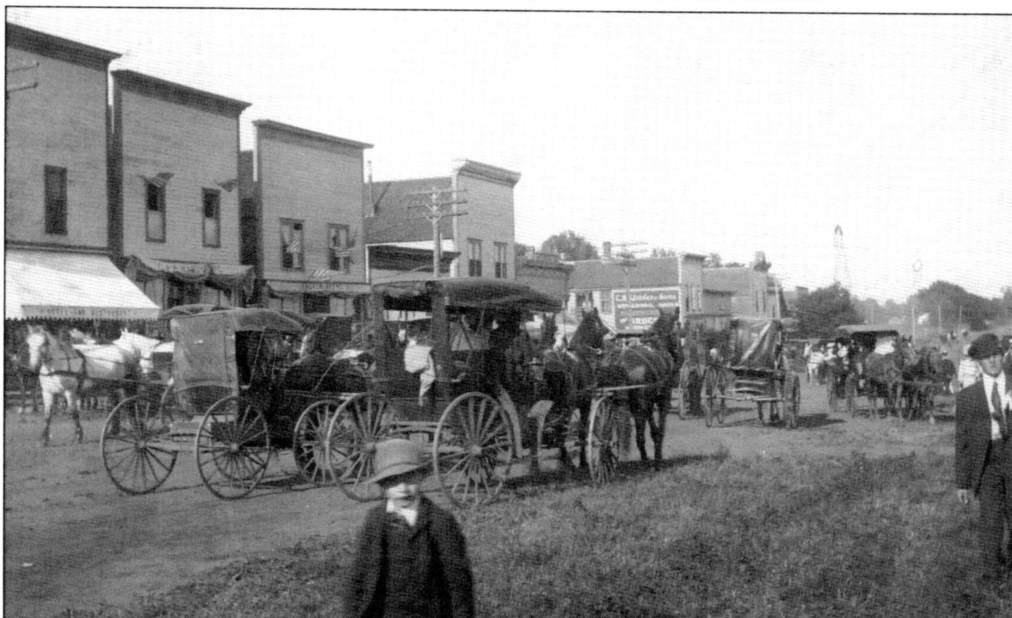

This photograph shows a busy day in Rutland. Bert DeGroote opened a hotel and restaurant in 1900. Henry Gregory and John Sheridan purchased McClure's Hardware at the same time. Andrew Arent Jr. operated a successful drugstore, which included paints, wallpaper, and a soda fountain. In the distance is an advertisement for the company E.A. Wilder and Sons, which ran a general merchandise store for several years.

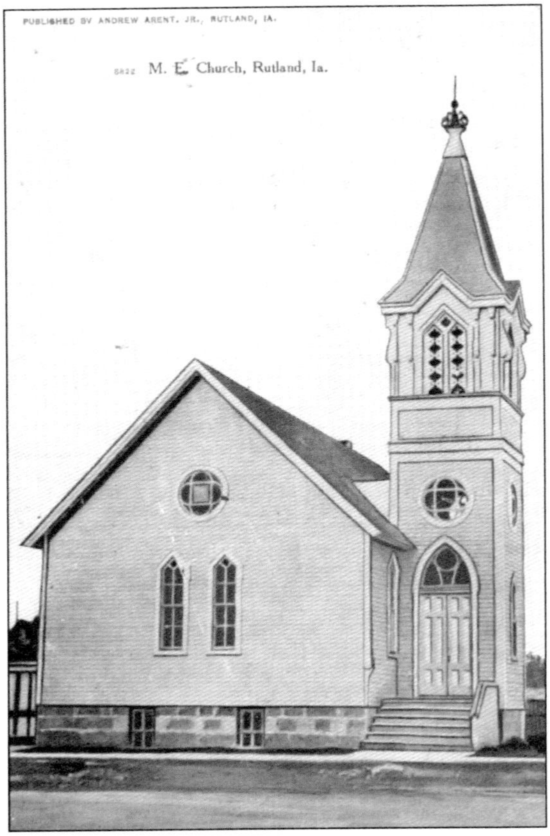

The First Methodist Society of Rutland was organized by Reverend Rowen in 1872. Members of the congregation built a church in 1890. Older residents recalled that limestone blocks that were used to build the foundation were cut from the riverbed south of town. Early members included the Barclay, Bean, Marsh, Sherman, Bair, and Ames families. The church is still in use.

Rutland School was organized in May 1868. Classes at first met in a small cabin. A new school was built in 1871 and served until 1900, when a two-story wooden building took its place. In 1934, the district erected an up-to-date brick building. It was 1936 when the first senior class graduated from Rutland High School. Rutland operated as an independent school until 1959.

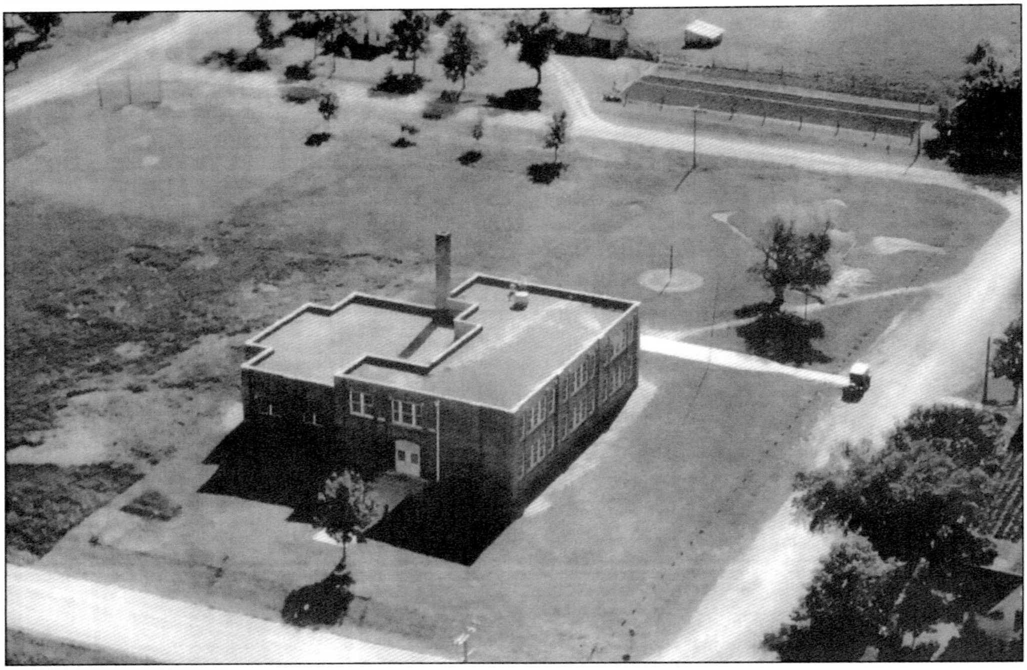

In 1878, Chris Lund and J.O. Nasset opened a small store one mile east and one mile south of the present town of Thor. They offered basic items such as sugar, coffee, nails, candy, cloth, and tobacco. A post office, established in 1880 under the name of Verbeck, was housed in the store. The post office was moved to the new town of Thor in 1882.

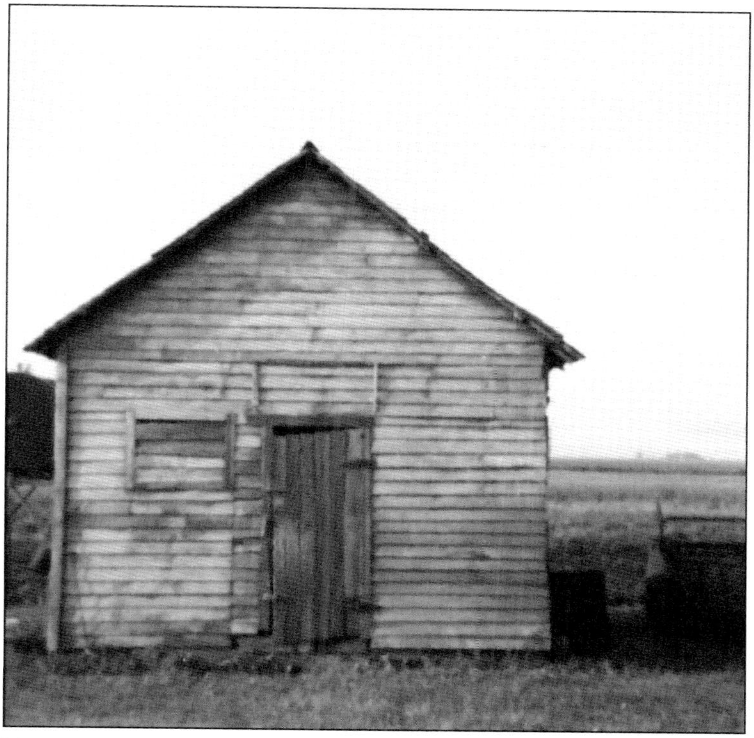

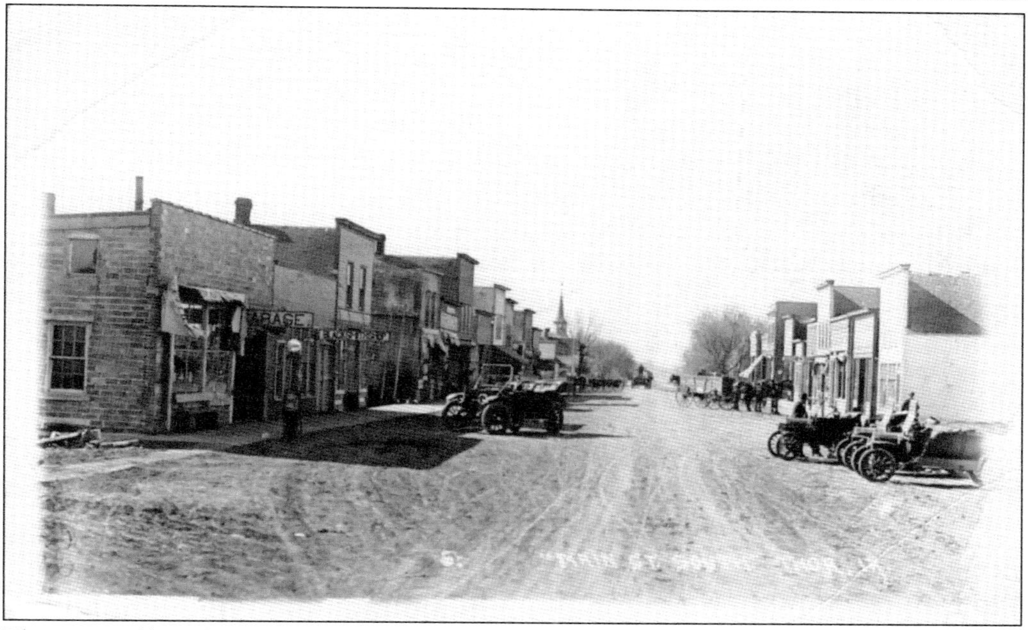

Thor, named by Ole Willickson, was laid out in 1881 by the Chicago & Northwestern Railway. Some of the early businesses were Olson General Merchandise, Sam Guddall General Store, Thor Lumber, Opheim and Lenning Hardware, Thor Savings Bank, Hotel Bartholomew, Mokelbust Meat Market, Digerness Blacksmith, Thor Cooperative Creamery, Mickelson Garage, and several restaurants. The town experienced a fire in 1934 that destroyed much of its business district.

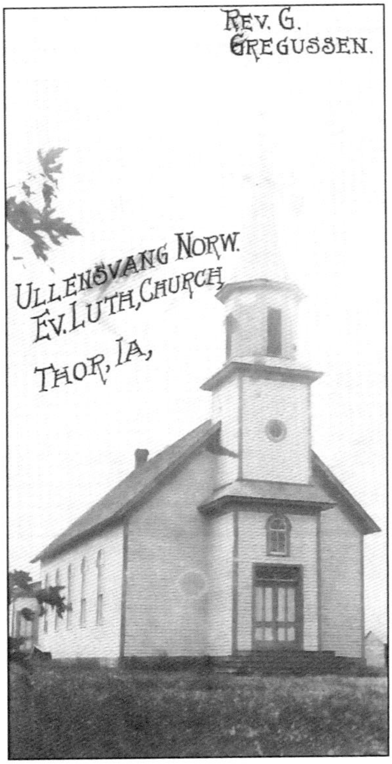

Ullensvang Norwegian Evangelical Lutheran Church was organized in August 1872 in Carrie Olson's home southeast of Thor. The building shown at left was constructed in 1881 on Section 28 in Norway Township. In 1905, it was moved into town. The church caught fire and burned in 1941. The congregation immediately planned a new building that was dedicated the following year. It is still in use.

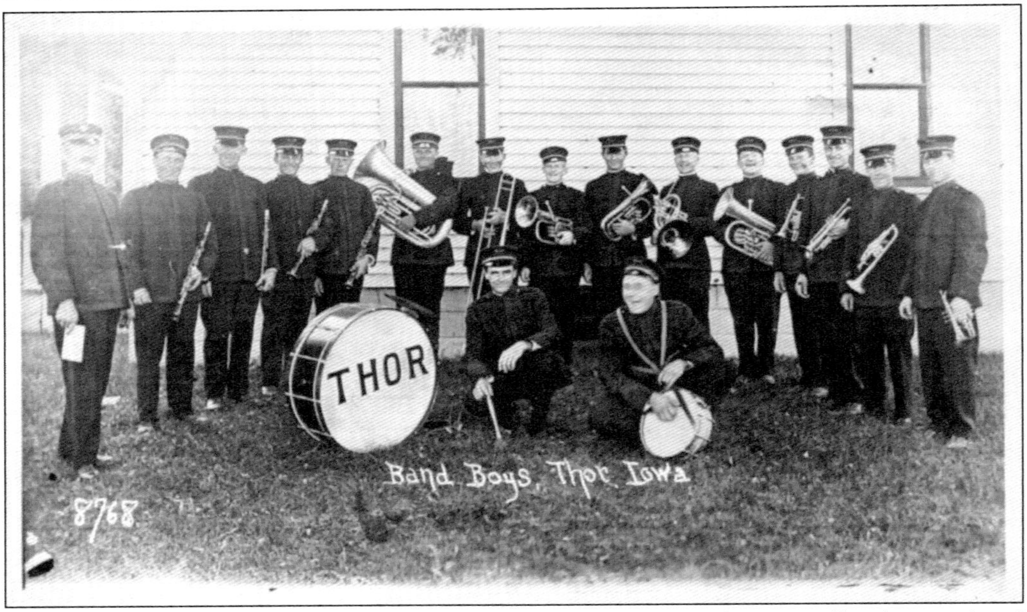

Thor had a town band for many years. The band drew large crowds, especially when it played at the town hall. From left to right are (first row) Peter Knutson and unidentified; (second row) John Sandvig, Tom Mickelson, George Olson, unidentified, Lewis Orsland, unidentified, Elmer Olson, George Sovde, two unidentified, Conrad Sovde, Rudolph Sandvig, Jake Onnereim, Ben Olson, and Percy Mickelson.

Thor Lumber and Grain Company was organized prior to 1901. The firm dealt in grain, lumber, coal, brick, tile, stucco, lime, cement, and grass seed. In 1900, the company handled over 175,000 bushels of grain. Officers of the company were Chris Lund, president; Sam Guddall, secretary; and S.K. Groth, manager. All three men were very active in the life of the town.

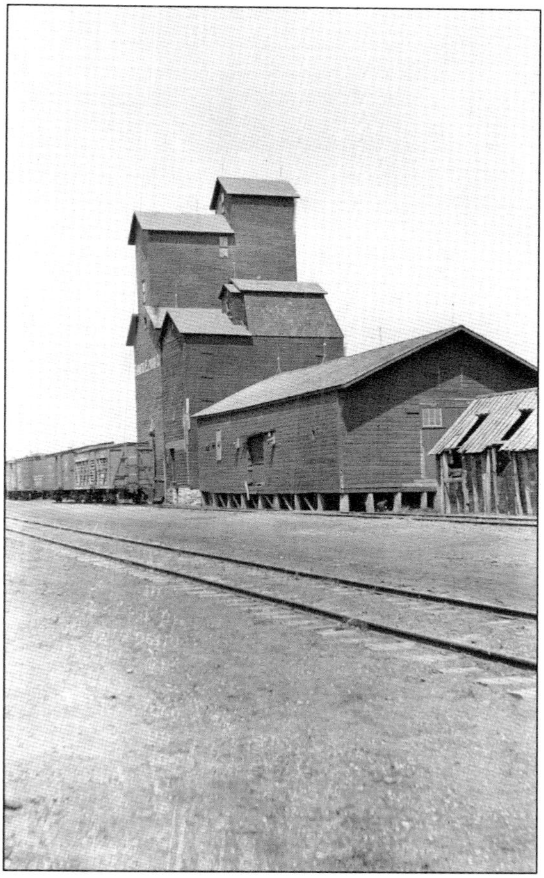

Henry Hanson operated a variety store on Ann Street. One of the features that children especially enjoyed was the selection of penny candy. They made their choices slowly and carefully as they had worked hard for their pennies. After the 1934 fire, which destroyed much of the business district, Henry moved his business to his house (shown). He also worked as a painter, cobbler, and paperhanger.

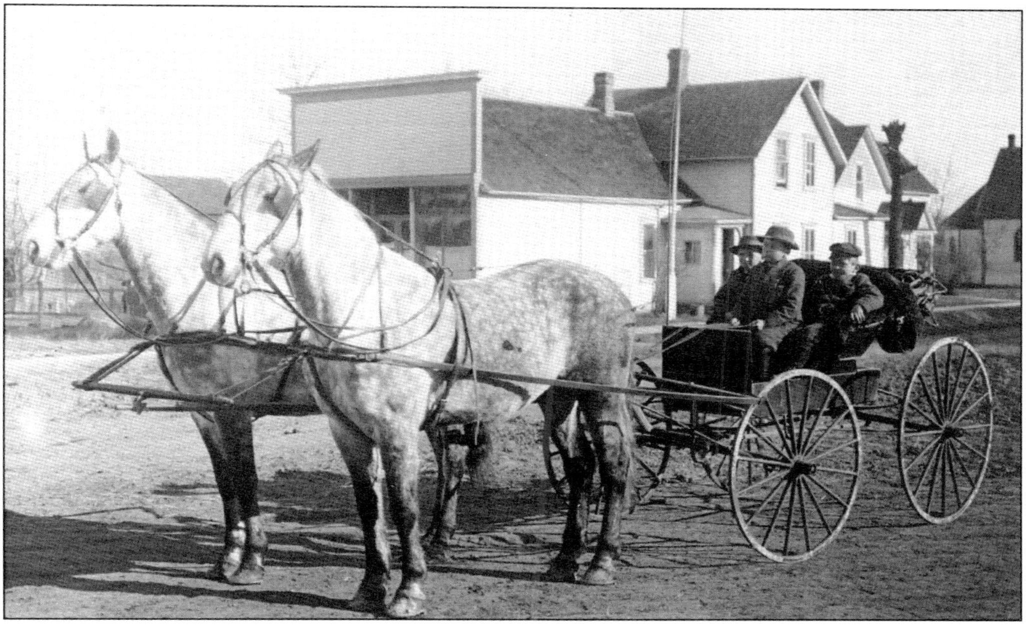

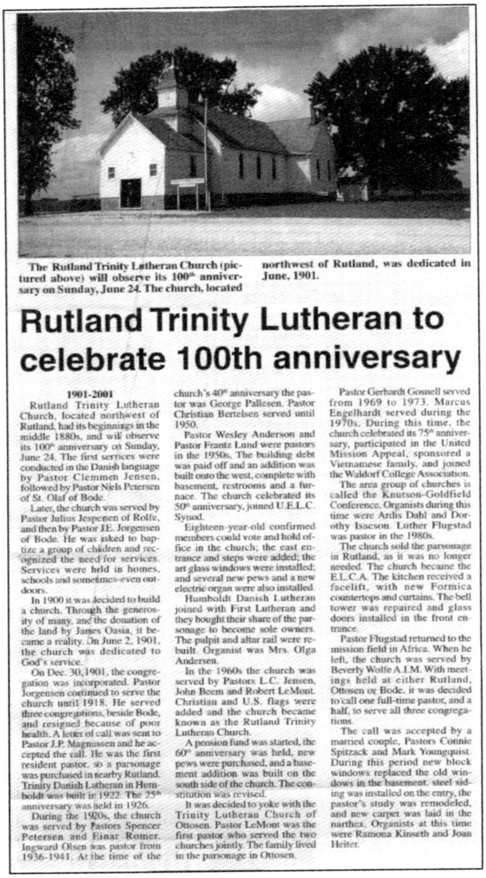

The Rutland Trinity Lutheran Church (pictured above) will observe its 100th anniversary on Sunday, June 24. The church, located northwest of Rutland, was dedicated in June, 1901.

Rutland Trinity Lutheran to celebrate 100th anniversary

1901-2001

Rutland Trinity Lutheran Church, located northwest of Rutland, had its beginnings in the middle 1880s, and will observe its 100th anniversary on Sunday, June 24. The first services were conducted in the Danish language by Pastor Clemmen Jensen, followed by Pastor Niels Petersen of St. Olaf of Bode.

Later, the church was served by Pastor Julius Jespersen of Rolfe, and then by Pastor J.E. Jorgensen of Bode. He was asked to baptize a group of children and recognized the need for services. Services were held in homes, schools and sometimes even outdoors.

In 1900 it was decided to build a church. Through the generosity of many, and the donation of the land by James Oasia, it became a reality. On June 2, 1901, the church was dedicated to God's service.

On Dec. 30, 1901, the congregation was incorporated. Pastor Jorgensen continued to serve the church until 1918. He served three congregations, beside Bode, and resigned because of poor health. A letter of call was sent to Pastor J.P. Magnussen and he accepted the call. He was the first resident pastor, so a parsonage was purchased in nearby Rutland. Trinity Danish Lutheran in Humboldt was built in 1922. The 25th anniversary was held in 1926.

During the 1920s, the church was served by Pastors Spencer Petersen and Einar Romer. Ingward Olsen was pastor from 1936-1941. At the time of the church's 40th anniversary the pastor was George Pallesen. Pastor Christian Bertelsen served until 1950.

Pastor Wesley Anderson and Pastor Frantz Lund were pastors in the 1950s. The building debt was paid off and an addition was built onto the west, complete with basement, restrooms and a furnace. The church celebrated its 50th anniversary, joined U.E.L.C. Synod.

Eighteen-year-old confirmed members could vote and hold office in the church; the east entrance and steps were added; the art glass windows were installed; and several new pews and a new electric organ were also installed.

Humboldt Danish Lutheran joined with First Lutheran and they bought their share of the parsonage to become sole owners. The pulpit and altar rail were rebuilt. Organist was Mrs. Olga Andersen.

In the 1960s the church was served by Pastors L.C. Jensen, John Beem and Robert LeMont. Christian and U.S. flags were added and the church became known as the Rutland Trinity Lutheran Church.

A pension fund was started, the 60th anniversary was held, new pews were purchased, and a basement addition was built on the south side of the church. The constitution was revised.

It was decided to yoke with the Trinity Lutheran Church of Ottosen. Pastor LeMont was the first pastor who served the two churches jointly. The family lived in the parsonage in Ottosen.

Pastor Gerhardt Gosnell served from 1969 to 1973. Marcus Engelhardt served during the 1970s. During this time, the church celebrated its 75th anniversary, participated in the United Mission Appeal, sponsored a Vietnamese family, and joined the Waldorf College Association.

The area group of churches is called the Knutson-Goldfield Conference. Organists during this time were Ardis Dahl and Dorothy Isacson. Luther Flugstad was pastor in the 1980s.

The church sold the parsonage in Rutland, as it was no longer needed. The church became the E.L.C.A. The kitchen received a facelift, with new Formica countertops and curtains. The bell tower was repaired and glass doors installed in the front entrance.

Pastor Flugstad returned to the mission field in Africa. When he left, the church was served by Beverly Wolfe A.I.M. With meetings held at either Rutland, Ottosen or Bode, it was decided to call one full-time pastor, and a half, to serve all three congregations.

The call was accepted by a married couple, Pastors Connie Spitzack and Mark Youngquist. During this period new block windows replaced the old windows in the basement, steel siding was installed on the entry, the pastor's study was remodeled, and new carpet was laid in the narthex. Organists at this time were Ramona Kinseth and Joan Heiter.

Religion was important to early citizens of Humboldt County, as shown by the number of churches built in rural areas. At one time, country churches included seven Norwegian Lutheran, one Danish Lutheran, one German Lutheran, one Methodist, one Danish Methodist, one Danish Baptist, one Congregational, and one Methodist-Presbyterian. The church shown is Rutland Trinity Lutheran Church, which was built on land donated by James Osia and dedicated in 1901.

Rutland Bridge, built about 1881, collapsed from the weight of Ed Braby's threshing rig in August 1913. His crew had finished work at Jared Heim's farm and was moving into town. As Lawrence and Lloyd Braby started over with the rig, the bridge began to swing and then gave way. The separator fell on one side, and the steam engine turned completely over. Neither man was seriously injured.

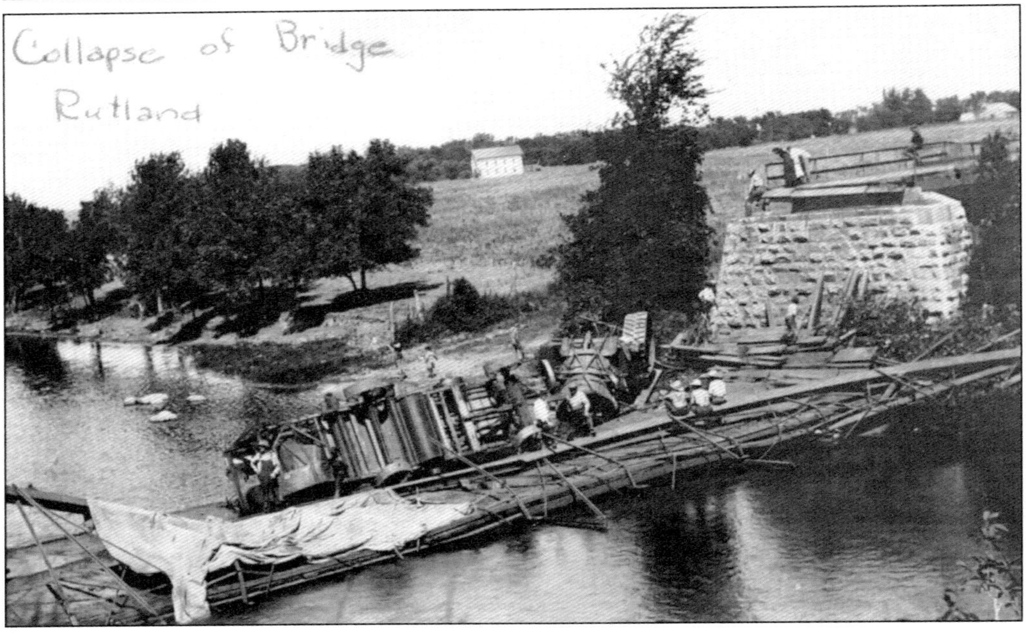

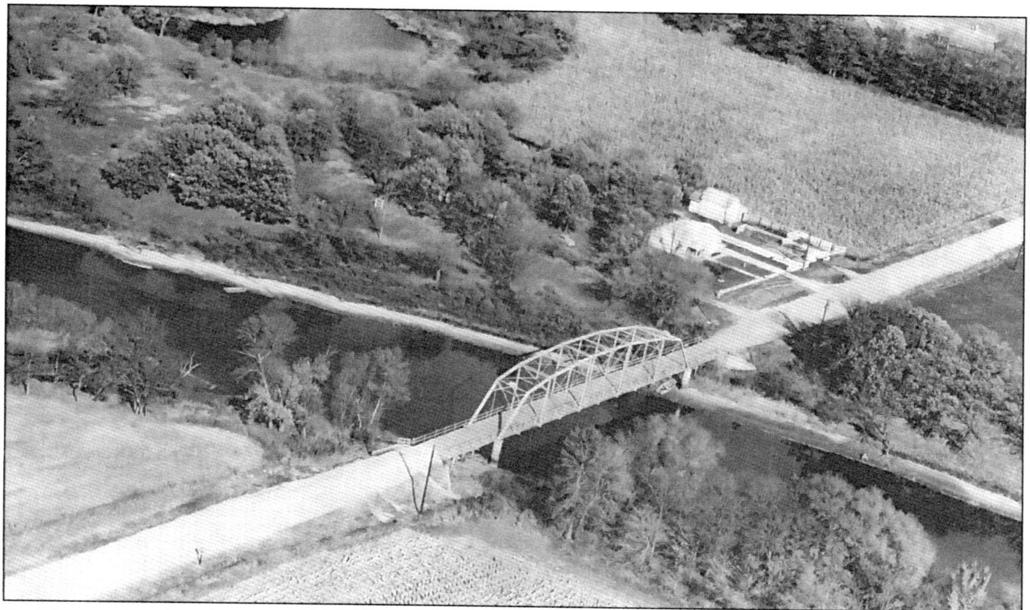

Berkhimer Bridge, located northwest of Humboldt, was built in the fall of 1899 near the ford on Mathias Berkhimer's farm. It was an important connection between Humboldt and towns to the west. Farmers in northern Corinth Township, northeastern Weaver, and southern Rutland Township had a more direct route into town. The cost of the bridge proper was less than $3,000. This century bridge is still in use.

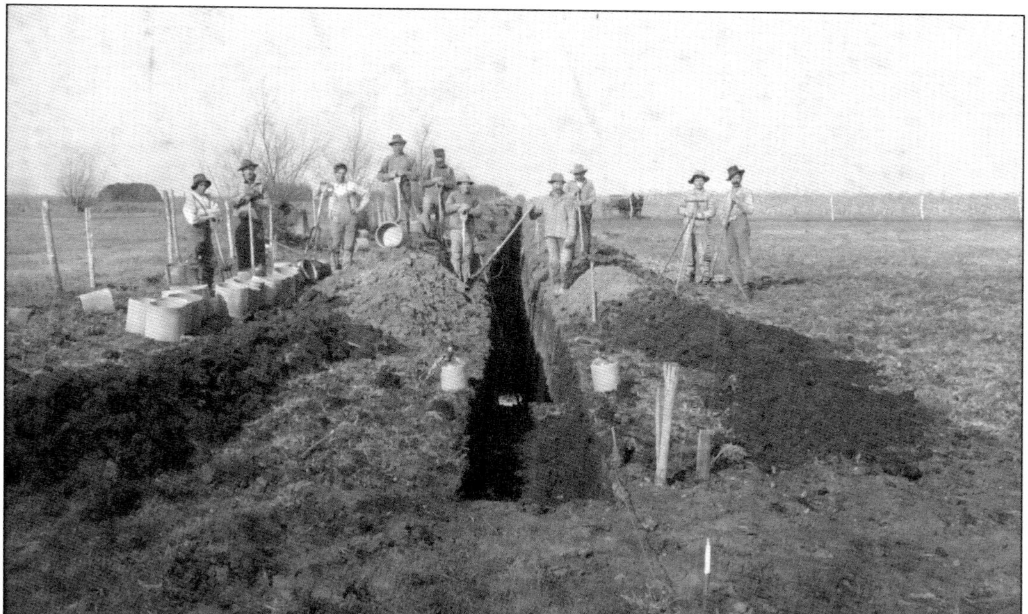

Humboldt County once contained many marshes and sloughs. The soil was productive but needed to be drained to make it farmable. Tiling was accomplished with a dredge boat and also digging by hand. In the early 1900s, many men worked as a tiler, which was hard, dangerous work. Ditches could collapse and bury them. Some were severely injured or died as a result.

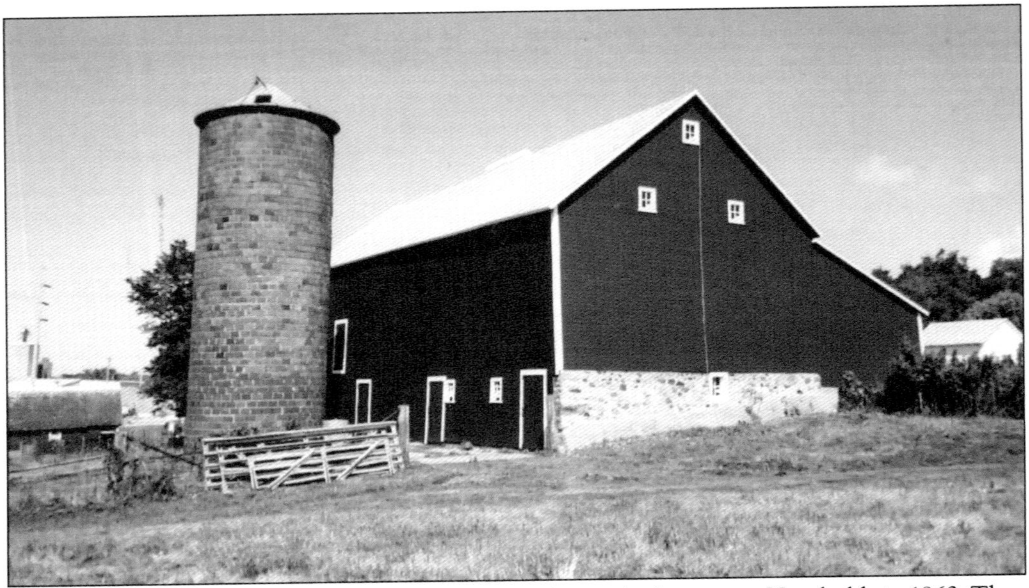

John G. Lorbeer Jr. and family were part of Taft's colony, which came to Humboldt in 1863. They settled on a farm 2.5 miles south of Dakota City. He built a barn using fieldstones in the foundation. It was large enough to hold nearly 40 milk cows as well as four teams of horses. Present owners Harold and Gladys McBurney restored the building in 2003.

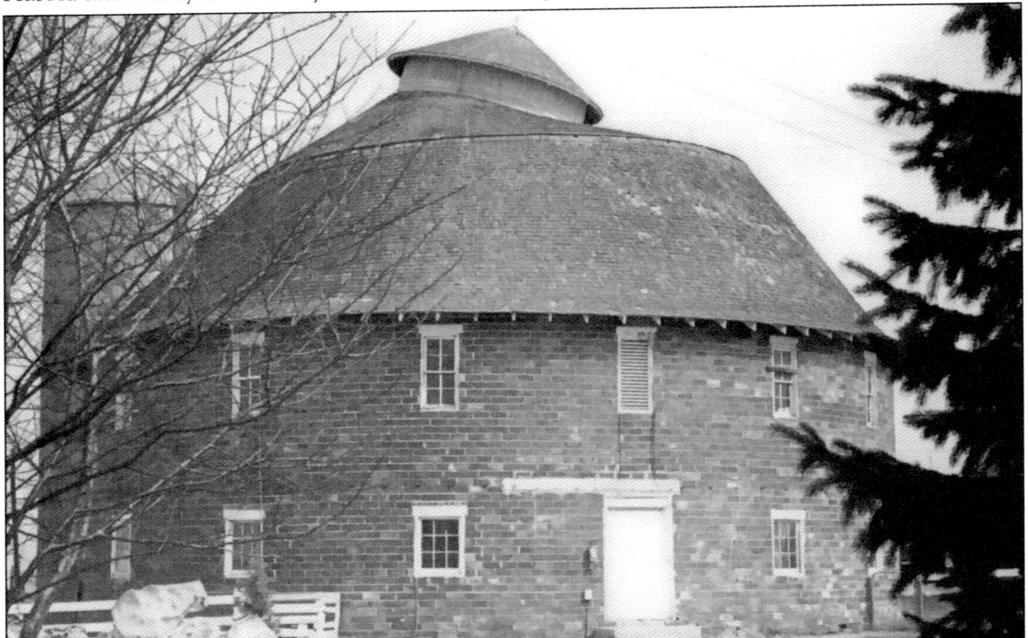

This round barn was built in southwest Delana Township about five miles north of Humboldt. It was built about 1916 by owners Ted and Albert B. White who were successful businessmen in Humboldt County. Built of clay tile, it had a diameter of 60 feet. There was a manger on one side for dairy cows and one for horses on the other. It was torn down about 1977.

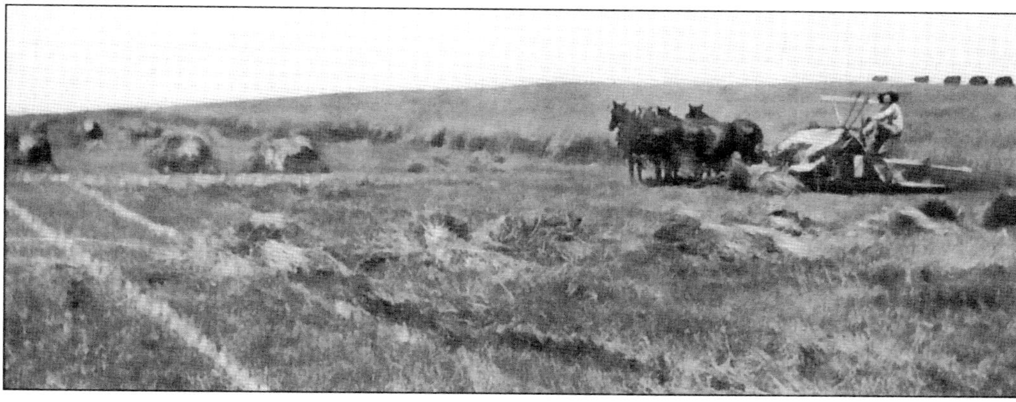

Threshing was an important part of farm life and meant lots of hard work for all involved. First a farmer cut and bound oats into bundles. He then stood four bundles upright in a group and placed one across the top to keep them dry. On threshing day, the engine fireman started building steam early in the morning. Neighbors brought hayracks and teams to haul bundles from the field to the separator. Some men stayed in the fields and pitched bundles onto hayracks. Others helped pitch bundles into the machine. Men who stacked straw had the most uncomfortable job, as sticky chaff would find a way inside their clothing. Neighborhood wives joined together and prepared a large noon meal. They spent hours baking and cooking to feed a hungry crew, which they did without electricity or running water.

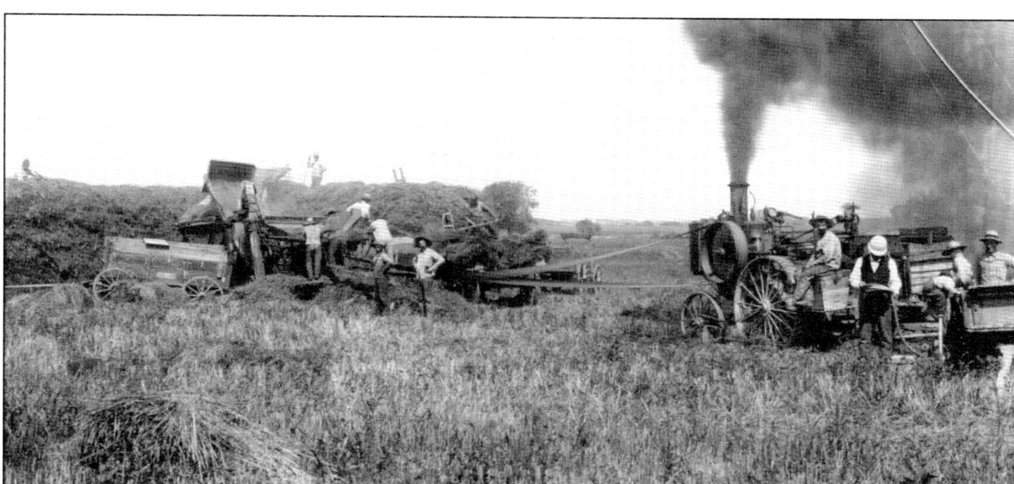

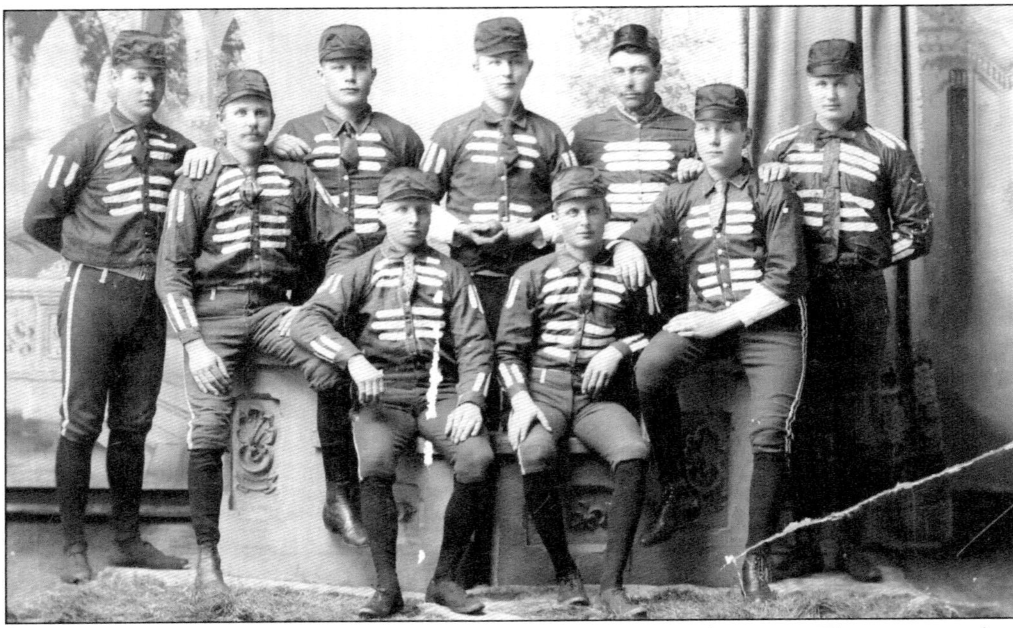

The Beaver First Nine baseball team was probably organized in the 1890s. The team members had attended country school together in southern Beaver Township. In June 1896, they played a Humboldt team, which included Clayton Foster, and won by a score of 25 to 5. Beaver players included Gustav Thompson, Hans Gangestad, Lars Fevold, Severt Thompson, Thomas Thompson, Ole Soppeland, Ole Gangestad, J. Cunningham, and J. Soppeland.

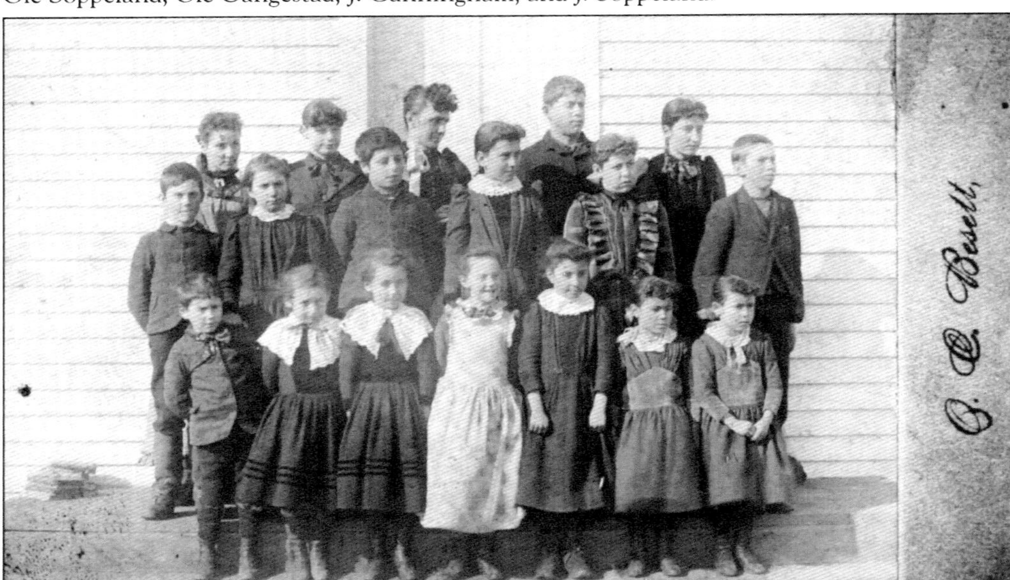

Pictured is South Maple Grove School in 1891. From left to right are (first row) George Lovrien, Mary Berte, Christina Berte, Helen Lovrien, Rose Cran, Alma Rollins, and Ada Rollins; (second row) Charles Lovrien, Daisy Bair, Sam Ferguson, Susie Bair, Pauline Rollins, and Robert Rundlet; (third row) Helen Bair, Addie Ferguson, Anna McKitrick (teacher), Charles Rollins, and Edith Entwhistle.

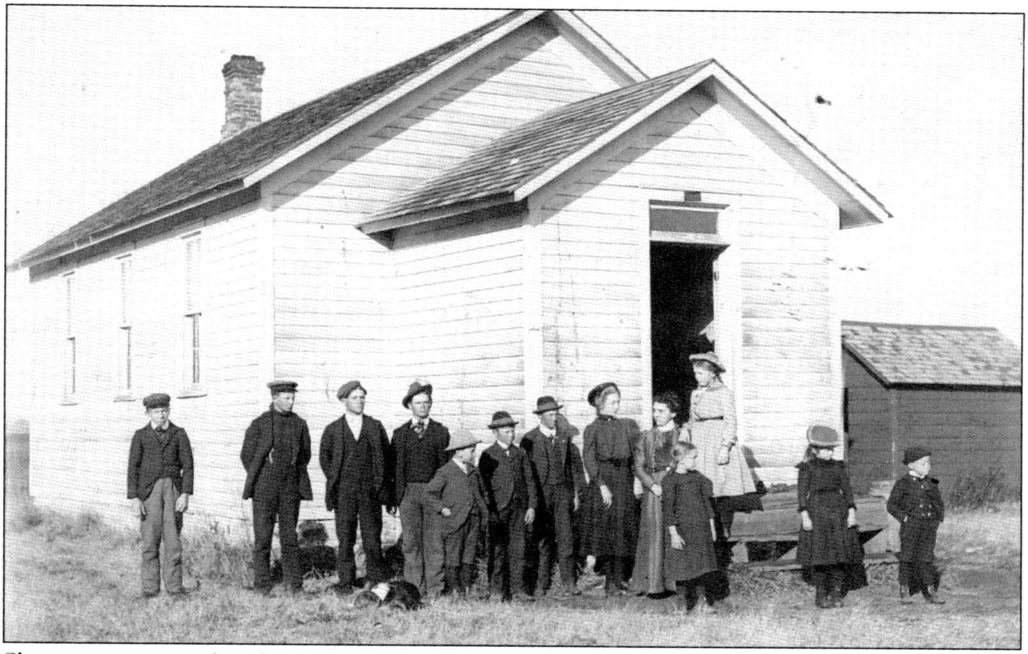

Shown is a group of students in 1891 standing in front of the Henry Blomker School located in southeast Avery Township. It was one of three schools in Independent Byron School District. The teacher that year was Lizzie Johnson. The first through eighth grades were well educated in the three Rs: readin', 'ritin', and 'rithmetic. These buildings were located every two miles so all rural students could go to school.

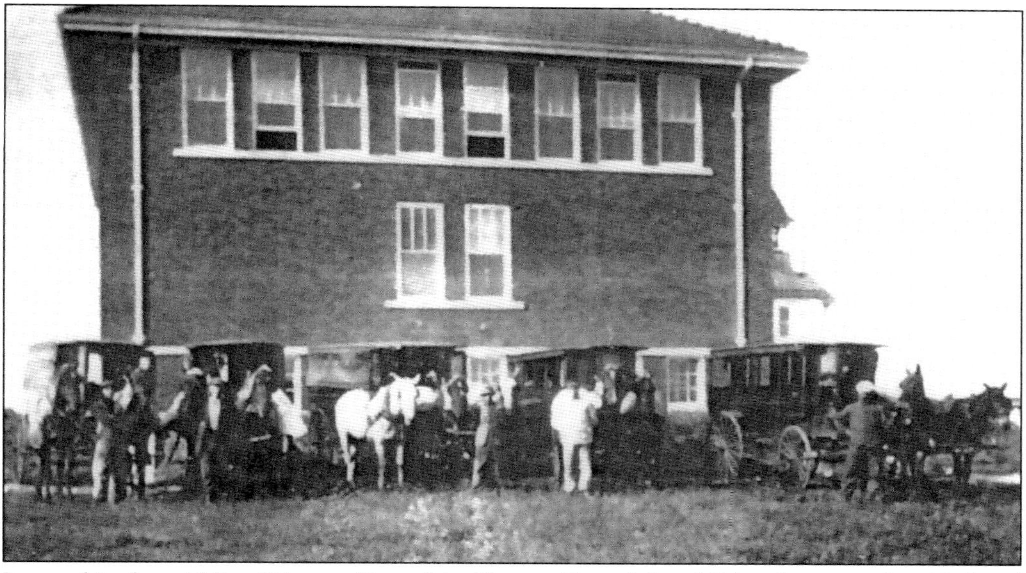

Located in the middle of Vernon Township, Vernon Consolidated School organized in 1915 and was the third consolidated school in Iowa. The building was ready for classes by 1916. In 1920, Rural Klasse and Aliene Schipull were the first Vernon graduates. The district provided buses, which were horse-drawn in the early years. The school even had an orchestra for a few years. Vernon merged with Renwick in the mid-1950s.

Find Your Place in History.

www.arcadiapublishing.com

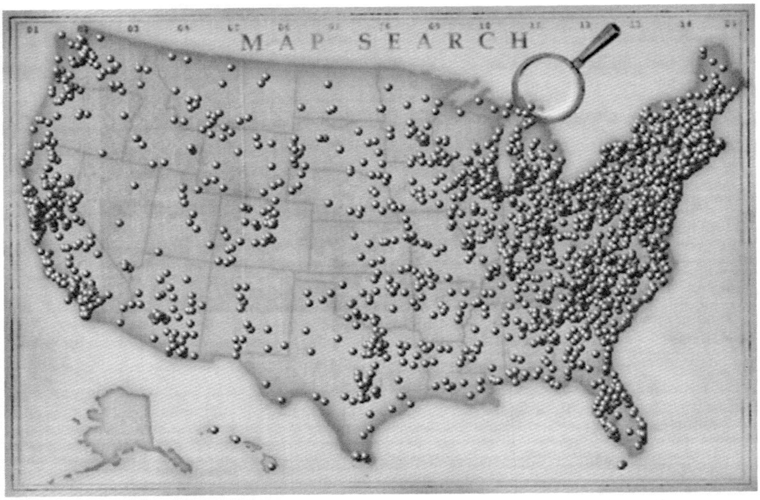

Discover books about the town where you grew up, the cities where your friends and families live, the town where your parents met, or even that retirement spot you've been dreaming about. Our Web site provides history lovers with exclusive deals, advanced notification about new titles, e-mail alerts of author events, and much more.

MADE IN THE USA

Arcadia Publishing, the leading local history publisher in the United States, is committed to making history accessible and meaningful through publishing books that celebrate and preserve the heritage of America's people and places. Consistent with our mission to preserve history on a local level, this book was printed in South Carolina on American-made paper and manufactured entirely in the United States.

This book carries the accredited Forest Stewardship Council (FSC) label and is printed on 100 percent FSC-certified paper. Products carrying the FSC label are independently certified to assure consumers that they come from forests that are managed to meet the social, economic, and ecological needs of present and future generations.

FSC
Mixed Sources
Product group from well-managed forests and other controlled sources

Cert no. SW-COC-001530
www.fsc.org